OPERATION OGRO

OPERATION OGRO

The Execution of
Admiral Luis Carrero Blanco

by Julen Agirre

TRANSLATED FROM THE SPANISH, ADAPTED

AND WITH AN INTRODUCTION BY

Barbara Probst Solomon

Quadrangle / The New York Times Book Co.

Design by Tere LoPrete

Library of Congress Cataloging in Publication Data

Agirre, Julen.
  Operation Ogro.

  Translation of Operación Ogro.
    1. Carrero Blanco, Luis. 2. Assassins—Spain—
Personal narratives. I. Title.
DP271.C37A6613   364.1'524'0946   74-26013
  ISBN 0-8129-0552-0

*For the countless men and women who
have died in Spanish prisons*

CONTENTS

QUESTION: You say you were mistreated?
ANSWER: Yes, sir.
THE COURT: You may say you were mistreated. You may not say how you were mistreated. We are not trying the police here.
QUESTION: Do you feel you have freedom to answer here?
ANSWER: No, sir.

There were points at which Colonel Ordovas relaxed his grip on the proceedings. During one of these, Eduardo Uriarte told of having been arrested and having seen another prisoner, Enrique Guezalalaga, shot by a policeman who was handcuffing him with one hand and holding a pistol in the other. "As Enrique fell," Mr. Uriarte said, "the policeman shouted, "It was an accident." Enrique said, "An accident . . . of course . . . of course . . . murderer!"

RICHARD EDER, excerpt from story
on Burgos military trial of ETA,
The New York Times, December 9, 1970

INTRODUCTION

Operation Ogro is the actual taped account of the four young Basques—Txabi, Iker, Mikel, and Jon—who came to Madrid, lived in the city for about a year, carefully picked their target, Admiral Luis Carerro Blanco (whom they considered their key enemy in the Spanish Government after Generalissimo Francisco Franco) and assassinated him on December 20, 1973 by dynamiting his car to the height of the fifth floor of the Madrid Church, San Francisco de Borja.

Perhaps the assassination of Carrero Blanco will be remembered as the end of an era—Portugal will have a revolution on April 25, the Greek dictatorship will fall the following summer. During the same tumultuous summer, Generalissimo Francisco Franco appears to be dying. His regime, the last vestige of the fascist dictatorships that dominated Europe during the 1930s, has been, in U. S. State Department usage, destabilized. Although the aging dictator partially recovers, one thing is certain: the careful success to power Franco had firmly mapped out has been shaken. Spain is on the verge of political chaos. To what degree it was that these four Basques altered the course of modern Spain, only history can decide.

The center of the stormy Spanish political beehive is Madrid, capital of a Spain unified by the force and will of the 15th-century Roman Catholic rulers, Ferdinand and Isabel. Indeed the city itself with all its Byzantine political intrigue is one of the main characters of Operation Ogro. Traditionally, Barcelona, in Catalonia, is regarded as the home of the left, while the Basque country, the most Catholic and conservative part of Spain, is thought of as having the most intensely nationalist resistance to the regime (even Basque priests were executed by Franco during the Civil War), and Madrid is considered to be the home of the Spanish oligarchy. Madrid's heritage is aristocratic; the Catalonian and Basque regions are highly industrialized and middle class. Since Franco's victory in the Civil War in 1939, Madrid has always stood as a symbol of his regime, the seat of his Government, the Castilian yoke that has politically oppressed the other provinces of Spain.

Though the fear and distrust of the capital that many Spaniards express is something of an exaggeration—the population in Madrid is now very mixed, made up of people from all the provinces of Spain—still, the fear that the young Basques in Operation Ogro feel in going to Madrid is very typical and very real. As the seat of the Government, the city is dominated by the police. Its location in the Sierras, at the center of Spain, makes escape to the French and Portuguese borders difficult. The odds against a successful political assassination anywhere in Spain were as great as the odds against the assassination of Hitler or Mussolini when they were in power. In Madrid the odds seemed impossible. Moreover, before Carrero Blanco's assassination, ETA had never operated outside the Basque country. Madrid was literally "another country" for the young Basques. Operation Ogro left the Spanish police stunned.

Ironically, though politics "happen" in Madrid, it is what happens in the Basque country that has been, during the last decade, a constant touchstone for the political changes within Spain. By the end of the Civil War in 1939, two of the richest and most industrial regions in Spain (Catalonia and the Basque Provinces of Vizcaya, Guipúzcoa, and Navarra) lost the partial autonomy granted to them under the Spanish Republic. Both regions suffered severe repression from the Franco regime—their languages and local customs were forbidden. But then, all of Spain seemed weighed down by the doubly deep gloom of poverty and political repression. After World War II, while the rest of Europe rejoiced and recovered, Spain still remained a forgotten country. In those grim and haunted years between 1940 and 1960 there was a continuous Spanish political underground, but the penalties for resistance were heavy, and the country seemed to remain a frightened silent tomb filled with somber, desperate people.

By 1960, with the advent of tourism, the migration of Spanish workers into Europe, an improved economy, and the industrialization of Spain, Madrid (the site of some of the worst battles of the Civil War) was changing overnight from a sleepy desert town to a supermodern capital, and indeed, had become the fastest growing city in all Europe. Hemingway's Puerta del Sol had been replaced by the Calle Serrano as the new center of the city. Spain, despite Franco, the church, the army, and the police, was going modern. This modernization in the sixties changed the underground resistance to an above-ground "opposition." A younger generation with only the dimmest memories of the Civil War had grown up. They wanted their part in modern life. Old-line fascism suddenly seemed outmoded. By the late sixties there were so many defectors from the official regime (men who now regarded themselves as part of the new opposition, whether for reasons of conviction or political opportunism) that it became difficult for sophisticated political observers to fathom just *who* remained within the official regime. The critical questions asked in Madrid were: What is possible after Franco's death? How do we get there? Just how solid is the army, police, church? And, how solid is the Spanish succession? All factions of the opposition wanted amnesty for political prisoners, restoration of partial autonomy for Catalonia and the Basque countries, the reestablishment of trade unions and political parties—in short, the basic freedoms of a democratic society.

But even more, all parties opposed to Franco wanted amnesty for political prisoners. The opposition still had to remain underground. Fear silenced the general population. By the end of the Civil War there were about one million dead, one million in exile and another million in concentration camps. In his 1946 *Report from Spain,* Emmett John Hughes estimated the number of prisoners in Spanish prisons as being "probably not less than 150,000." Nearly all Spanish families have had some of their men spend part of their lives in prison. Affluent Spaniards frequently preferred to send their children abroad to be educated—sending them to a Spanish university too often led to their being imprisoned for years on account of political activities. Prison is a part of the Spanish way of life—Spain leads the West in political arrests. Amnesty for political prisoners, some of whom have been imprisoned since the end of the Civil War, is a gut issue in Spain.

The Burgos trials in December 1970 enabled the opposition to emerge publicly. The trials were a political watershed and the first significant test of possibilities for the post-Franco era. In the suspense-filled trial, which began on December 7 and ended with Generalissimo Franco's commutation of the death sentence just before New Year's Eve, the political acronym ETA (Euskadi Ta Askatasuna—Basque Nation and Freedom) became known throughout the entire world. Fifteen members of ETA were on trial for involvement in the death of a policeman, but principally for being ETA. True, there had been countless political trials in Spain prior to the Burgos trials. But something about these trials, the image of young men and women, students, priests, and workers, handcuffed, with plugs in their ears, at times blindfolded, obviously tortured, in addition to the peculiarly feudal barbarity of demanding for some of the prisoners, double-death sentences, was simply too much for modern Europe. The defense lawyers maintained that the only evidence against the accused that appeared in the 5,000-page indictment was contained in the confessions of the accused themselves—secured after long months of solitary confinement, severe torture—and later repudiated. It was a murky trial.

Modern media played their role. The regime now had to cope with an onrush of European journalists as well as TV cameras. There were mass demonstrations in West Germany, Italy, and France. The Pope joined Spanish bishops in protest; significant members of most European governments also clamored against the trial; even Americans such as New York's Mayor Lindsay, and Senator Edward Kennedy protested. The trial was so heated that at one point one of the judges drew his sword against Juan María Bandres, one of the sixteen lawyers for the defense. Iker, one of the narrators of *Operation Ogro,* quite correctly points out that in the Burgos trials the defendants brought the Spanish Government to trial.

In its origins in the early sixties, ETA was a modern version of the Basque movement for independence, and ETA militants were regarded as freedom-fighters. Most Basques are in sympathy with the Basque struggle to become a nation. By the time of the Burgos trial, ETA had become more "Marxist-Leninist" in its political theory, and one of its chief battlegrounds, as *Operation Ogro* indicates, had become the huge industrial plants in Viscaya. In a country without legal parties, without elections, and without legal trade unions (except the official Government syndicate) the unionizing of the factories and the politicizing of Spanish workers was the one tangible battleground for the diffuse Spanish opposition. Factory strikes and university protests were the two areas where the modern opposition could first show its real existence. In the Burgos trials, which involved workers, priests, and students, with modern media looking on, events suddenly crystallized.

There was mass support for ETA in the Basque country: An unprecedented 150,000 Basques demonstrated against the trial. And there was heavy support in neighboring Carlist regions as well as in Madrid, and Catalonia, Valencia, and Seville. The added issue of separatism seemed to unite all of Spain for ETA (Galicia and Catalonia also have strong separatist tendencies). Those with a sense of humor in Madrid remarked that only in Spain could an issue like separatism ignite such spontaneous unified response. After the Civil War, Basque nationalists set up a Government-in-Exile in Paris which exists to this day (though it is not related to ETA). Although many modern Spaniards consider separatism economically unfeasible, most have gut sympathy for the Spaniards' inalienable right to be individualistic.

During those weeks of the Burgos trials, the impossible suddenly seemed possible. For the first time since 1940 the regime appeared uncertain of itself. Spain seemed almost at the brink of another civil war.

ETA had an added attraction: It had not been in existence during the Civil War and was not part of Spain's stormy left-wing history; thus many groups on the left who had bitter memories of anarchist or communist struggles, betrayals and so forth, had no such feeling toward ETA. Consequently, the Burgos trials for the first time united the opposition, whereas on the right there suddenly appeared a visible crack in what had appeared to be a monolithic regime. The death sentences could not be carried out. Priests, students, communists, socialists, Catalans, Galicians, Madrileños, and Basques had stood behind ETA, whereas there were clear splits within the official regime itself. The army split into hawks and doves. Young lawyers from Madrid, Barcelona, and the Basque country found that they were able to put the regime on the defensive.

The next heavy blow for the regime fell on September 1971 when the liberal and left wings of the Roman Catholic Church, having gained ascendancy over the ultraconservatives, announced their separation from the regime and affirmed their support for social reform and human rights. Then, even more extraordinary, the church formally denounced itself for the sins it had committed against the people of Spain by taking sides in the Civil War. They even went so far as to declare that they considered themselves to have been on the wrong side during the Civil War, and that it had been a war between opposing political interests whose chief victims had been the Spanish people.

This fractured the regime to its foundation. Though Franco has held the supreme power, the Spanish church, the army, and the police were the powers that sustained his position. Now the church had destroyed the regime's ideological claim that the Civil War was fought for Catholicism. Franco could no longer claim to rule Spain "in the name of God and the Cross."

At the same time this change was taking place in the church, the shape of the opposition was also being transformed. The country was becoming less religious, but violent anticlericalism was also dead. The new opposition joined radicalized priests and demonstrated against the regime by locking themselves in churches and monasteries. A new class of dissident priests appeared. In the traditionally Catholic Basque country ETA encouraged the dissident Catholics, and in *Operation Ogro* the Basques discuss the possibility of helping a prisoner escape from Zamora, the Spanish prison set aside for punishing clerics.

In the past five years, I have interviewed members of the whole spectrum of political groups springing up in Spain. Most of the younger generation suffer from the political vacuum created by the Franco regime. They know very little about the Civil War period and almost nothing of what happened to their own exiles. They respond to such phenomena as Che Guevara and the Palestine Liberation Organization with unexamined enthusiasm (ironically, the Franco Government also supports the P.L.O.). But ETA evokes the greatest admiration of most groups. ETA was an example of a "real" underground, and as freedom-fighters they were the heroes of all the student movements. Even the communists (who fundamentally are against such revolutionary tactics as those used by ETA) diplomatically expressed their sympathy for the extreme repression in the Basque country and specifically for tortures suffered by ETA prisoners. Ninety percent of the political prisoners in Spain are Basques, the majority of whom are connected with ETA. The most common expression heard was "the poor boys from ETA." I asked one very wealthy Basque woman (the wife of a Basque industrialist) why, since she was deathly afraid of communists and since ETA is far more revolutionary than the Communist Party, why she was so elated each time members of ETA "won." She thought for a moment. Clearly her sympathies with ETA had little to do with ideology. "I am Basque," she finally replied, "and even if I don't always agree with them, you must admit what they do, they do *well*. They are not like those café leftists who talk, talk, talk. Besides, if I had a son or a daughter of university age, he or she would surely be in ETA and could be killed," she paused, "and, I am proud of ETA."

The same phenomenon obtains among Basques outside Spain. I interviewed some members of ETA living in exile in France. They were all university students. We met in a café and as soon as I entered the three students got up and rapidly we walked through the back streets of the city; most of the interview took place as we walked. Eventually, in a totally different area of the city, they chose to sit down in a nondescript café remote from the student quarter. They were neatly dressed, extremely bright, middle-class students (one planned to be a mathematician, another an architect).

The myth ETA sought to break was that the Spanish police were invincible. Prior to Premier Luis Carrero Blanco's assassination, in the thirty-four years of the Franco regime, there had been no attempts made against the lives of any of the leaders of the regime.

But why Carrero Blanco? Franco's greatest weakness was his fear of losing power. Consequently, the dictator ran his country virtually single-handedly. When his own party, the Falange, appeared too strong, he braked its power by bringing into prominent positions members of the Catholic lay organization, the Opus Dei (an amorphous group of technocrats). In turn, as they grew strong, he removed their key figures from the Government. The one man Franco did trust was Admiral Luis Carrero Blanco. Though not a member of the Opus Dei, it was his advice to Franco that led to that group's gaining power. Aside from being the only man Franco actually confided in, Admiral Luis Carrero Blanco was the one man who seemed to have enough power to glue Spain's political future together. Under Franco, he was the arch symbol of the regime. The Spanish oligarchy counted on Carrero to assure their easy passage into the post-Franco era. But Carrero Blanco himself clearly wasn't the same as Franco; the oligarchy needed a second pillar to maintain itself. In the mid-sixties it was Carrero Blanco's plan to have Prince Juan Carlos head the Spanish succession, with himself as the prince's advisor. The prince was considered an ineffectual future "boy king" who had "sold his father" (the Spanish pretender, Don Juan living in exile in Estoril, Portugal) "for a crown." It was a clever move politically. Juan Carlos would be in the public eye, while behind the scenes Carrero Blanco would manage everything, keeping the real power in his own hands.

Luis Carrero Blanco, born in 1913, was a rather colorless man, whose most prominent feature was his bushy eyebrows, which is why the Basques nicknamed him "Ogro." He was given to obsessions about early Christianity and wrote on these various historical preoccupations under the pseudonym Juan de la Cosa. He had a somewhat simplistic view of the world as divided into forces of good (those with God) against the forces of evil (communists, masons, anarchists, and Jews). He was a man of rigid habits and had an extreme distaste for all intellectuals. He was known for saying he "would rather die in an atomic explosion than live in a world dominated by communists." Carrero Blanco was a figure out of Spain's melancholic, super-authoritarian past. With the exception of the ultra right and General Franco himself, in Spain there was singularly little grief displayed at the time of his funeral.

In Bayonne, France, on December 28, 1973, eight days after Carrero Blanco's assassination, hooded members of "Commando Txikia" gave their first news conference to the foreign press to explain the rationale of Operation Ogro and how they did it. Though there were some political round-ups in Spain directly after the assassination, the police were not able to make any significant arrests. Despite the regime's angry demands for extradition of members of ETA at large in France, Belgium, and other European countries, since the end of World War II no European country has handed back political exiles to Spain. Whether the police in Belgium and France could not find the members of

ETA, or, as Spain suggested, did not choose to find them, was never clarified.

At the end of July 1973, the Spanish edition of *Operation Ogro* was published in Paris. Of course the book was banned in Spain, but it was selling briskly in France, and Spaniards, in France for summer holidays, rapidly brought the book back home. Excerpts were printed in the Barcelona newspaper, *Mundo*. The injury to the pride of the Spanish police was enormous. Not only had they been unable, in six months, to make any arrests—now all of Spain could read how four young Basques, with extraordinary insolence, had outwitted the invincible Spanish security system. Six weeks later, on September 13, a bomb exploded in a Madrid cafeteria generally frequented by Madrid policemen. Twelve people were killed. Two members of ETA, known as Tupa and Tanka, were arrested, tortured, and charged with the crime. ETA, whose policy is always to claim credit for their acts of terrorism, disclaimed involvement in the Café Rolando bombing. The fact that no policemen were in the cafe at the time of the bombing was picked up by Spanish newspapers. The Barcelona newspaper *Vanguardia* described the bombing as having an odd cast. Many in Spain suspected ultra-right-wing involvement in the bungled bombing. The French Government, in a diplomatic gesture, agreed to ban the sale of the Spanish (Ruedo Ibérico) edition in France—but soon after it permitted a French (Editions du Seuil) edition.

On September 16, Dr. Genoveva Forest, a psychiatrist and the wife of the famous Madrid playwright Alfonso Sastre, and seven other prominent intellectuals were arrested. They were charged with being a "link" between the Communist Party and ETA and with having aided ETA in the cafeteria bombing.

According to police, the homes of these prominent Madrid and Barcelona intellectuals were used as ETA hiding places, such as those mentioned in *Operation Ogro*. Ironically, none of the intellectuals arrested in the bizarre turn of events was of Basque origin. Genoveva Forest was accused of having co-authored *Operation Ogro*, and apparently the chief evidence, according to the Madrid police, was her possession of a copy of the manuscript (after *Ogro* was published), and the single reference in *Ogro* to a Madrid doctor. What clearly shocked most Spaniards was the regime's further attempt to charge Dr. Forest and several

other of the arrested intellectuals with actual participation in the
assassination of Carrero Blanco, and its demand that they be
sentenced to death. Clearly any linkage between the Communist
Party and ETA (two groups not noted for their mutual admiration, a fact that clearly comes out in *Operation Ogro*) seems
absurd. Spain suddenly seemed a rudderless country, veering
from one senseless political arrest and trial to another. The
regime seemed paralyzed by Franco's decline and by revolution
in nearby Portugal, and the police acted with the fury of the
impotent. But what shocked Spaniards most, as well as the world
at large, were the reports of torture that were being smuggled
out of Spain by international lawyers in what was becoming
known as "the Sastre affair."

In a letter released in France and Sweden, written by Dr.
Forest, she reported being kicked and beaten in all parts of her
body. The prisoners were held incommunicado the first twenty-six
days. Dr. Forest was told she would be thrown out of a window,
and the world would be told of her suicide. When she vomited,
she was forced to swallow "the mess." According to reports in
Le Monde, she and the other women prisoners were repeatedly
raped. Among the other prisoners were the prominent Catalan
feminist and labor lawyer, Lídia Falcon O'Neill; her husband,
the writer Eliseo Bayo Poblador; Antonio Duran Velesco, a labor
leader; María Paz Ballesteros, a television actress; her husband,
the producer Vicente Sains de la Pena; María del Carmen Nadal,
a teacher; and her husband, Bernardo Vadell Carreras, an airline
pilot. Later Alfonso Sastre also turned himself in. All have apparently been tortured. International protest against the tortures
seems to have had some effect on a badly shaken and confused
regime. As of this writing in April of 1975, the case appears to be
stalled.

When my publishers asked me in November 1974 to do the
American translation and adaptation of *Operation Ogro*, I went
back to France at their request and interviewed several of the
Basques connected with the Basque publishing house of Mugalde,
the original edition's co-publisher with Ruedo Ibérico of Paris. At
that time they released to me some additional information not
originally contained in either the French or Spanish versions of
Operation Ogro. Among the additional material is the cassette
of the short-wave radio police communication just prior to and

after Carrero's assassination. (This had been taped by the Basques in Madrid at the time of the assassination.) I was also able, in the American edition, to make certain place names, sentences, and sequences of events more coherent. In the American edition, the original interview format with the questions posed by the journalist Julen Aguirre to the Basques has been omitted as being redundant. Txabi, Jon, Iker, and Mikel tell their own story. Any speculations giving personal characteristics to the four young Basques are strictly my own deductions based on what they have to say about themselves on the tapes and on my general impressions gathered from interviews with other members of ETA. The asides on the main characters, as well as information inserts are strictly my own interpretations and are to be taken as such.

In the editing of this book, I am particularly indebted to the publishing house of Mugalde, and to Ruedo Ibérico, and *The New York Times* for giving me access to their files. I would also like to thank Martha Hawthorne for the list of Basque political prisoners, and the *New York Review of Books* for permission to draw on my article, *Shaking up Franco's Spain* (February 21, 1974).

B.P.S.
April 1975
New York City

PROLOGUE

The time is December 20, 1973, Madrid, around 9:30 A.M.
Henry Kissinger has just left the city after a whirlwind political
visit. The trial of the Carabanchel 10 (ten members of the illegal
trade union movement in Madrid's Carabanchel prison) is scheduled to begin that morning in the Palace of Justice. The police
are cruising the city, checking for workers demonstrating against
the trial. The police are talking over their radio:

"The workers appear to be working normally. H-20 over."

". . . I'm going to give that homo a punch—is there a Dominican
college here, Ruiz de Alda?"

"Nobody has heard of that college, there is only a church . . ."

"Forget it, forget it."

"Corner of Claudio Coello. There seems to have been a very heavy
explosion here. Over."

"Coming in 20. We are busy here with the business of the bull.
The municipal police are trying to kill him, but he doesn't die.
See if somebody can bring us heavy arms so we can kill him.
[Apparently a bull had gotten loose in the streets.] This way, he's
not going to die . . ."

"Nothing new at the University City. Very few students. In the
school of *Bellas Artes* they haven't erased the graffiti [apparently
political] we saw yesterday. Okay, over."

"Coming in 18. Go to Claudio Coello and Maldonado to see about
that explosion."

"R-20 over. Did you get the report?"

"Have you gotten to the scene?"

"Not yet."

"Send over some of the cars in the vicinity . . . Z-40, K-20. See if they've gotten there . . . Can we get any information on the explosion?"

"H-20 wants to find out what happened, what caused the explosion? It was a gas explosion on Claudio Coello!"

"Good, H-20 has the message."

"R-22. Can you tell us if the President's car that went by here suffered any damage?"

"No. Nothing happened to the President. There are five or six cars that have been damaged. Two badly. It appears that the wounded have been taken to Montesa Hospital . . . water is spilling over . . ."

"Has anything happened to the President of the Government? Yes or no? His car must have been in the vicinity . . . They are trying to locate the President's car to make sure everything is normal . . ."

"Nothing seems to have happened to the President's car . . . it appears to have passed . . ."

"Okay. I haven't seen anything more than what happened. I haven't been given any more information. I will try to verify what information I can."

"R-20 over. Please see if you can inform us as to whether anything has happened to the President's car . . ."

[Car interrupts with report of another accident.] "She fainted. Got hit on the head. A little girl."

"No, got it, no. I thought one car . . . but the escort car . . . not his. One of the traffic policemen told me his passed by already."

"Okay, over."

"I think the bull has hit a pedestrian."

"The explosion (Claudio Coello) appears to have demolished the entire street."

"Are there wounded?"

"Appear to be several. Appears to have affected several cars. I can't give you any information about the other thing."

"Can you find out if anything has happened to the President's car?"

"We have no information. We will check on the wounded at Montesa . . ."

"Send over some armed police to move back the crowds. Smells of gas and there is danger of a second explosion . . ."

[Voice suddenly appears to be more urgent.] *"Go over, go over to the President's house in Hermanos Bécquer and find out if the President's car is in front of the door. Over 16."*

"We will check it out."

"Yes, check it out. To see if anything has happened to the President."

[This car appears to be at scene of accident.] "According to what they tell us, one car got directly hit and is on the roof of the church. The firemen are just coming down. Car had three occupants. Over K-20."

[Voice suddenly gets hysterical.] "It seems that the car that rose, that the explosion sent to the roof . . . is the *President* of the Government's car!!! I can't yet confirm—it appears he is dead!"

"The car on the roof is the President's car! It appears that he is dead!"
[Confusion]
"Yes, I have got the message. Others are confirming it."

"Do you know what roof?"

"Claudio Coello corner of Maldonado. Number 1 Maldonado Street."

"Have checked out the situation. It is true, the car that was sent to the roof was the car of the President of the Government. It appears he, his chauffeur, and one escort are dead."

Another voice suddenly gasping. "I have just seen them carry out the President of the Government on a stretcher. But he is still alive! He is alive!"

"An ambulance is taking him . . ."

"We are at the site of the explosion."

"There are a lot of journalists and cameramen."

"*Don't* give out any information until the superior chief says something."

[New voice, hysterical.] "Inform the commanding officer, that Colonel Sanchez Alcalde and Colonel Davila both are requesting concretely, both are requesting concretely, that they be informed with exactness . . . if he is a cadaver, yes or no, in order to be able to inform his Excellency, the Chief of State."

"Cadaver, cadaver."

"No, no, *you* can't say that. The commanding officer must tell us. You must inform him that he must call and speak to the director."

"The police doctor told us cadaver."

"Considering the importance of the event it is the commanding officer or director that must give the information, to his Excellency, the Chief of State . . . and to the prince!"

THE SPANISH GOVERNMENT STUPIFIED BY PERFECTLY PREPARED ASSASSINATION . . . AN ACT WITHOUT PRECEDENCE (*Le Monde*, December 22, 1973)

PROOF THAT FASCISM NOT INVINCIBLE IN THE ENCHAINED PENINSULA (*Liberation*, December 26, 1973, France)

SPANISH RIGHTISTS DISRUPT FUNERAL OF SLAIN PREMIER (*N.Y. Times*, December 22, 1973) . . . "When the Archbishop of Madrid, Vicente Cardinal Enriqūe y Tarancón, a moderately liberal churchman, entered the central government building where Premier Carrero Blanco lay in state in his admiral's uniform, he was called assassin by members of the crowd. There were calls that he be put against a wall and shot . . . 'Death to the Communist priests,' many shouted. 'Death to the Reds.' 'Long live Spain.'"

SPANISH PAPERS CHARGE FRENCH SHELTER KILLERS (*N.Y. Times,* December 28, 1973) . . . "If a Paris newspaper can interview an ETA chief, it is difficult to imagine that the French police cannot do it."

SPAIN SEEKING TEN BASQUES FOR MURDER OF PREMIER (*N.Y. Times,* April 8, 1974) . . . "It is believed that Spain has asked the French to extradite eight persons and Belgium two. Neither Government has indicated willingness to comply."

OPERATION OGRO

CHAPTER ONE

Some Useful Information Is Given to Operation Ogro

Txabi started the tape; "ETA was given a secret news report that in Madrid Luis Carrero Blanco went to mass every morning at 9 in a Jesuit church on Serrano Street.

"In the beginning," Txabi added, "it was a piece of information like many others that come our way—nobody placed much hope or importance in knowing where Carrero went to mass—but we finally decided that one of the militants of ETA should go to Madrid and check out the report. The militant found out that the Madrid information was accurate. In addition, it appeared that there wasn't much guarding of Carrero. It might even be possible to kidnap him. That's the real way the idea of kidnapping Carrero came about. It would have been more logical first for us to have planned to kidnap Carrero and then to find the means of doing it. But life is always a little topsy-turvy, and in this case, we did it backwards. So, with this information as a base, a small group of militants began to analyze the situation. Clearly, Carrero was the key man in the regime. He was the man who for many years had prepared the way for the continuation and perpetuation of the Franquist regime. Carrero was now the real guarantee of this regime. He was precisely the man we should try to kidnap. He was actually one of the few people—perhaps the only person— with whom we might obtain the liberation of Spanish and Basque political prisoners. More than 150 members of ETA were in prison with sentences over ten years each. The summer before, three militants were killed by the police. Just recently more than 70 Basque militants had been taken in Galdakano. The repression was fierce and brutal."

Jon broke in, "The organization's first plan was to kidnap Carrero Blanco. Since the Burgos trial in December 1971 the organization has made a priority of getting imprisoned militants out of jail. We didn't have much faith in prison escapes because, aside from the fact that the militants are scattered throughout many prisons, we lacked the kind of structure in the rest of Spain —outside of the Basque country—that would have made such a tactic practical. We didn't see any possibilities of success along those lines. As an alternative we thought of kidnapping somebody important—but not an ambassador or a consul. Not enough impact. It had to be somebody who had a great deal of weight within the Spanish government. When the news about Carrero's going to the mass was confirmed, we decided that he was the ideal choice."

Iker continued, "In line with ETA's concern for liberating prisoners, we gathered information for a long time. In the case of the Basque worker–priests who were incarcerated in Zamora clerical prison, a prison escape was attempted from the inside, with support from the outside. It didn't work."

"We had a lot of underground information," added Txabi, "but our problem was that we lacked a sufficiently strong organization and time to develop what we needed—the right place and the right contacts. For example, imagine managing a prison escape, say, in Extremadura. To start with, you'd have to have the means of getting to Madrid. That would take two or three hours, which would be very risky, with the police guarding the roads. Because we Basques don't know areas like Extremadura, that adds to the danger. In addition, we had the problem that any Basque activists in Spain proper would immediately be recognized by their Basque accents as soon as they made contact with people from the area. Prison escapes are rough to pull off—there are a thousand problems that make it not a very practical solution."

Jon spoke again. "The trouble has always been that Spaniards outside of the Basque country don't really understand the Basque problem. Each time we actually established some contact with people from Madrid or Barcelona, it didn't work. Spaniards— even the Spanish opposition—don't really understand us Basques. For example, the problem we presented of the necessity for armed resistance to the regime simply was beyond the comprehension of opposition circles in Madrid and Barcelona. And as far as talking about a national problem, they see it from a completely different point of view. They don't really understand that the Basque country has suffered from its own unique form of repression. This is, without a doubt, one of the results of Franquist

A. Home of the Ogro
B. Studio of the "sculptor"
C. The Church of San Francisco de Borja
D. Arab Embassy
E. British Embassy
F. American Embassy
G. Original site chosen for kidnapping
H. Bridge over the Castellana

**AREA MAP OF
OPERATION OGRO**

propaganda. Ninety percent of the political arrests in Spain are of Basques. This is a truth that Spaniards don't want to hear about—and that's the way it is."

Mikel broke in, "Spaniards have an enormous incapacity to understand that Euskadi *is* a country, and, as such, it has a right to its national liberty."

"In general," added Txabi, "the oppression of minorities is not understood by those who don't suffer from it. This is a reality that we have to live with."

He continued, "During the fall of '72 our commando—which consisted of the four of us—had been given the information about Carrero's going to mass. We limited ourselves to trying to carry out what the central committee of ETA asked of us. We didn't even know who had given the information to ETA. Of course, in Madrid, as in many other cities in Spain, we have informants. ETA has an information network—other political information gets to ETA by the same means that information was leaked to us about Carrero Blanco."

Txabi went on, "In general, ETA has a lot of support in the Basque country. But there are Basques who help and others who don't. And there are Spaniards who help and others who don't. When we receive some political information, two members of the commando of four go to check it out."

"Just two of us," Jon broke in, "Mikel and I went on that first trip to Madrid. Though we have ways of getting information reports on what is going on in other Spanish cities, ETA has no real organization outside the Basque country. So we were on our own in Madrid. We had no contact with other left-wing Spanish groups who would have been ready to help us in our plan for armed resistance—or if there was any such group, we didn't know of their existence. Once in Madrid, we rented, on our own, several rooms in a pension. We carried with us false papers and false identification cards. All our false papers were in order. As we were only going to spend a few days in the pension, we managed to avoid giving the owner any real explanation about who we were. Madrid is complicated. In all the pensions and hotels, they ask a lot of questions."

Jon paused, then continued the tape.

"It was in the beginning of December, '72—the first or second of December—because I remember that as soon as we finished

in Madrid, we came back to Euskadi to spend Christmas vacation with our families. As soon as we got back to Euskadi, we
reported on the Madrid situation to ETA. Then we joined our
families for the Christmas holidays."

Jon paused again, as though remembering back.

"I had only been in Madrid once before, and it was a long time
ago. Mikel had never been in the city. I remember we arrived
during the Madrid afternoon—around 6 or 7 o'clock. It was
already dark, December dark, and I was startled by all the noise,
the traffic jams, the lights of Madrid, the mobs of people milling
in the streets. During that entire week in Madrid, I always felt
dizzy—and disoriented. The distances in Madrid seemed enormous to me, the air unbreathable, filth in all the streets . . ."

Mikel interrupted, "I also had an awful impression of Madrid.
Everything was very different from Euskadi. The people in the
streets were fancily dressed, completely different from the way
we go around here. They wore jackets, ties . . . and the men had
moustaches. Christ, to me, they all looked like they were policemen or informers."

Jon went on, "Their moustaches made a big impression on me,
too. All different styles—small ones, military cut, Fascist cut—
those moustaches were the first thing that caught my attention.
After a while it all began to look normal to us. But I still remember that first terrible feeling of arriving in a strange city. You
don't know your way, you are lost—disoriented. But—bueno—we
managed to locate ourselves in a pension. The next day we went
out early. We went to a bar and we asked for a telephone book.
We looked up the name—Carrero Blanco—and we found it right
away in the telephone book. He lived in Hermanos Bécquer. In
number 6, I think. Christ, it seemed incredible that it was all that
easy—somebody that important in the telephone book! Anyway,
with that done, we looked at a subway map and figured out the
location of his street, and we figured out that it was near the
church. This made us think that the information about his going
to the Jesuits' church was probably accurate.

"We walked over to the church," Jon continued. "During the
walk over, Mikel and I made plans where to meet later, and then
we separated. Each of us reconnoitered the church separately.
The church was very big. A real Jesuit temple. I remember that
as soon as I entered the church, I walked over to the middle—

slightly to the right-hand side. Mikel entered the church a few minutes later. He placed himself behind me—just in case I ran into trouble. We were a little afraid. The church could have been very well guarded. Without our realizing it, they could have observed the people who entered the church. They might search us and ask for our papers. Anyway, it was past 9 and still no Carrero. When the mass was over, people started to leave. That was when I saw him. He was accompanied by a man of around 70. Anyway, he looked very old—his hair was very white, his build small. Carrero passed directly in front of us. I was standing staring at the altar, and Carrero passed right alongside me. I recognized him as soon as soon as he came close to me—even though I had only seen pictures of him in the movie newsreels and in the newspapers."

Mikel interrupted Jon, "Yes, the same for me. Although we had in addition the closeup of his face that the central committee of ETA had given us. And we also were aware that he always went alone to the church. Our information was that he didn't take any visible security measures—anyway, none that could be observed."

Then Jon said, "At any rate, we took a great deal of precaution, because it could very easily have been that our informant hadn't realized all the security measures that Carrero could have taken. And for that reason, we moved cautiously. Also, the first day, we ourselves hadn't seen how and in whose company Carrero had entered the church. Because we had only seen photographs of him, we didn't recognize him from the distance. But when Carrero was leaving the church, I realized immediately which one he was. I watched him talking to the old man, and after that I followed him—at quite a distance—but without losing sight of him. At the bottom of the church stairs he said goodbye to the old man; then he got into his car with a second man who carried a briefcase— and they drove in the direction of Calle Serrano. Christ, we were elated. The information given to us about Carrero was accurate!"

"The next day we went back, and this time we saw him enter the church—we noticed that he arrived in a black Dodge," Mikel said.

"Mikel stayed outside the church, watching for his arrival, and I was posted inside the church," Jon added. "It was easy for us to observe Carrero's movements from the outside because there are several bus stops around there. One is just in front of the church

—on the sidewalk in front of the American Embassy. The other
bus stop is in Hermanos Bécquer, practically on the corner of
Bécquer and Serrano, and I think there was another bus stop on
Serrano itself, a little further up the street."

"But during that period, that day, we really didn't know much
about anything," Mikel said. "We didn't know the area. I saw
people in front of the church, waiting at a bus stop, and I joined
them there, and also waited. There were several 'grises'—Spanish
security police—talking—they weren't paying attention to anything. ["Grises" is the nickname given to the civil military police
because of their grey uniforms. They are the police used to break
up political demonstrations, for arrests of students, etc., and are
much feared.] A lot of cars went by—but there were very few
people in the street. At 9 . . . no, it must have been two or three
minutes after 9 . . . I saw the black Dodge pull up. The driver
double-parked it. Carrero got out. Another man also got out—the
same one who had accompanied him the first day. He was dark,
wore glasses, medium height, strong; he was the one who carried
the briefcase under his arm. They walked up the church steps and
into the church. The chauffeur stayed behind in the car. A little
later, a municipal guard walked over to the chauffeur—the two
of them clearly made a habit of greeting each other. Then a
bus passed by, and I was thinking that perhaps there were people
observing us—maybe on the street—and five minutes had already
gone by—so I got on the bus and got off at the next stop. I returned and walked into the church. Then I waited in the background—near the holy water at the entrance of the church. The
mass was half finished."

"Before Mikel had entered the church, I had already seen
Carrero came in," Jon continued. "He walked slowly—he was very
calm—he looked like a big landlord type—typical businessman.
Behind him came the man with the briefcase from the previous
day. He walked right past me, but paid no attention to me—but
when he got more or less to the place where I was standing he
moved to my left and sat down in one of the pews. He sat near
the center aisle. Meanwhile, Carrero kept walking up the central
aisle. He walked up to the front pew, but finally selected a seat
in the second or third pew. After sitting down, he got up again,
and followed the mass standing up. He stood very rigidly, con-
centrating. I watched every move he was making. Later, during

communion, he went over to the *prie-dieu,* which was directly in front of the altar. I followed him. I remember that I was standing to his right. I was totally absorbed in my own thoughts. When I kneeled down in front of the altar, without my realizing how, somebody came up behind me—practically glued to me. I was thunderstruck, because I was looking at Carrero. I had already recognized him. I was next to him—thinking how easy it would be for me to do something. If I had wanted, I could have even fired two gunshots at him—I had a pistol tucked into my belt. After that, I never carried the pistol on me, because we realized how risky it was to walk around armed. We could have been stopped and searched for a million and one reasons—identity papers, a routine street check by the police—so we decided not to carry pistols with us when we went to church. Those first few days, though, we did have arms. Still, nothing happened to us. While I was kneeling at the *prie-dieu,* I kept thinking—Franco, Carrero—they are immortal, they are 'untouchable.' I myself had always assumed that a man like that would be almost impossible to kidnap. I had always heard the same familiar story. The Spanish myth was that to get Franco or one of his entourage was out of the question. Everybody always said, 'Those types—impossible!' " Jon paused, then went on. "I was brooding about that when, all of a sudden, I looked up, and I realized there was this guy behind me, practically glued to me on my left side, almost so close to me that I got the idea he wanted there to be more distance between me and Carrero. He must have been about 30, maybe a few years younger. Very tall; blond, I think. Anyway, the guy looked at me with a sort of fresh, almost insolent stare. I felt shaky. I returned to my pew, then I lost sight of him. After mass was over, Carrero joined the older man from the previous day . . ." Jon paused a long time.

". . . and they left the church together. The man with the brief-case followed behind Carrero at a prudent distance. They then went through the same routine as the previous day. At the bottom of the church steps the old man said goodbye to Carrero and went into his own car. I think it was a red Morris. A tough young guy—about 25—was already inside the car waiting for him. He looked like a bodyguard. I saw that same bodyguard several times after that, but I don't really know who the old man was, what function the bodyguard had. But that's who I assumed they were. Then the Ogro, followed by the man with the briefcase, got into his Dodge."

Jon was quiet for a few seconds. Then he added, "You know, we called him Ogro because he looked exactly like an ogro—bushy eyebrows, hairy. He was very impressive, on the scary side."

"From the beginning we called him Ogro, and it became a sort of code between us—it was our code name for the operation—'Operation Ogro,'" Mikel added.

Jon continued, "The same day, while the Ogro was speaking to the old man on the stairs—before they separated—we noticed that they always spent a few minutes together talking, before they said goodbye to each other. I noticed that the old man always stood with his jacket buttoned, and kept his hand inside his vest. That meant he was armed. I figured he must be Carrero's secretary and bodyguard."

Mikel commented, "That same day, we figured out the route of Carrero's car. His habit was to have his chauffeur drive down Serrano and turn left toward Juan Bravo; that was the same route we saw the day before, and he repeated the route this time. We tried to appear offhand, casual. We started to walk along Serrano in the opposite direction. While we were crossing Diego de León, Jon nudged me. The Ogro's car suddenly passed in front of us. The chauffeur drove the car across Serrano, and parked on Hermanos Bécquer. Because of the one-way streets in Madrid, the car must have gone in a circle, come back up Serrano, and then returned to Carrero's home. We realized that instead of going directly to his office, Carrero first would stop off at his home."

"By this time," Jon went on, "we had figured out Carrero's route, and we studied it, walking the streets, in order to familiarize ourselves with the neighborhood. Serrano, Juan Bravo, Claudio Coello, Diego de León, Hermanos Bécquer. Then we went to a Madrid bookstore, bought a plan of Madrid, and studied the zone with the map."

"Yes, all those things made our job of observation much easier, and knowing the terrain well was very important later, when we changed the plans from kidnapping to assassination," Mikel explained. "In the beginning, we only tried to study the car route from his house to the church, and to watch how he exited from the church. It never would have occurred to us to follow him afterwards. We assumed he was going to his office—which would have been very far away. This bit of information about his daily churchgoing meant we were going to have some chance of direct action . . ."

"Right!" Jon exclaimed. "The next day, we checked out the church again, and sure enough he followed the same route. The schedule was exactly the same. We felt good. We had the main thing checked out: The information that had been given to us about Carrero was correct. Now we could take advantage of what had been first-rate information."

"This first December visit to Madrid was very short," Mikel said. "By the twentieth of the month, I was back in Pamplona— home for Christmas. During this initial period in Madrid, we went to mass at 9 every morning. We took turns. One day Jon would stand outside observing everything going on—the arrival of Carrero, the chauffeur's movements, the people who entered the church after Carrero—the whole works—while I observed what was going on inside the church. I stood behind the man with the briefcase; by this time we called him the 'bodyguard.' Other days, I stayed outside, and Jon was inside."

"That way," Jon went on, "we could see many things that gave us a good idea of the situation—that when Carrero entered, only the bodyguard with the briefcase came with him. But some days the young blond man substituted for the bodyguard. He wore a very elegant blue jacket. So we figured there were a minimum of at least two bodyguards—even though it was possible that there was perhaps one or more already stationed within the church. I often saw several other young men inside the church. They went to take communion, and they went regularly. There was one young man—I couldn't be sure whether it was always the same one—but this young man—about 20 or 30 years old—always placed himself next to me, separating the Ogro from me. I don't know if it was a coincidence, because during this phase I was always scared, and everyone looked like a policeman to me. It is possible that it was only a coincidence. I never saw him leave the church with the Ogro, and later on we never saw him again. When I went near the *prie-dieu* it was always crowded with people. As there were so many people kneeling, I had to stand in line to wait my turn. I was scared, because this young man was always behind me, practically glued to my side. Under those circumstances I was scared—he made me nervous."

"The times I entered the church myself, I never saw those young men," Mikel added. "True, there were young men, but they were just ordinary people taking communion. It was an hour that a lot of young people went into the church, and many of them didn't even wait to hear the mass. They came and went rapidly. Naturally, what happened is that every moment we were filled with fear, and we observed everything and everybody. Several times I placed myself in the line right behind the bodyguard. He had a habit of standing up and watching Carrero, sometimes with his arms crossed in front of him, and other times with his arms folded behind him, his hands joined together. One of my fantasies, as he was standing just in front of me, was that with his arms folded behind him I could instantly reach out and handcuff him, completely immobilizing him. I thought about that one a lot of times. Imagine—he was so close to me that when I kneeled down on the bench behind the bodyguard, I was so close my nose practically touched his hands."

Jon added, "We checked out that Carrero arrived each day at the church at the same time—one or two minutes past 9 in the morning. Very punctual. For the 9 o'clock mass. And afterwards he always followed the same route with the car. Except Saturday and Sunday, when he never went to that church."

Txabi suddenly broke into Jon and Mikel's account of their first Madrid visit.

"No," he said. "Carrero never went on the weekends. Occasionally, during our second stay in Madrid, we went to church on the weekends—but we never saw Carrero. On the second trip, all four of us went to Madrid."

"Another item that we took note of was his car plate number," Jon went on. "It was a black Dodge—PMM 17 416. We always assumed that it was a bullet-proof car."

"The morning mass in early December tended to be on the empty side," Mikel remembered. "Later, in spring, there were more people. During the winter, I once counted thirty-one people in the church, another time a little over forty. The number never got up to fifty. And for a church of that enormous size, it looked empty. It had wide naves and an extremely high dome. Everything echoed—doors, women's high heels—and when people went into the confessional box, that made an eerie noise, too.

"Most of the people tended to gather in the front of the

church. Of course, there were always some scattered in other parts. In general, they were very old people, and an occasional elderly priest. I was almost certain that several of the priests belonged to the military because several times I saw them getting into cars that belonged to the Army Landed Forces."

"Yes," said Jon, "there were always some old people. And some of them knew the Ogro—they always greeted him. In addition, there was a military man and somebody I couldn't identify.

"During that period in Madrid, while we reconnoitered the church, Mikel and I were already thinking of possible ways of kidnapping Carrero. We knew we had been sent to Madrid by the central committee of ETA with the idea of formulating a plan for the future kidnapping of Carrero."

"From the very beginning, we realized that the action had to occur inside the church," Mikel said. "Given the zone, a zone filled with policemen, embassies, consulates, diplomatic missions, and so forth, with 'grises' in all the doorways, we had to plan to work inside. Too much traffic outside the church—it would have been impossible for us."

"Yes," Jon continued, "we calculated that as soon as the first shot was heard, there would be an immediate rush of grises in the area. At that time, we thought we might have to use guns. At first, we thought the plan would have to be executed from within the church. And I remember that Mikel and I talked about the problem as to whether the noise of gunshot could be heard outside the church. I thought it could. But he said that with the traffic noise, the thick walls of the church, and the heavy curtains at the church door, the sound would be muffled."

Mikel elaborated: "But those were our own private speculations. Actually, neither Jon nor I knew at that time what the organization was going to decide in view of our report. Finally, one extremely cold morning—one of those Madrid mornings when the cold and the wind from the Sierras freezes everything —we decided to go home. We suffered from the cold because Jon and I had come to Madrid traveling on the light side. No overcoats—practically naked! Nothing more than a sweater apiece. Not even a suitcase, and it wasn't worth our while to buy coats, because we were short of cash. So, one of those cold, freezing mornings, we took the Talgo rapid express back to San Sebastian. We went back home. To the Basque country."

CHAPTER TWO

The Second Group of Commandos— Iker, Jon, Mikel, and Txabi Their Daily Life Their Investigation for the Kidnapping of Carrero

"The four of us—Jon, Mikel, Txabi, who was the one in charge, and I—arrived in Madrid in the beginning of February [1973]," Iker started.

Mikel continued, "We didn't remember the exact date, but it coincided with the kidnapping of the Basque industrialist, Huarte, in Pamplona. We arrived late at night in Madrid and read in the next morning's newspapers about Huarte's kidnapping. We didn't know that ETA was going to kidnap Huarte, because each commando works independently. But we figured out that the organization must have sent us to Madrid just before the Huarte kidnapping in order to avoid possible problems we might have had with police controls."

"We didn't know anything about the Huarte affair, nor did we have a clue, technically, how it was carried out," Iker said.

Txabi added, "However, the political circumstances that motivated the kidnapping of Huarte were as follows: There were huge factory strikes in Torfinasa, many economic problems, and bad working conditions. The workers had presented their case through legal channels, which was the official government syndicate. Aside from the official syndicate, all other trade unions in Spain have been outlawed since the civil war. The workers did their bit by going out on strike. But, as usual, the official syndicate demanded that the strike be stopped before negotiations began. The workers knew how the government syndicate would act. They formed their own groups, and appointed their own members, threw out the official syndicate representatives, and started to talk directly to the factory owners . . ."

"They asked for sympathy strikes and the support of other opposition groups," Iker added.

Txabi explained, "This appeal was made by the Workers' Commissions, and channeled to other opposition groups. Propaganda was distributed in Imenasa and Indecasa, which belong to the same chain of factories. But there was little group solidarity. ETA pressured the Workers' Commissions to make a bigger protest and show more solidarity. Finally, there was a call for a general strike."

"The strike caused a lot of layoffs. In Torfinasa the strike had been going on for forty days—the workers were exhausted," said Mikel.

"ETA waited for the day when the general strike was called. The general strike never came off. That's when ETA decided to intervene militarily," Txabi continued.

"One should understand," Mikel emphasized, "that this wasn't an action precipitated by ETA. ETA came in when they saw that all possibilities for group action and solidarity had stopped. ETA saw military action as a new form of political protest within Spain. They thought they'd have a greater chance of success. The regime, with its antiquated capitalism, is very adept at putting down traditional forms of protest, but when confronted with this new form of action, we were sure they would be completely unprepared. What the other opposition groups haven't understood about ETA is that this did not mean that ETA wanted traditional forms of protest dropped. Direct action and traditional action are not necessarily in opposition to one another. Even though many opposition groups didn't understand our position, the people in the Basque country did know and understand what we were doing—which gave us a great deal of popular support."

"The kidnapping of Huarte was a success," Txabi said.

Mikel pointed out, "If there had been more cases like that of Huarte, the factory owners and their boards of directors would genuinely panic, and there would be more concessions to workers' demands within the factories. Everybody knows that after the Huarte case there was a lot of unease among the factory owners, and demands by the workers suddenly were met more promptly. After the Huarte case, many factory owners began to have their own private bodyguards. We also learned from the Huarte case a great deal about the reactions of the workers. They did what they had to do. They kept quiet and accepted what they had won. If they had made any overt demonstration of joy, or support, or solidarity, they would have been lost. All the Government's repressive measures would have fallen on their shoulders . . .

"This is exactly what happened after the execution of the Ogro. Fairly recently, while I was at work, one of the workers said to me, 'How great that was, the execution of Carrero. That's giving it to Franco. What a pity that the people didn't take to the streets . . .' He said all that with the best of intentions, but he was wrong. If the people had expressed themselves during that period, naturally they would have been killed. There would have been bad reprisals. The people did the best they could. They bought cider and privately celebrated in their own homes. Christ, here, in this town the stores ran out of cider. It was the same all over Spain.

"This doesn't mean that the people are marginal to the struggle, but merely that each form of protest needs its own tactics. And in this the people are smarter and know more than is obvious from the surface," Mikel explained.

"Look," Iker said, "the Huarte affair was a victory. The workers got their demands met, the layoffs were rehired—something that rarely happens in Spain. When a Spanish worker is laid off, his only legal recourse is to protest to the official labor board, and there, in the majority of cases, even though the worker might win the case, the factory still has the choice of whether to rehire him, or give him instead a technical pittance. The latter is what generally happens. And it has happened to many of us. But this time, ETA had Huarte over a barrel."

"The Huarte case was also a good example of the innate justice of the people," Txabi pointed out. "They first used every legal method of obtaining their rights. Then the workers tried to strike; then there was a general backing of the strike—but nothing worked. Finally, there was revolutionary action in support of the workers' demands. The capitalists and the Government always use violence against the workers. They use it every day. They have the police and the military at their disposal, and they used them in armed battle. Why should we, therefore, limit our own resources? We have to employ all the revolutionary means at our own disposal to gain our own victories. The only way we have of really giving them a blow is by using these tactics against their own brutality. We hit them where it hurts—which is why we get the roughest treatment.

"Look," Txabi continued, "ETA asked for 50 million pesetas (about $1 million) for the release of Huarte—and we got it, but this was a secondary factor. The most important thing was that we got the support of the workers. About the money—clearly, a group like ETA needs money to carry out our struggle. Where *should* we get it? This is our form of taxation against those multi-interests that exploit the workers. Why shouldn't we have demanded money from Huarte, who is one of the richest men in the 'Spanish state?' It was our form of fine, and it seems to me damn small, considering everything. After the Huarte case was over, it turned out that the idea of fining Huarte $1 million was very popular—then the people lamented, when they realized how rich Huarte was, that we hadn't asked for more!"

Txabi paused. Then he went on to describe the main sequence of events. "Now, right after the Huarte affair, we arrived in Madrid. If we made an exchange—Carrero in exchange for freeing the political prisoners, this would have meant an enormous victory, because of all the political consequences that would have followed. Of course, we couldn't figure everything out. But we saw that it would have forced Carrero to radicalize himself more —in one direction or the other. It would break the equilibrium of the regime, creating an enormous conflict within the regime itself. It always could have happened that the Government itself, in spite of Carrero being the key figure, wouldn't have wanted to show this sign of weakness—even though in reality it wouldn't have been a weakness, and it would not have given in. If that happened, we would have had to execute Carrero." Txabi paused. "For the same reasons that in the end we did execute him, because the execution in itself also had a goal and clear political objectives.

"Beginning in 1951, Carrero was practically the head of the Government within the regime. Carrero symbolized more than anybody the idea of 'pure Francismo.' Without allying himself directly with any of the Franquist groups, he clearly was the chief person who pushed the Opus Dei into power. He was a man without scruples, absolutely determined to build up his own power within the regime.

"He built up a network of informants and confidants within the ministries, within the military, within the Falange, and even within the Opus Dei. His police (the information service of the President of the Government) managed to put themselves within the whole Franquist apparatus. This way, he managed to become the key element of the regime and the prime link in the political maneuverings of the Spanish oligarchy. And, in addition, he managed to make himself indispensable because of his experience and his capacity for political maneuverings. And, no one else had managed, as he had, to maintain the internal equilibrium of the Franquist regime.

"The Spanish oligarchy counted on Carrero to assure the passage of the post-Franco era without any internal convulsions. In my opinion, it was clearly more important, from the point of view of attacking the 'Spanish state' to execute Carrero rather than kidnap him. Therefore, the idea of taking Carrero as a hostage was with the plan in mind of freeing political prisoners, and the second plan had in mind the future political consequences for Spain."

Jon took over. "What happened is that the political objectives and consequences were maybe even more important than an immediate objective. For example, if we obtained the exchange prisoners, and Carrero was freed after that, this would have changed many things in Spain. If the Government had had to accede to a general amnesty, this would have created an enormous crisis, and Carrero wouldn't have had any other solution except either to go in a more right-wing direction or to open himself a little to more liberal ideas. He couldn't have stood still. This would have created a disunity within the regime itself. If the Government would not have acceded to an exchange of prisoners, they would have had another problem."

Txabi interrupted Jon. "We wanted to show the whole opposition that there was a possibility of destroying the regime by armed battle."

"We know that when you kill the head of any system, somebody else is substituted," Iker explained. "But damage has been done. Look what happened to us. Eustakio, one of the heads of

ETA, was killed. This caused tremendous damage within ETA. This was also a change of the Government's repressive tactics toward us. Clearly, they didn't want another Burgos trial—a public trial. They prefer now to eliminate one by one the heads of ETA, and kill them instantly, before taking them prisoners, which would mean a trial. We know for certain that they killed Mikelon, Iharra, and Txikia once they were wounded. They shot them on the spot," Iker paused. "Our idea of Carrero was that the Government has created an image of such invincibility by their repression that any mass action using arms, violence, on the part of the workers would be impossible, and that they have convinced the people that the only way they have of liberating themselves is by cooperation with the system. This is the idea of the Pact of Liberty."

[Communist Party pact involving alliances with middle-of-the-road and conservative groups in the regime. ETA wanted to "radicalize" workers. Communists wanted, as in France and Italy, a piece of the system.]

"We realized," Iker continued, "that some of the other opposition groups might not go along with our manner of freeing their prisoners, but we didn't give it too much importance. When the time came, they could choose. We thought that many prisoners, given the chance to go free, with or without the permission of their political groups, would take it. They'd leave the prisons. An operation like this one doesn't consult with anybody. Once the organization decided to go through with the idea, the organization picked a commando of four persons, and sent them to Madrid to study the possibilities and to see what was necessary for the action."

"The first thing we did," said Txabi, "was to look for a room to rent. We needed a permanent place to live in Madrid as long as necessary without running into any problems. While we were looking for an apartment, we split up into two groups and took temporary rooms in two different pensions. The four of us came to Madrid prepared with false documentation—just like Mikel and Jon on their first trip."

"First we tried to use rental agencies, but we immediately saw that this wasn't going to work out," Iker said. "We made several errors that we'll explain later on. Without experience, it's easy to make mistakes. We soon realized it was better for us not to approach the rental agencies. It was very possible that they were controlled by the police. They might pass on a list of apartments to the police that they rented. We were afraid that our false papers, if investigated, might not hold up. So we decided to rent a place ourselves, directly. There were a lot of apartments free— the question was how we were to go about renting one."

"We couldn't rent as students," Jon said. "We saw in the agencies that they only rented apartments to students for Princesa, Moncloa—the outskirts of the university city—but that zone didn't interest us. That's precisely the area where all the students hang out—the 'Latin quarter' of Madrid. It is filled with police informants, and police are constantly breaking up riots in that neighborhood. Walking down Princesa you get the feeling that the area is glutted with student political conspiracies. There are other neighborhoods where landlords don't want to rent to students. They want white-collar workers or minor members of the bourgeoisie. They are afraid that the students are going to give a lot of parties, or ruin the furnishings, or won't pay their rent. So they prefer white-collar workers. But we couldn't pass ourselves off as workers, because of the type of life we had to lead. Even though we intended to be very discreet—no parties or things of that sort—still, we clearly couldn't be workers because we didn't have a fixed schedule of leaving in the morning and coming home at midday and at night. One day we would go out at 7 in the morning, another day at 11. Another day, two of us would go out at 6 in the afternoon; and later in the evening, we often had to go out to buy things . . ."

Txabi clarified the type of work they planned to do. "Two of us planned to follow Carrero, and two would stay behind in the apartment. Because this sort of schedule would be hard to explain to a landlord, we said that we were workers, but of a professional class: an economist, a technical engineer—things like that—and that only one of us was a student."

"We finally found the apartment by reading an ad in the newspaper," Jon explained. "We went, and we liked what we saw. It was a large apartment, plenty of space, well ventilated—a little far from the center of Madrid, but with good transportation. So we immediately signed a lease with the landlord. We had a lease for one year—one of those leases where you put down a deposit, pay something each month, and have the eventual right to buy the apartment. We would have had our choice, eventually, of continuing to rent the apartment or buying it outright. To have bought it outright was exorbitant, almost 2 million pesetas—about $40,000—for a simple furnished apartment."

Iker said, "Even though few people actually buy the apartments, the only way the landlord could ask such a high monthly rent of 8000 pesetas—$140 a month—was by making the lease with a clause to buy. This is the way landlords get away with asking high rents. Even though it was furnished—which was very important to us—considering that it was in a working-class neighborhood, far from the center of Madrid, it was extremely expensive."

Mikel added, "Madrid landlords are shit—real speculator types. We knew we were easy game. When they see you are young and alone, they charge whatever they can get away with—a high rate of speculation. They ask one month extra as a guarantee; when you give it to them, then they say they need two months. Very avaricious." Mikel paused. "I can't imagine being like that."

"Therefore, our alibi was that we led a student's life—but when the super or anybody asked us, we always replied we were professionals—in the 'liberal' professions, and we made them understand that this was the reason we had such irregular schedules," Txabi recounted. "I was a technical engineer. My work was to install and inspect factory machinery. I didn't have a fixed schedule, because I didn't work in one factory, but was sent from one place to another. One day I finished my work in eight hours; other days, it might work out that I had to spend two days at home. Or, I might suddenly be called away from Madrid to inspect machinery in some factory outside Madrid. At any rate, I described the sort of work that could account for my irregular schedule."

Jon said that he was an economist who worked for the Bank of Bilbao, in Bilbao: "But I had been transferred to Madrid in order to take some specialized courses in market investigation. I was paid my regular salary, but during this time, I was taking courses. Therefore, we invented professions of the sort that are popular these days, which use a series of words that everybody knows exist, and don't appear to be strange—but nobody knows the exact meaning of those words—for example, marketing!"

Iker said he was an industrial designer and worked in government industrial development industries. "A friend of mine in the Industrial Ministry gave me plans to copy, and I copied the plans either in my office, or at home; that is what I told everyone."

"I was the student," Mikel said. "It wasn't very clear what I studied. The important thing was that if anybody asked, I would give them a vague explanation of what I was studying and doing. What I had planned to say is that I was doing my thesis in the field of scientific investigation—but nobody ever asked me what I was doing."

"These were all false answers for the porter and the super, in case they asked something," Txabi said. "We didn't have too much contact with the super, but he was convinced that we were all working hard and had occupations. If they asked anything in the neighborhood stores, we had our alibi prepared."

"The super realized that we weren't working-class types; we were well educated," Jon added. "The neighbors saw that we had several cars among us. They thought we were affluent, and that we had finished our studies . . . that we were young men on the threshold of making our careers in Madrid."

"In the beginning of the second stay in Madrid, we had many difficulties. We were new in Madrid; we felt like outsiders. Everything was so different from what we were used to. We could make a lot of mistakes," Mikel remembered. "Later, we became accustomed to the city. In the end, we even felt sad to have to leave. I want to go back one day. I feel close to Madrid now."

"The biggest difference," said Jon, "between Madrid and Euskadi is that in Euskadi we work with militants of ETA or close sympathizers—with people whose support is unconditional. When there's trouble and we can't stay in our own homes in the Basque country, we can always be taken in by people who themselves are legal residents—we are protected. The Basques help pass on information to us and get us from place to place. They'll transport us in their own cars. In Euskadi we were backed up by tremendous support; in Madrid we had only ourselves. We were alone, isolated."

"When you have nobody backing you, and you are alone in a strange city, it all becomes very difficult and scary," Txabi mused.

"God, I felt the same thing. Being alone, having no Basque support is what hit me the most emotionally. I felt, every day, 'I am in a mousetrap'—if anything happened to us, there was no escape route. We didn't know a soul," said Mikel, echoing their fears.

"As soon as we hit Madrid we tried to acclimatize ourselves to the Madrileño atmosphere," Txabi continued. "We changed our way of dressing. In Euskadi young people our age dress in pants, a shirt, and a sweater thrown over. Our habits, our ways of acting in the Basque country were all very different. We were sure the way we were, people could instantly take us for Basques, that we were recognizable. As soon as we opened our mouths, they could tell we were Basques. When we had to invent explanations for ourselves, our accent was an enormous problem. Our false papers said that we were from Burgos and Palencia, but people instantly said to us, 'Ay—You're from Bilbao.' Spaniards identify Basques with Bilbainos. They think all Basques come from Bilbao, because it's a big city. Our accents constantly gave us enormous problems of this sort."

Mikel agreed with him. "It sure did create problems. We had to say that we had worked in Bilbao, or that when we had been young children we had lived in the province of Vizcaya, because our fathers had gone there to work. All these explanations made our lives much more complicated."

"Another big problem," added Txabi, "was that we didn't know Madrid; we walked the streets completely lost. During the first part of the second stay, we spent a great deal of our time simply learning the city. We always met in the Gran Vía, very frequently in the same café. This was a mistake. It was a neighborhood where one could easily bump into other Basques or the police. One day we bumped into a crowd of Basques—they all knew us! This was dangerous. After that experience, we immediately changed our meeting place. We finally decided not to have any one café or place for our rendezvous.

"We didn't know anybody, really, in Madrid, nor did we want to have any connection with people who lived in Madrid. We wanted to avoid, in case of the kidnapping, any relation with the police. We knew that members of the police could come to the house where we were living. If the police later asked the super or the neighbors questions about us, with the descriptions the neighbors and super could give them, the police would be able to make fairly accurate drawings of our faces. That was one of

the reasons we didn't want to see anybody. We were better off
if we managed to avoid bumping into people—it would be impossible for the police to find us. The police didn't have the
vaguest idea that we were in Madrid . . . nor that we existed;
we were invisible."

Iker agreed. "To this day, the police have no idea who we
really are. For them, we are still incognito—a mystery. Everything the police say about their proof and information is false."

Txabi underlined the point, saying, "The police had no idea of
our existence. For this reason, we were much better off alone—
without anybody's help. We deliberately made no attempt to see
anybody, not even Basques we knew were in Madrid. We were
determined to remain invisible."

"We gave false explanations of our whereabouts—both to our
families and at work. The proof that they were good explanations
is that now we are still here, in the Basque country," Jon explained. "There were several reasons why we didn't want help
from other people in Madrid. First, Basques, or people from other
opposition groups who would have wanted to help us, could have
become frightened once they realized the danger of what we were
planning to do. Second, even though we knew that people in the
Basque country are used to this sort of direct action, and we
knew that when Basques get caught, they act well, we didn't
know how people in Madrid would react in the sort of situation
that involves an armed struggle. They have no experience with
this type of action. And this isn't the sort of operation that can be
an education course."

Iker said, "We thought that after the kidnapping the police
would arrest all the Basque students in Madrid, and round up
other Basques living in Madrid. Clearly, the police were going
to make enormous efforts to locate the Ogro. If we were known
to other Basques in Madrid, the police could easily have tracked
us down."

"If the operation went off without any mistakes, the best
guarantee of our safety was to be totally unknown to the police
and the Madrileños. The police wouldn't know where to look,
or for whom. This gave us a sense of security. We knew that we
were living our lives on an island—isolated—on an island nobody
knew existed," Mikel recalled.

"We knew from the beginning that even though it was much harder, we had to do the whole job ourselves," Iker added. "It was our only chance."

"Our isolation made for many hardships, obstacles . . . sometimes it got comical," said Txabi, his mood changing. "One day, while Jon was walking along the Gran Vía, a guy he didn't know came up to him. He called Jon by his real name and said, 'Ola, qué tal?'—'Hi, how are you?'—So Jon had to reply that he, Jon, wasn't really Jon. And to make it look more legit, Jon showed him his identity papers. The Basque looked a little puzzled, but he finally went away."

Jon broke in, "I didn't recognize the man—actually, I thought he was from the police. I told him I was from Bilbao—but that I wasn't me and that I wasn't from ETA—he had asked me that, too. Imagine! All this took place in a cafeteria filled with people. The man stood talking to me in an extremely loud voice—and, I must admit, even now I haven't the vaguest idea who the hell he was. I didn't recognize his face. I'll bet that since Carrero's execution he's wondered about that meeting—plenty!"

"A lot of people, joking, always told us that we were from ETA —people in the street—a Madrid joke," Mikel added. "In the beginning, we were pulverized, but after a little while, we got used to the Madrid sense of humor. In the Basque country, nobody jokes with you about belonging to ETA."

"In Spain," Txabi said, "as soon as they hear a Basque accent they start to kid you about being from ETA."

"That's right," Jon agreed, "Spaniards assume that all Basques belong to ETA—and above all, Basque students—'Oh, a Basque, well, well, and so how is the ETA?'"

"What drove me wild," Iker went on, "was the way Spaniards pronounced ETA—they don't say 'ETA'—they say 'la ETA.' Everybody in the neighborhood where we lived teased us about *the* ETA. When we went to buy food or go to the laundry— somebody would always say, 'Here they come—the boys from la ETA.'"

"Finally," Jon said, "we handled it like any normal person who wasn't from ETA would have. We giggled and made jokes ourselves. We got along great with the neighbors, and the people in the local stores. Like in the grocery store, the owners wanted to fix up Mikel with the young cashier. We knew that if any armed action took place in Euskadi, our neighbors would have teased us —'Look—they did it, the boys from la ETA.'"

"In the beginning," Iker interrupted, "I was startled, scared. Txabi was the one who always went to the butcher. But one day he wasn't home, so I went. When I walked into the butcher's, the butcher looked up and asked me, deadpan, 'Well, have they already expelled your pal from la ETA?' I was stunned. I thought, Wow, what the hell is going on? We're fucked. Everybody knows the truth here!'"

"At the same time that we were learning to live with the Madrileños—and their crazy wit—and learning the city and trying to adapt ourselves to their crazy hours, their habits, and so forth, we started to make a plan for Carrero's kidnapping," Txabi said. "We had no set deadline for the execution of the plan. After we had made careful preparations and everything was in order, we could pick the day. We were determined to make sure that all our arrangements were foolproof: we wanted to make sure that it was going to work."

"We worked hard. We wanted to do everything as quickly as possible—but we wanted to do a good job. If we couldn't do the job well, we were willing to spend more time in Madrid," Iker said.

"We worked extremely systematically," Jon explained. "We watched the church, the church zone, Carrero's movements, his bodyguards, and the police. We timed Carrero's auto route. We timed the traffic lights, the amount of traffic, and how much this varied from day to day. Everything that was necessary to coordinate the action."

"This took us about a month," added Iker, "because there were some days that we didn't go. We watched the situation almost continuously, because occasionally there were changes that we wanted to take note of."

"In this sort of operation, it isn't necessary to be on the spot all the time," Txabi explained. "Consistency is far more important. Almost every day we spent half an hour, or an hour, at the church. Nearly every day we observed the church from 8 to 10 in the morning. Then we spent the rest of the day on related projects. We were on the lookout for information, specifically on Madrid, that could be valuable later to ETA. While were planning the kidnapping, we kept in mind what would be useful for other operations."

"We would give anything if in Euskadi we had the sort of facilities they have in Madrid. Christ! Madrid is a gold mine. All sorts of things that can't be found in Pamplona, Vitoria, Bilbao, or San Sebastian that would be useful for ETA are obtainable in Madrid. We bought tons of handcuffs in Madrid. In Bilbao this would be impossible. In Madrid this was an easy purchase. We would go into a store and ask, very assertively—very sure of ourselves—for handcuffs. They assumed we were policemen," Mikel commented, bemused.

"We were extremely well dressed—so it made sense that they thought we were policemen. We always had a phony explanation ready, but we never had to use it. The store was near La Puerta del Sol," Iker remembered.

"While one of us went into the store, the rest of the group waited outside, next to the Puerta del Sol subway stop. This is right near the main police headquarters. I was startled, seeing slews of policemen going out of the doors of the main office. Hombre!" exclaimed Jon. "It was very easy to spot the plain-clothesmen. They were always dressed very elegantly, in the latest fashion. Jackets with a very modern cut, flashy ties, and they wore their hair on the long side. I think they thought it was easier for them to infiltrate into political movements dressed that way. What a menagerie, what a zoo! They looked like department store dummies—like the dummies in the display windows of cheap stores."

"We also learned a great deal about the police—their methods, their internal structure, how they went about things. We got some information in a very haphazard manner," Iker explained. "When we rented one of the apartments, we casually met a military man who by accident gave us a real helping hand. He gave us an address where, when we said we were friends of the military man, we were able to get information on the police." Iker paused. "I know this part sounds vague, but we can't tape exactly what happened at that point."

Mikel said, "We got a lot of printing material in order to make propaganda, and, specifically, we got hold of some useful material that could be used to make false identity papers. We also learned new techniques for falsifying papers, and we bought great inks and stamps—marvelous stuff! While we were living in Euskadi we were always over our heads in work. We all led lives of 'militants.' In Madrid, we had a lot of free time, and we used it to learn many new techniques."

"Normally," Iker explained, "none of us carried pistols. But we did have guns, and from time to time we carried them."

"While living in Madrid we decided that this was a strictly personal choice. We had no regulations on the subject," Jon said. "Two of us thought it was better to go armed. The other two thought that it wasn't a good idea. In Euskadi, one of the main reasons most of ETA travels armed is that they can be easily recognized. There are a lot of police controls near the Basque frontier where you have to show your papers. You need to be prepared for quick action. But in Madrid, it's difficult for the police to hunt out members of ETA. In Madrid, the real risk is that we could have gotten caught up in a street demonstration and accidentally picked up by the police. This made it risky to carry guns. This happened to us once—but not during a street demonstration. When President Campora of Argentina was in Madrid, there was one of those quick, spontaneous street gatherings. We were coming out of the subway, not thinking of anything in particular, when, suddenly, we were surrounded by grises and plainclothesmen. We quickly turned around to walk in the other direction, and we found ourselves directly in the path of TV cameras and news cameras that were focused on us. One of the TV cameras got a closeup of us. At first we were startled, but we instantly realized it had nothing to do with us. Still, incidents like that scare you. You could panic and start running. The police could grab you, and if they searched and found guns, it would be serious. That was one of the main reasons we generally went unarmed."

Mikel broke in with the dates. "It actually took us from January to the middle of February to have the plan of action well laid out. By the end of February we also had a good plan of the zone marked out. Jon, you tell about it—you were the one who made the plans. Jon spent his days with pencil and paper, making drawings. Jon, explain it—all about the zone, the church—the whole lot."

CHAPTER THREE

The Area—
The Plan of Action

"Okay, the zone you already know," Jon said, referring to the maps. "Barrio de Salamanca—upper-middle-class neighborhood, embassies, and the church, which has a Jesuits' residence attached. Inside, the church is one unit. You can get to all parts of the church without going outside. Everything interconnects from within. One part is a school, or something like that, because there were always kids around there, and the rest is the church. Christ, that church is like a monstrous slab of concrete, swallowing everything around it. And, sitting on top of all that concrete, an enormous dome. No beauty, that church. The main entrance to the church is on Serrano. There is an iron gate between the church and the sidewalk. Behind the gate, there are four or five huge steps. Then there is a wide landing, which is the place the Ogro used to stop and chat with the old bodyguard. The main door is almost always closed. Then there are two lateral doors, perpendicular to the main door, one on each side of the landing, which are also almost always closed. These doors usually were used as the entrance to the church. It is much clearer on the map. When you go through those side doors, you enter a small, squarish, dark room, about 9 feet by 9 feet. After that, you go through a second door, which has a curtain, to get to the main part of the church. The squarish antechamber acted as a buffer, which made it impossible for the noises of the street to be heard in the church. The church is an unusually cavernous building." He paused. "I remember, it had three naves, one central nave, and two lateral naves. The central one was wide—with two rows of separate pews, separated by a long center aisle. There were no pews in the lateral naves, only confessional boxes along the walls of the church—three or four confessional boxes in a row. That was the darkest, most obscure part of the church. The central nave was separated from the lateral naves by five columns . . . yes, I

FLOOR PLAN OF
SAN FRANCISCO DE BORJA CHURCH

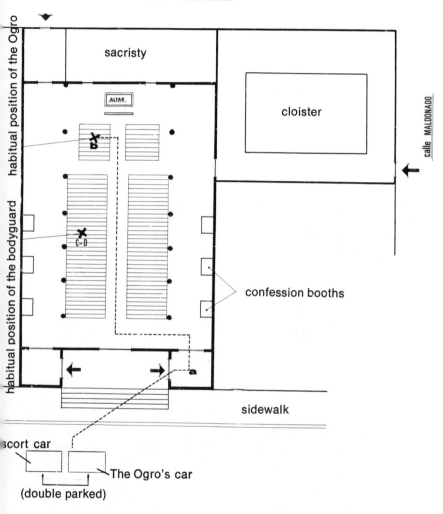

calle CLAUDIO COELLO

habitual position of the Ogro

sacristy

calle MALDONADO

cloister

ALTAR

B

C-D

confession booths

habitual position of the bodyguard

a

sidewalk

scort car

The Ogro's car
(double parked)

Usual route taken by the Orgo

A. Site planned for the eventual kidnapping between the two doors (first plan)

B. Original site for the eventual kidnapping; (entering simultaneously through the four doors, covering them from the inside and overpowering the bodyguard with militants C and D—second plan) believe there were five. The altar was in the center of the far end of the church. There were two doors next to the altar, one on each side between the altar and the sacristy. They were wooden doors which opened up directly into the sacristy. Well, I figured out that at least the left door led into the sacristy, because when I looked up, just the priests walked through that door. Then there was the altar table, and in front of that, the prie-dieu for taking communion. There was also a narrow balcony, about 15 feet high, which girded the entire church, with the exception of the altar. It was quite wide, though, at the point in the back of the church above the main door, which was the place the choir sang. There was also an enormous organ, and we thought that it would be an excellent place for us, with a gun with a silencer, to grab the bodyguard—just in case we had to subdue him. But what we wanted to find was the door for the choir. It was hard, finding that door. I remember that one Sunday there was a wedding in the church, and we mingled with the crowd of people attending the wedding. Iker was with me—he was trying to figure out a way for us to get up to the balcony, where the choir was singing and the organ was being played—but we couldn't find a way. We knew there was a door up there, but it was always shut." Jon paused.

"Later on, we found the door, but we were never able to open it, so we never had access to the balcony, where the choir was. On the right-hand side of the church, toward the front, there was a door that led through the cloister to Maldonado Street. There was a patio in the middle of the cloister, and there was a narrow terrace above, enclosing the cloister." Jon exclaimed, "Christ! Who would have thought, then, that this was where the car was going to land! Hombre!" Then he went on, "To get from the church door, through the cloister, and out onto the street— Maldonado—one had to pass through a long corridor. Before getting to the street door, there was a sort of office, for the super —but we noticed that nobody asked us any questions when we tried walking out of the church that way. Then there was another door that we discovered, which in the beginning we hadn't noticed—the door on the left of the altar, almost in the corner, which was hardly visible from the pews. This almost invisible door was the exit nearest to the Ogro. The Ogro always stood in the rows of pews on the left of the church. This door was so near to where the Ogro stood, we thought at that time we would use it to remove the Ogro from the church."

"We felt great the day we found that door!" Mikel remembered. "A few days after arriving in Madrid for the second time, Jon and I were walking on Claudio Coello, circling around the entire church. We suddenly saw that door—fuck! Where did that door go? I went inside. I went down several marble stairs to a small landing, where I saw a bulletin board on the wall with the schedule of the masses and a lot of other nonsense scribbled on it —and a wooden door. The stairway probably continued on down past the wooden door to a basement. I opened the wooden door, and Christ! Fuck! I found myself right inside the church! Right next to the pews, right next to the Ogro's pew! I swore to myself —what a holy communion! *La hostia!* Then I ran back out onto the street. I told Jon what I had discovered, and we spent the whole day talking about it. *That* was our door by which we had to kidnap the Ogro!"

Jon interrupted, "Okay, so those were the doors. Now we knew we had good exits to two different streets. Now, for the location of the pews, which was very important later for the actual moment we had planned the action. All the pews were located in the central nave. The rows of the pews occupied the whole central part of the nave. There was a central aisle running down the middle. There was very little space on either side of the pews, because the pews were placed right up next to the church columns. Christ, those columns were ugly—massive blocks of concrete—terrible taste! The rows of pews ended just past the middle of the church, near the place where the door to the cloister was, which was also just about where the line of columns ended. There was an aisle about 5 feet wide separating it from the block of pews near the altar. The pews near the altar were much narrower; there was also more space on either side of the pews, because there were no columns in the block of pews near the altar. Therefore, there was a very easy access from either side of those pews. You can see by the map the route the Ogro always used to get to the second pew which, as nobody sat in the first row, in reality was the third—and also the exits we had in mind for the kidnapping. But the first block of pews was smaller, much more together, much nearer the altar—this was the place most of the people normally sat."

Mikel broke in, saying, "It is also important to mention something about the streets. Serrano has heavy traffic and is a one-way street in the direction of Puerta de Alcalá—there are a lot of police watching Serrano, precisely because the American Embassy is also on Serrano, just across from the church. There are three grises at the front gate of the American Embassy—this is in addition to whoever is inside, which we didn't even know about. We didn't know what the Americans had inside their embassy— maybe even machines? And a little farther down—the British Embassy, also with three grises at the front entrance. Then there is the Calle de Maldonado, which is one-way in the direction of Serrano. On the right-hand sidewalk of Maldonado, by the church, there is only that one doorway leading to the Jesuits' cloister. And on the other sidewalk there is a garage—and a private property with an iron gate in front of it. Right there, cars were always parked in a crowded hodgepodge. No easy space. The other street was Claudio Coello. One way, in the direction of Diego de León. On the right-hand side there were a lot of houses. Some of them were very old. And on the left-hand side was the Jesuits' building, with two doors. One door was the getaway door we mentioned before. The other door was near the corner of Maldonado, and we thought that it led to a warehouse of the Jesuits—we saw them unloading packages there."

"There was nearly always an ambulance—do you remember that?" Jon asked. "The ambulance puzzled us because it was always parked in the same place on the street. It wasn't a very modern ambulance—a sort of antiquated truck, of the kind you practically never see nowadays, and we never learned what the ambulance was for."

"On Claudio Coello you can park on either side, and it is important to point out that this zone is very difficult for parking. There is an enormous concentration of vehicles in this area, and a lot of cars are double-parked. Nobody pays attention to the double-parking. There are a lot of people in cars who circle the area. I always felt like they were looking at me, but actually they were waiting for people to move their cars and leave a free space so that they could park their own cars."

"Yes—what Mikel just said is important," Iker broke in, "It happened to me several times, particularly at the end of our stay in Madrid. When one of us would go inside to mass, and the other one would wait outside in the car, the one in the car always got edgy. There were so many people in cars in that neighborhood trying to park, and staring at the parked car, that even if you knew all they wanted to do was to park their own cars— well, it scared you. Suppose one of them was from the secret police? Actually, when the 'operation' took place, that *is* what happened—we did have a scare."

"Diego de León was the other street we still had to check on," Jon said. "This is a two-way street—the cars go toward Velásquez one way, and in the other direction they go down toward the Castellana, crossing Serrano. This was the street that the Ogro used to take to get to his house on Hermanos Bécquer. Well, there were also grises stationed in front of a bank, and a little farther down there were three or four grises who used to congregate in front of the houses next to the Ogro's—these houses belonged to the diplomatic corps. Oh, and I forgot that on Serrano, a little farther up, there was a newspaper kiosk."

"That's right—the kiosk!" Mikel interrupted. "I nearly blew it in that kiosk. ETA was still holding Huarte hostage. It was Txabi's and my turn to watch the church. We wanted to buy *El Diario Vasco*—a Basque newspaper—to see if there were any pictures of the kidnappers and to get the latest news on the case. I was the one staying outside the church, in charge of watching the Ogro. I didn't want to let him out of my sight, and I was a little absentminded, so, without thinking or looking at what the kiosk was selling, I asked for *El Diario Vasco* and *La Gaceta del Norte*—two Basque newspapers—and when they told me that the kiosk didn't carry local, provincial Basque newspapers, I quickly realized what a dumb thing I had done. I was stunned, scared, and didn't know what to do. Even though the news vendor didn't notice anything, I felt—Christ! Now they know everything! In our case, it was a terrible error, because it was very important for us not to call attention to *anything* Basque. We had to be above suspicion. If they were going to see us hanging around that neighborhood frequently, it could have been serious. The news vendor could have said something to Carrero's chauffeur, or to the civil police, because all those guys surely knew each other."

"Often we were afraid that Carrero might turn out to have more bodyguards—one or two more. All we ever saw for sure were the two men who took turns, the old man and the man with the briefcase," Iker said.

Txabi added, "The bodyguard always kept his eyes on the Ogro; he never paid attention to himself. He always kept his arms folded behind him; it would have been easy to handcuff him and knock him out. We realized that he always looked a little absent-minded, like he was sure of the situation. The only thing he did do was occasionally to watch if someone young went into the church—but he never paid any attention to himself, or what could be going on around *him*."

Mikel changed the subject slightly. "We prepared the action among the four of us. We kept verifying data. We got new data, elaborated on it, making plans as to what we would do later on."

Iker said, "We knew it was a complicated action, which needed several commandos. The four of us could make the preparations. But then several more commandos would be needed to collaborate with us. With this in mind, we knew that we needed to have several apartments ready for them when they arrived—high-rent apartments in which they could live, just as we did, as anonymously as possible."

"Yes—because this involved taking a church—a church with forty or fifty people inside—in order to take one man hostage." Jon paused. "We didn't want a bloodbath, butchery—we were determined that this action was going to be *clean*—with no victims—and if we could do it without firing a gun, even better. We were going to need people who could manage the people in the church and manage the police, and who could manage the Ogro and take him with them. We calculated that we needed eight people inside the church. Besides others outside in the cars—and others who could act as a coverup. This meant we were going to need in Madrid at least eight more militants—and we had to find places to house them."

"We had to rent several apartments," Mikel explained. "It wouldn't have been a good idea to have eight people living together in one apartment. The best would be to rent apartments for four apiece. In this phase we were still thinking of a total of twelve commandos being involved, which would have meant three apartments in all—the one we already had and two more that we were going to need. We wanted to rent them as quickly as possible because in this way we would arouse fewer suspicions. The problem wasn't one of suddenly coming to Madrid, renting a place quickly, and going into action. For this sort of operation, the longer time one had the apartments rented before the action, the better. A long rental would be less suspicious."

"This was when we decided to rent two more apartments," Txabi added. "We wanted apartments with the same advantages as the one we lived in—furnished; good, high rent; as comfortable as possible. The only difference is that we rented these two in the center of Madrid. We wanted downtown Madrid for several reasons. First, because the militants who were going to join us would be spending very little time in Madrid; they would be coming in at the end, and would have less time to learn the city. They'd need to learn the city quickly, to be able to find each other easily, and to move around without risking getting lost," Txabi explained. "For this type of work we needed apartments that were centrally located. Easy access at all times, in case anything suddenly happened. Besides, in the center of Madrid it is easier to appear anonymous. Also, because apartments in the center of the city are more expensive, the high rent implies that the people who live there are middle class, respectable, and above suspicion."

Jon began to muse again. "I remember that I rented one of the apartments of a high army official, grandson of a titled aristocrat, a general of the 'Spanish state.' Years ago he was also one of the chief officials of the regime. I remember that I got along very well with him and that at the end he behaved extremely well with us. When I left the apartment he returned the deposit to me. We have no complaints to make about him. We became friendly with him, and on the last day I lived there he gave me a cigar. I asked him about the political line of the Spanish army, and he told me that there were three generals that were called 'blue' generals— they were Iniesta Cano, Garcia Rebull, and another one that I don't remember now. And then, on the other hand, there was Diez Alegria, and the majority of the young officers, and also some generals who were of another 'tendency'—'apolitical,' he said. Professional soldiers. They defended whatever government happened to be in power."

Mikel laughed. "Yes, *apolitical*—defending *whatever* government happens to be in power. Bullshit! Like in Chile!"

"That's what he *said*," Jon insisted. "And that they were ready to obey any regime—because they were at the service of the Government. But that they were inclined a little more toward supporting a republic. Indeed, he intimated that one could say that they were pro-republicans. Well, he *said* that. He also told me that he was a champion marksman, had won many prizes, and was a champion fencer. In karate, he had got up to the black belt —which is the top in karate. He knew judo, too—Christ!—Who knows how many trophies he had!

"When I rented the apartment, I told him that I was working for the Bank of Bilbao. I said we were all in market research. That at present I was working for the Bank of Bilbao—but that we all worked on a freelance basis, by contract. I remember that when I signed the lease, he took me to a room in his house where he had machine guns, two precision pistols, a big musket, an old short musket, and an ancient harquebus—I think it was an harquebus. He was completely surrounded by arms!"

"In brief, a *slightly* violent man—a *little* on the violent side, right, Jon?" asked Txabi ironically.

"But he was *simpático*," Jon insisted. "He was a great conversationalist. I only saw him a few more times. We paid for the apartment through the bank."

"The other apartment was also good—a first-rate location," Txabi added. "It was the most expensive of all. I rented it myself. We pretended to be a group of sociologists and economists who were going to come up to work for the City Hall in Madrid—to do research for them. We said we normally traveled a great deal throughout Spain. I told the landlord that some of our group was in Valencia, but that they soon would be arriving in Madrid."

"Though the four of us did the renting, we always made it clear that others were to join us," Iker emphasized. "So, one day one of us would use the two new apartments. Another day, another one of us. We took turns. I think I am being clear . . . somebody always occupied the three apartments . . . we rotated and took turns. In one apartment we were sociologists, and Txabi was the one who signed the lease. In another one, we were bank economists, and Jon was the one they knew."

"Our work gave us a good alibi for not being continuously in residence—with the exception of the first apartment, which was where we really lived—what we did later was to stay two days in the second apartment, three days in the third—and then be away on business for, say, fifteen days," Txabi elaborated.

"We had to do it this way—all the apartments were very expensive, and it would have looked odd if we were willing to pay such high rent to maintain empty apartments. This was the main reason we went through the *commedia del arte*," Mikel said.

Jon added, "We had to do a real number. Our theatrics weren't so essential in the beginning, but they were going to be needed for the end, to really carry out our plan of action. Mikel had a wig that made him look like a playboy. It completely altered his face—Ooof! It was an awful bother—always having to calculate how we were going to appear and as 'who' in each different apartment—I don't even want to remember that part of it," said Jon, the one who always seemed to remember the bad smells, the filth, the troubles.

"Sometimes we left one apartment and spent some time in one of the other apartments for the express purpose of having the super see us. Generally we would ask him to do some small favor for us—a pretext, so that he would be sure to see us," Txabi continued, with his usual calm. "We didn't really have any enormous problems with the janitor. But there was one who had the keys to one of the apartments, and who was very fussy. He seemed to want to stick his nose into everything. We didn't ask him for his extra set of keys; we didn't want to arouse suspicion. Since there was nothing in the house that could compromise us, we didn't bother with him. But a couple of times, when we slept in that apartment, we heard the door open. We'd get out of bed, in our underwear, and suddenly we'd see the super peeking around our door! He'd say, 'Oh, I'm sorry, I thought there was nobody here.' But we didn't run into any real big problems."

"Look," said Jon, getting back to his own special nitty gritty, "we also tipped the super very well—that hurt me, I must admit, in my gut. That really hurt."

"We never overdid our relations with the supers—precisely to avoid questions. Just what was strictly necessary in order not to alienate them and look totally unfriendly—but no undue familiarity with them." Txabi stuck to the facts, leaving the emotions to Jon.

Then Iker interrupted. "There *was* a tense moment, once, between that particular janitor and us. This was when we forgot to tip him for one month. Then we were in the doghouse. The guy gave us a look—like drop dead. Then, just before the end, a little before the 'action,' he came up to wish us a Merry Christmas. We gave him 40 duros [about $4] and he melted like butter."

"That one struck us like a bit of an informer," said Jon again. "I remember how one day he saw me coming in at 10 at night. I hadn't realized he was standing there. I went in and pressed the elevator button. While I was waiting in the dark I suddenly turned around and looked in the direction of the hallway. Everything was black, except for a tiny red light. That was the super, who was inside his janitor's cubicle, smoking a cigarette, observing everything I was doing. For a moment, I thought he was watching me but I later forgot about it." [In Spain, supers and *serenos* (men who have the keys to all the buildings on each street) are a major problem for the opposition. *Serenos* usually are retired policemen. They play a significant role in helping the Spanish police check on the movements of the population at large.]

"I think he was an ex-policeman—he didn't look on the level to me," Iker said.

"This was a very odd apartment house—there was a strange assortment of people living there. A marquise upstairs, a count downstairs—all of them types from the regime. With well-known last names. People very well situated economically," Txabi went on.

"Do you remember the marquise the day the gun went off?" asked Iker. "Jon, by mistake, nearly polished off the marquise! His gun went off accidentally. *He* was the one of us who always kept telling the group we had to be extra careful, we couldn't treat guns as toys—and then it was *Jon's* gun that went off!"

"That was a very funny bit—but we can go into that later," said Jon quickly. "Otherwise, we are going to mess up the narration." He paused briefly, then continued. "We have now described the apartments, the apartments that were intended to shelter all the militants involved at the time of the action. We intended, once the action was carried out, to abandon the apartments. We always thought of the possibility that the apartments could be discovered later. That's why we tried to leave only clues that were convenient for us to leave. We wanted at least one of our phony clues to be picked up by the police. Now for the most important part of the operation—the planning for what was going to happen immediately after 'the action' was of paramount importance and was going to take a lot of planning and security. We had to take extreme security measures. It would have been fatal to commit any errors."

"By now," said Mikel, "I think we've made it clear how we were feeling our way step by step, according to our needs as they arose. But now it would be better if we tell how we had originally planned 'the action.' Txabi, you were the one in charge, so why don't you tell about it?" Mikel stopped. He wanted Txabi to talk. Txabi was the leader.

CHAPTER FOUR

The Projected Kidnapping
The Crisis of the Plan

Txabi began, "In the beginning, when we studied the problem, we realized that there were three possibilities. The first was to take the Ogro when he left his house—at the moment when he went down Hermanos Bécquer, then would turn right toward a small street that leads to Serrano, just before going toward the church. We originally had planned to kidnap him on this street. In the 'Marseillaise' fashion—taking him in a sandwich between two cars going in opposite directions. One crossing his car in front, and the second car crossing his car in back, in such a way as to stall his car right in the middle. But we were afraid that if the Ogro's car was bullet-proof, and if the bodyguard was armed —and we were sure he was, and was no ordinary policeman, but a trained bodyguard capable of putting up a good fight, one who wouldn't allow himself to be defeated easily—this would mean a direct confrontation. With little chance of success for us. In effect, the chauffeur, with the help of quick reflexes on the part of the bodyguard, could then smash the Ogro's car into one of our cars, rendering ours useless. If our car was smashed, a getaway would be impossible for us. The street was narrow, without any room to maneuver about, and cars were parked on both sides. In addition, there were several boutiques on the street that always had delivery trucks parked in front. So we quickly discarded that plan of action. But we already had another plan in mind. When the car reached the church, usually the bodyguard got out on the right side, because he always sat next to the chauffeur. Then Carrero, who would exit by the left door, would go up the stairs followed by the bodyguard—who was always at a distance of 12 or 14 feet, a prudent distance. Obviously he wanted to avoid personal contact with Carrero, and remain at just the right distance from him for security reasons. Carrero would go up the stairs and would walk over to the right lateral door of the church

—he always entered the church by that door. He would push open the door and would walk through the small dark room that Jon described earlier, the square antechamber. What we had in mind, although we didn't make too much of a plan, was to kidnap Carrero in the small antechamber, before he could reach the door that opened into the main part of the church. But we also saw the problems.

"It would have had to be done with split-second timing in order not to allow the bodyguard time to reach Carrero (I've already mentioned that we considered him to be an extremely well-prepared and able man). Because it was at the beginning of the mass (it always appeared that the bodyguard was more alert at the beginning of the mass than after it got going), the bodyguard could have responded with quicker reflexes than we could manage. There would be a second possibility of a direct confrontation. We could have ended up having to shoot, and because the chauffeur wouldn't yet have relaxed his attention by doing what he would do later—reading the newspaper, talking with others—he also could quickly give an alert. We thought that if the action took place ten minutes later, with everybody a little off guard, there would be more chance of success. We then completely discarded this second possibility. Finally, the third possibility was to interrupt the mass. To kidnap Carrero and get out. How did we conceive of this taking place? At the beginning, the bodyguard always remained in the rear, toward the middle of the church and on the left. Our idea was the following: Two militants, dressed as priests, should start showing up at the church, as if they were walking in from the street. They should do this for a week, making themselves very visible, constantly frequenting the church. They should place themselves near the bodyguards, up until the point that their presence in the church would appear to be a normal custom, so that nobody would consider them to be suspicious.

"It's logical for priests to go to mass every day that way. The two 'priests' would come in at the same time that the Ogro and the bodyguard walked in; on *that* day, the priests would stand directly behind the bodyguard. One of them would carry a club and the other one a gun—and both of them would be in charge of neutralizing the police. Another two would come in behind them to protect and cover the doors and other places of access.

They would carry a machine gun. Their assignment would be to prevent people from leaving the church and to prevent people who were entering the church from exiting. We thought that the action would last two minutes—during that time, we wanted to prevent any movement within the church. The two people who were guarding the lateral doors would enter the church and place themselves well—in such a way that the bodyguard wouldn't suspect that anything unusual was going on. As long as the bodyguard could see nobody coming near the Ogro, he didn't worry. It was normal for people to stand around, waiting for their turn in the confessional booths. We would have two more men discreetly waiting in the background to guard the doors—then, at the same moment, one 'priest' would neutralize Carrero's bodyguard. We decided that the best time was ten minutes after 9."

Txabi gave the details—coolly, explicitly: "We still had two more commandos who were going to be part of this action. One was going to come in by Maldonado Street and the other by Claudio Coello. Their watches would be synchronized, and all of them would come into the church at precisely the same moment. The commando of Maldonado Street consisted of one militant with a machine gun who was going to guard those doors for obvious reasons—not to let anybody leave, and to detain those people coming into the church. Then, three other militants would enter the church—running—they'd cross the aisle between the pews—and grab the Ogro. Two of them would overpower him— they would carry only one pistol each—meaning they'd have one hand free and could act quickly in case they met with resistance from Carrero. The third man, carrying a machine gun, would have the job of *intimidating* the people around Carrero, controlling them. This would also permit the commando in charge of overpowering the Ogro total freedom of action.

"At the same time, another commando would come in from Claudio Coello Street. Everything was perfectly calculated so that the two commandos would appear at exactly the same moment in the church. The Maldonado Street commando would have to make a small detour before reaching the church. This commando had to go through the cloister, while the commando from Claudio Coello Street had to go down a flight of stairs before reaching their door of the church. The Claudio Coello commando consisted of two militants—one with a machine gun, who would remain at the door, on guard, watching—not letting any people leave the church and allowing no movement within the church— and a second militant armed with a pistol. He would run toward the Ogro to be on the spot at exactly the same moment as the militants who were in charge of grabbing him.

"All this would be happening simultaneously. In brief, there would be four people covering all the exits and another two in charge of overpowering the bodyguard (this might easily have involved killing him, even though we only intended to give him a blow on the head to knock him unconscious; this might not have worked, and we might have had to shoot him). The two militants in charge of overpowering the bodyguard would then go back and join the others who were guarding the back doors. These were the main church doors near Serrano, so the chauffeur or another policeman might arrive at any moment from that direction. But we thought it would be difficult for anybody on the outside of the church to hear what was going on inside. For one thing, it's an extremely high building, and sounds inside the church tend to disappear, to go up into the dome. Also, the thickness of the walls and the tapestries would deaden any sound inside. The noise of street traffic was also going to be of help. So, in effect, there were six people in charge of kidnapping the Ogro —a total of ten militants for the action planned inside the church.

"Outside, we had planned to have three cars waiting. One large car, with room for six, would be ready, with the engine running. This was the car that the commando in charge of kidnapping the Ogro planned to use. Four men, the Ogro, and the driver—a total of six. This was the getaway car, with the Ogro. Another car, parked directly behind the getaway car, also in Claudio Coello, also with the engine running was for the men guarding the church door. We thought that nobody in the church would try to leave by the Claudio Coello door, and the militants could get out that way. The second car would follow directly behind the first. Its mission was to keep the first car covered for as long as possible. Inside that car would be the driver, one of us, with a machine gun ready in case of trouble."

Iker broke into Txabi's meticulous explanation: "So, in case anybody pursued us, our second car would cover the getaway car. And, if worse came to worst, it could crisscross and impede any car following us from passing. At *any* price, we had to guarantee the escape of the car containing the Ogro."

Txabi went on, "Finally, there was a third car. This car would remain parked on Maldonado Street."

"No," Iker said, "the third car was going to stay on the corner of Claudio Coello, because Maldonado was one way, going in the opposite direction, and since we had to go toward Diego de León, we decided to park it just behind the ambulance."

"No," disagreed Txabi. "As I remember it, we even considered letting this particular commando get away through Serrano."

"*No*," Iker insisted. "We talked about parking that car on Maldonado. And going backwards—in reverse—but then we thought that another car could interfere with this, and we decided to leave the car on Claudio Coello."

"Okay, then—on Claudio Coello," Txabi conceded. "So," he continued, "the third car was to remain on Claudio Coello, and the five remaining people were to get into the car there. The 'priests' were the last ones. They would be the last group—they were to stay behind and cover the getaway of the others—the 'priests' would be the last ones to leave the church. They'd have to lock the doors behind them and scatter small suitcases near the doorway—as a signal to the people in the church that the suitcases could explode with bombs if they went near them. This was a point we had not yet fully analyzed. But something would be necessary to prevent people from being able to react. This would give us enough time—say, a minute—to help us make our getaway . . ." Txabi paused a moment, then continued. "We calculated that the entire operation was going to last around 2 minutes. We knew that the operation had to be quick, sudden, abrupt—to prevent people from being able to respond in a coherent fashion. This was the time schedule for the capture of the Ogro. Then we needed one more minute to start the getaway. Everything had to be done with split-second timing."

"We thought a lot about people's responses," Iker explained, "but we didn't expect them to react in a very coherent way, really. We figured the surprise factor would play a major role in keeping them confused. From our experience—from other things we have done—people's reactions tend to be passive. At most, they become hysterical. Then, it's enough to give them a slap across the face to calm them down. But, generally, they don't even move. I don't know whether it's the instinct of self-preservation, but in general the tendency is for people to be passive at a time like that."

"In the beginning, we thought it would have been very easy for the whole thing to take place without any shots being fired," Jon said. "We wanted very much for it to be a *clean* 'action.' We thought nobody outside the church would realize what was going on inside. That while all this was going on inside, the policeman outside, even the chauffeur, would remain calm."

"Look here," said Iker, who was now beginning to talk more about Operation Ogro, "if the people outside had known what was going on inside the church, it would have made the action very complicated. The problem of escaping would have been entirely different. Given the area we were operating in, this would have meant a direct confrontation with maybe a dozen grises and the secret police, too. Plus scores more who would arrive on the spot immediately!"

"The first car that was going to leave was the one carrying the Ogro," said Jon, summing up the plan, "and the one immediately behind it was to be the car used to cover the getaway car. Five people were going to be in the third car—the driver and four other militants, who would drive to the place where they would remain hidden. These five men would go directly to their shelter."

"What we planned," Txabi explained calmly, "was to have the Ogro's car go to a predetermined place—and there we would change cars, abandoning the original getaway car. The car acting as a cover would wait to see that the change of cars was accomplished—and would then go its own way. The militants in the cover car weren't to be informed as to where we intended to hide the Ogro. This we planned just in case they got caught and weren't able to escape.

"We planned to take the Ogro to the shelter—'prison,' 'cage,' 'refuge'—we called the 'place' by many names . . ."

"These refuges weren't the same apartments we had been living in," Jon explained. "We planned to abandon our apartments at the start of the 'action.' We intended to go to different apartments, also rented, but much safer. We expected the police to mount a huge dragnet, very strong, to find the Ogro. For example, they'd set up roadblocks throughout the city. There'd be a large-scale military hunt. We needed places that were invulnerable to even a perfect manhunt on the part of the police and the military. We needed places of people who were *completely* above suspicion—people connected either to the regime or to the military . . ."

"We don't want to detail this," Txabi interrupted, "because it could be used against us—but I can say that they *were* places of maximum security. I'll admit that we were imaginative and used good psychology in our choice."

"This was a completely thought-out project," added Mikel, who had been sitting quietly, "lacking only in one thing—and that's why we didn't go ahead with the plan. We didn't have support, we didn't know Madrid well enough, and we had a small accident . . . we had to change apartments . . . and we didn't have time to find another apartment. The accident . . . occurred one week before the intended action . . ." Mikel's voice suddenly began to sound vague.

"We even had an apartment we were going to use as a hospital! It was fitted out like an emergency room. It was a normal apartment, with beds—and with the sorts of things that were vital to have in case of an emergency—for quick first-aid treatment or for giving a blood transfusion. We also had on call a medical doctor —one of our militants. This doctor didn't know anything about Operation Ogro. He only knew that we were going to call him for an action outside of the Basque country. His mission was to go to Madrid, wait in the emergency unit—and then to go back to the Basque country," added Iker, who was always good at filling in the James Bond–like details of the operation.

Then Txabi continued, speaking firmly, "We planned to give the Government forty-eight hours. There was a lot of discussion on this point. Some of the militants wanted to give them seventy-two hours, but the ETA leadership decided on forty-eight—with no extensions. During this period, the Government had to free all the political prisoners we wanted them to free. As to where they were going to send the freed prisoners—this was going to be the Government's problem. But I *can* say that there was, at the very minimum, at least one country with whom ETA talked that was willing to accept the prisoners. Okay. Now—let's get on with it! There were two possibilities. Either the Government would free the prisoners, or they wouldn't accept our offer.

"Let's talk about the first possibility. This was the best solution, because there wasn't much vigilance on the part of the police that would prevent us from freeing the Ogro. We planned to use the same car to free the Ogro as the one finally used to take him to the refuge. This car model would have been impossible to track down—there are just too many of them in Madrid. So let's talk about the second possibility. We would kill Carrero and leave the body abandoned—in the same car. In order to free Carrero, we wanted two conditions met. One, free the political prisoners we had chosen to be freed. Two, make public our own communication from ETA explaining to the general public our reasons for taking the action. We would demand that this communication from us be dispersed throughout the entire Spanish state by the official Spanish Government, using all the means at their disposal. The text of this communication was later to become a part of the manifesto that ETA published in August."

"The object of this communication," Jon explained," was to get through to the general population—to break through the Spanish censorship—nothing political *ever* appears in our newspapers! We wanted to make clear what the Basque struggle for freedom is about, and what ETA is struggling for. This is especially important for the provinces of the Spanish state outside of Euskadi. The Spanish state's propaganda gives the impression that ETA is not interested in what goes on in the Spanish state outside of Euskadi. Our communiqué to the people was to tell the *truth*."

Now Txabi broke in, saying, "But to get on with describing what happened—in either of the two outcomes, freeing Carrero or killing him, we planned to abandon our refuge. The refuge was planned for maximum security. But the maximum security would work only if we were to use the refuge for a very short time—at the most, three days. We know this may be difficult to comprehend, but we *cannot* give you more precise details. It was an excellent refuge—and I can only say that it required, most of all, a great deal of imagination in the planning of it." Txabi paused. "After we were done—with the Ogro, dead or alive—we planned to go to a third apartment, in order to wait for the right moment for us to leave Madrid and go back to Euskadi."

"Once the action was done, and when we were all in our different refuges, we had arranged a good communications system," said Jon. "In order to coordinate the different refuges, a militant of ETA was going to come to Madrid. This militant would have a perfect alibi for being in a hotel in Madrid—he had the sort of work and social relations that would make his stay in Madrid normal."

"Naturally," interrupted Txabi, "this militant wouldn't know where any of the refuges were. We would have set up other points of communication with him. Actually, his real role was in getting us back to the Basque country—he was in charge of getting all the militants back home again. In the third phase of this operation, between the Basque country and Madrid, we had two more apartments ready. It was important, once we were back in Euskadi, that each one of us could give a good reason for being absent from Euskadi. Two of these apartments would be necessary for supporting the alibi."

"What finally happened," Mikel said, "was that in the end we were not able to go ahead with the plan for the kidnapping. Because of that, the militant in charge of getting us back to Euskadi never found out what he was supposed to do. And the extra members of ETA who were supposed to come to Madrid never did find out about the 'action.'"

"The way we do things in ETA," Jon said, "is that when ETA decides on a plan of action, the commando in charge knows what it is about, and only in very rare cases are other militants informed of what is going on. In our action, finally, no other group was informed. They knew something was up—that something important was going to happen in Madrid—but they didn't know what. Naturally, after the execution of Carrero, they realized what had happened." Jon paused, then went on. "After Carrero's execution, some of the Madrid newspapers reported that some people knew in advance about the execution and the kidnapping plan . . ."

Txabi broke in quickly, saying, "The members of ETA who were supposed to go to Madrid *didn't* know anything—in fact, it was only at the very end, just before the action, that they were told to be prepared for an action. What happened is that *during* the action it turned out that there were some other members of ETA in Madrid. This coincided with the arrests of some members of ETA in Euskadi who were forced to tell the police about an ETA meeting in Madrid—this probably gave the impression that those ETA members were connected to our operation—but actually, they didn't know anything about it. It was precisely our total isolation from the rest of the world that made our operation successful."

"Only the four of us designed our operation," said Iker, backing up Txabi. "It was an enormous effort—an effort that, at least as far as kidnapping Carrero was concerned, in the end didn't work out."

"Well," mused Mikel, "after all—it was good experience for us. I *never* worked like I did that summer—it was a bitch! We gained tremendous experience. That's always useful . . . if it hadn't been for that accident . . . the one I mentioned before . . . it might have worked . . ."

"We had everything ready!" said Jon, ". . . the hospital, the apartment, the apartment where the commando was to go after the church getaway, the apartment for hiding the Ogro, the two provisional apartments, the cars . . . in short, everything, except the refuge for us, for later on. We had a plan in mind for that refuge too, but the accident interfered . . ."

Txabi broke in now, saying, "We had the apartment—the refuge—already rented. One night the apartment was robbed by gypsies. The *sereno* interrupted the burglary. He fired some shots into the air, and the whole neighborhood was awakened. The owner of the apartment was informed of the burglary. She spoke to the police before we saw her the next morning—we had been in another apartment the night before. When we came to the house, the owner informed us that the police had told her that we, as lessees, had to file a complaint with the police. It turned into a very risky situation for us. The fact that guns had been fired, between the *serenos* and the gypsies, just a few days before the action, and in that area—something that rarely happens in Madrid—could have made it very dangerous for us to be there after the action. The police could have made some odd tie-up between the two events and reinvestigated the apartment. So, immediately after that happened, we decided to dump that apartment," Txabi concluded.

"Also," said Jon, "the next day the owner came into the apartment with her brother. The brother said to Mikel, 'Oh! What a coincidence! You're Basque! I have a brother living in San Sebastian!' Our eternal problem," sighed Jon, ". . . he recognized our Basque accents."

"So *I* said," added Mikel, " 'No, I'm not Basque—I'm a Valenciano.' "

"That was one more thing that made us nervous, and it made us sure that we'd have to leave that apartment," explained Jon.

"That was during the most critical period of all," Mikel continued. "It was a crazy situation—about those vagrant gypsies—but, for us, it was decisive. That burglary complicated everything. At first, we thought we'd just have to postpone the action for one or two more weeks, until we had a new refuge. That was at the end of May. We had planned to go into operation the first few weeks in June. But—that was when Carrero was named President of the Government! After that, we had to figure out if this would mean changes in his daily routine. Suddenly, Carrero started traveling to different sections in Spain, and we rarely saw him at mass. It was getting close to the eighteenth of July . . . that was our deadline for this plan. After the eighteenth, the Government goes into recess until the end of August. We kept on looking for a new refuge; finally, we found a place. But by that time, Carrero had gone away on vacation! For maximum security, this new refuge would have to be used and abandoned in a very short space of time—no more than a few days. Anything else would have made it too risky. With Carrero gone, it was of no use to us."

"Our plan had snafued," said Jon.

"We stayed in Madrid another month and a half—through the middle of July," said Mikel, taking up the narration, "but whenever we could, we escaped Madrid for the weekends. That summer in Madrid, without a breeze, dry, under the boiling Madrid sun—it felt like we were in the desert, or walking through an inferno. I don't know how they can take those temperatures there —well over 100°, the sun beating down. Whenever we didn't have too much work, we fled the Madrid oven. At that time, Iker and I were alone; one of us had to be in Madrid. So we flipped a coin to see who would have to stay in Madrid. I lost. I got Madrid! One day, walking through the center of the city, I went into a bar—the radio was blaring, and I heard that Luis Carrero Blanco had been nominated President of the Government! Fuck it! I wasn't sure at first if I had heard the news right. Nobody in the café stirred or made any comment. I bought the evening newspapers. There it was, the news about Carrero being President.

"I called Iker. I asked him to turn his radio on, to listen to the 7 o'clock news—it was then around 6—then we spent the rest of the late-summer Madrid night talking, conjecturing—what was all this going to mean? Would this mean that the Ogro would change his life style? Would he change houses? Would he live in the President's residence? We didn't even know where the President of the Government's house was located! Would he change his place of mass? We didn't think this likely, because it seemed to be a habit of many years with him . . . since the end of the Spanish Civil War. But what we did think was that from now on he would have more bodyguards. We mulled over a whole series of questions that didn't give us a chance to sleep. The next day we got up early. Iker remained at home cleaning up. I went to mass. I remember being surprised to see that the Ogro was there as usual. I sat very close to him. On the assumption that he wasn't going to go to mass that day, I placed myself near the front, and then he came in the same as usual. And this time, a little before the mass ended, a child approached him, gave him a kiss, and remained beside him until the end of the mass. Then a blond woman joined him . . . the same woman we had seen at other times. We learned later that it was his daughter. The three of them departed together."

"When we saw that he was still going to mass, we thought we had to hurry up and use the time as well as possible, because he might change his habits to fit into his new bureaucratic schedule," Jon said. "Now, from one day to the next, he might have to change his habits. We began to get anxious about the time span involved. We decided to go ahead as best we could before the eighteenth of July. If it couldn't come out as well as we had thought it out— well, then, it would be done a little worse. We knew the important thing was to get it done. We wanted guarantees, but the important thing was—to *do* it."

"We decided on the necessity of a minimum of conditions, and meanwhile, without calling too much attention to ourselves, we kept dropping into the church from time to time to see how things were going, and to take a quick look at the bodyguard situation," Txabi added.

"By then," Iker went on, "the Ogro began to go to church more irregularly. Around the same time we noticed that the main central doors of the church, which previously had been kept shut, were now opened wide and used as a main thoroughfare. This presented new difficulties. Noises could be heard from the street, and the interior of the church was now visible from the outside."

"We think they opened the main doors due to the heat," added Jon. "Later, whenever it rained and became cooler, the main doors were shut again."

"In Madrid, it *never* got cooler!" exclaimed Iker, remembering the heat. "So the doors of the church remained open most of the time. I was the one who first saw the church with the doors open . . . it was always *my* luck to get the bad news first. Fuck! And the day of the children! I also got *that* glorious bit of news. I was at the church when a bunch of children suddenly appeared from nowhere. They were suddenly inside the church. They had come in from another part of the building. Then they immediately went over to the confessional booths. Who knows? Maybe they were all preparing themselves for their communion. I suddenly saw all those children, and I nearly died in my gut. What could we do if those children started coming to the church every day? But later we found out that they would be coming only on Thursdays."

"We noticed, now, that the Ogro no longer came to mass with such regularity; he came less and less frequently as the days went by. By now he was busy with the Presidency and was taking trips outside Madrid," said Txabi, continuing his usual meticulous description. "Carrero's habits appeared changed. Until that time, he had had very little public life; he had remained in the shadows. Now he suddenly had become publicly far more visible. Like Juan Carlos, he could now be seen everywhere—everywhere but in the church! The summer holidays were getting close, too. We hoped Carrero would show up for a few days, that he would come back from one of his trips and reappear at the church. Then we could immediately send for the other commandos, who were already ready and waiting in their homes. But what happened is that Carrero *didn't* show up—so at this time we discarded the possibility of doing the operation before the eighteenth of July—and we decided to leave Madrid.

"We left Madrid," said Txabi, "because ETA had convened the Sixth Assembly, and since the operation was delayed, it was of interest to us to go to the Sixth Assembly. Earlier in the year, during the national Basque fete—*Aberri Eguna,* which is held in April—the police had killed an ETA militant, of the military section, in Algorta. Eustakio Mendizabal—we called him 'Txikia.' The leadership of ETA would not leave the martyrship of Txikia unanswered. ETA planned to respond. But the response to Txikia's death depended slightly on Operation Ogro—originally, Operation Ogro was to have taken place not long after Txikia's assassination. It was meant to take place at the end of May or the beginning of June. The schedule we had in mind was first, some immediate, quick action on the part of ETA in response to Txikia's death—followed then, of course, by repression by the Government—then, this would have been answered by Operation Ogro. If this schedule had worked, the two months would have been enough to make it clear that we had Txikia in mind. But as it turned out, it wasn't possible to organize a quick action in the month following Txikia's death. Because further delay of that action would have made the timing too close to Operation Ogro, the initial action was canceled.

"Another reason the first action on the schedule was canceled was that *two* ETA operations so close to one another could have influenced the extreme right-wing faction of the Government. They could have become intransigent about freeing the prisoners. We decided to abandon our plans to avenge Txikia's death and, instead, to concentrate totally—as our action—on Operation Ogro. Then, in June and July, we ran into all the difficulties in Madrid we've explained previously. It was then that we came back to the Basque country. We went to the Sixth Assembly of ETA", Txabi paused. "We went home."

CHAPTER FIVE

Return to Madrid
Execution Instead of Kidnapping?
More of Day-to-Day Life
Mishaps and Other Episodes
Breaking into the Armory
"Action" on the Main Military
Quarters in the Area
A "Gymnastic" Exercise
Abandoning the Kidnapping

"After the Sixth Assembly," said Mikel, "in September, only three of us returned to Madrid. The organization had decided that Txabi should stay in the Basque country until we could send a report. We would report on changes, on new possibilities—a rough outline. We decided to call our commando 'Commando Txikia.' That's why many people later thought Operation Ogro was our revenge for his death. But it was far more complicated. For one thing, the idea of Ogro was well under way before Txikia was killed. Also, it was much more complicated than simple revenge—too simple for Txikia's death. Our struggle is far more serious. When one of us dies, we don't simply avenge his death. We take him as an example, and continue his struggle. What happens is that the loss of a militant—Fuck!" cursed Mikel, "especially if he's your friend, shakes you—and it gives you more strength to continue."

"For example," seconded Jon, "in the case of Txabi—when he pressed the button that set off the bomb, he thought of his own dead friend."

"That's true!" burst forth Mikel, "because those two, Txabi and Josu, had lived together for a long time. Remembering Josu gave Txabi strength when he had to press that button!" said Mikel excitedly, jumping ahead of the narrative. "Txabi was responsible for pushing the button that made contact for the explosion that killed Carrero. After Txabi pressed the button, he came running wildly toward the car, yelling 'Josu! Josu! *He* gave me strength!' Josu was one of our militants whom the police shot in a house in San Sebastian. The story appeared in all the newspapers. He and Txabi were like brothers. And Txabi came running—when it was all over—he kept repeating, over and over, 'Josu, Josu gave me strength!' That memory of Josu—that's not sentimental bullshit! There *are* people who don't give much importance to things like people's names, their photos—all that is supposed to be irrelevant—but it's not true. It's easy to think that when you are on the outside. It's easy to see the bullfight from outside the ring, from the sidelines. Look," said Mikel, abruptly changing his tone, "I'm sorry if I seem to get excited on this point, but sometimes people are full of shit. Well," he continued, more quietly now, "we formed the Commando Txikia—and when we came back to Madrid in September, the first thing we did was to inspect the zones—for Operation Ogro."

Jon spoke up. "Soon after we arrived, Carrero showed up. Everything was different now. He had changed his system of bodyguards. Now, besides his own car and the bodyguard who always accompanied him, there was another car of the same make behind it. It was metallic blue. There were always four people in it. The chauffeur would stand near the door of the Ogro's car, talking to the Ogro's chauffeur inside. During mass the three other people would place themselves somewhere near the middle of the church, slightly nearer the right. The original bodyguard remained in the same place as before. A muscular young man, new on the scene, would stand next to another man, who looked like a secretary. A third man, also young—maybe 27—dark-haired, with a moustache—looked like a cop—would stand during the whole mass, either on one side or the other of the confessional boxes. We realized that the way things had developed, it would be impossible to carry out the action without a gunfight. It was impossible to control so many people. We hoped that eventually the guard around Carrero would be reduced in number," said Jon, coming back to the actual sequence of events.

Iker added, "Other times, instead of the bodyguard with the moustache, another bodyguard showed up—Inspector Bueno. Naturally, we didn't know his name then, but later on we read in the newspapers that he was called Inspector Bueno. When he came along, in the second car, only three other people came with him. That is precisely what happened on the day of the execution."

"Carrero's car was double-parked," Mikel added. "The cover car was parked behind it and, behind the cover car, also double-parked, was López Bravo's car."

[Gregorio López Bravo was the Foreign Affairs Minister in the 1970 "Opus Dei" cabinet. He was one of the chief spokesmen for the Opus Dei and a favorite of Premier Luis Carrero Blanco.]

"López Bravo had a Mercedes. In the beginning, a chauffeur drove it—then, later, López Bravo himself. Three limousines, double-parked! It looked like an official gathering," Mikel remembered.

"We saw López Bravo at mass every day. After mass the three cars drove along Serrano and turned into Juan Bravo," Jon said. "When they reached Claudio Coello, the Ogro took Claudio Coello, and López Bravo drove straight ahead, along Juan Bravo,"

"We never saw López Bravo before that summer," interrupted Iker. "I think he started to go to mass that following September . . . after he was no longer minister . . . some people thought he did this to suck up to the Ogro. He was at mass the day the Ogro was executed."

"We continued to go to the church. But nothing seemed to have changed. We began to think to ourselves that we finally had no other solution but to execute Carrero," continued Jon.

"Our observation of the Ogro began to be dangerous. We were only three people—the same three people. On the other hand, there were many police who had the place covered, and who were also watching the area. We decided to go less frequently to the church—only twice a week. We also took turns, so they didn't see the same faces in the area," Iker said. He paused, then suddenly switched the conversation to more mundane matters. "Our daily life was now very simple," he said. "We got up very early. We went to mass whenever it was our turn. We went out infrequently. Occasionally we went to the movies. We read a lot. It was normal for us to spend our lives with books. But, in reality— as a way of life—it was abnormal. It's a little peculiar that young men of our age should have been leading lives of complete sexual abstinence—a little like monks," sighed Iker.

"But we read all sorts of books," Jon added. "In our house, we had books of all kinds. The four of us had very different kinds of taste. For example, I read a lot of books on Marxist economic theory. I studied economy. I read Dickens, Russian novels, the whole lot. Mikel read books on guerrilla warfare. He also would go into fits of hysterical laughter over the Spanish comic strips *Mortadelo* and *Filemón*—two wild comic-strip characters. On the other hand, Iker read very little—he worked most of the time. He was always busy, fiddling around with techniques of making false papers and documents, things involving stamps, inks, and so forth—he was obsessed with all of that. He bought all sorts of special books on the subject. Every day he came home with new supplies, new inks, new methods of fabrication—that was his passion. As for Txabi, he was busy writing a book on political theory for ETA. It was a study of revolutionary violence—actually, we never read the book. Txabi also had a habit of sleeping a lot, particularly after meals. In the summer days, and early September, when we were dizzy from the Madrid heat, and the sweltering Madrid sun, we also slept a lot. Always dozing off . . ."

"We generally ate at home," added Iker. "If there was something very important that the four of us had to do in the city together, then we stayed out and had a quick bite in a Madrid bar. But most often we cooked at home. By cooking at home we saved money; also, the food we prepared ourselves was better. We were very happy with our cook," Iker admitted.

"Thanks, hombre!" exploded Mikel. "You never told me before how great a cook I was! You guys were not exactly the last of the great talkers. I had to dig compliments out of you with a cork-screw! Somebody listening to the three of you *now* might get the impression you are good talkers—but that's because of the cognac. Actually, you are types who sit in a corner for *hours,* without opening your mouths! You were like tombs . . . one has to have a lot of patience to be able to live with you types," Mikel said, and paused. "In Madrid, during the action, they were either monosyl-labic—I've already mentioned they weren't expansive types—or, when they weren't being quiet, they'd suddenly explode over some minor detail, and the shit would fly!"

"He's right," Txabi said evenly, "Iker and I, we were the quiet ones . . . but Jon and Mikel . . . they fought all day long. Despite all this, we managed to organize our days fairly well. One of us did the cooking, another washed the dishes, a third did the shopping for the household, and the fourth cleaned the apartment."

"We also stuck to a gymnastic routine," Iker added. "Some of us more than the others—but Jon always did gymnastics. For him it was almost an obsession. We had weights, pulleys, and, with all that, during that July and September, Jon developed very strong muscles. As he often wore a light blue jersey shirt, showing those big arm muscles, we called him Popeye the sailor man. Jon would get up early, take a glass of orange juice, then work out for one solid hour. Later, he'd have an English breakfast—bacon and eggs, toast and coffee—and, after that, the day and Madrid and our work started."

"We also had rifle practice," continued Txabi. "Our house was far away from the center of Madrid, and our building was the last one in our neighborhood. Near our house were empty lots—we had target practice in those empty lots. We had two different kinds of guns," he added, speaking precisely, as usual—"guns for the country and for the city. In our own neighborhood we used guns with compressed air, filled with buckshot. We practiced a lot with those guns to improve our aim. This particular kind of gun is very heavy, and you need a lot of strength in your wrist to manage it accurately. We practiced this. In the Sierras, though, we practiced with real guns—*Parabellum*. One or two hours away from Madrid, in the Sierras, it's easy to find places where you can shoot guns without fear of being noticed. We went regularly to the mountains, and nobody ever paid any attention to us. There are good mountains near Segovia. Also near Avila. All of the Sierras contain good terrain for target practice. Christ! If we only had those marvelous Sierras here in Euskadi—those long, rugged distances! The mountains without houses, without the sound of a human voice—hombre, if the Sierras were in Euskadi, how much easier it would be for us! Euskadi is overpopulated. The towns are so close to one another—you're always bumping into a local village—and a local villager, planting his cabbage patch," concluded Txabi.

"But in spite of the bad conditions in Euskadi, we do have target practice there, too—otherwise, we'd be lost," Jon added.

"But here," explained Iker, "it is very different—you know that in Euskadi nobody is going to denounce you. Many times we realized that a local goat herder or farmer heard us shooting, but we knew that nobody would say anything. In Madrid we were always more scared—we were alien to Madrid. Like, we had a bad time in Madrid, when we had our accidents . . ."

"I had the first accident," Txabi explained. "I shot my hand with a small bullet. It wasn't a dangerous wound, but it hurt like hell, and it could have gotten infected. We had to get the bullet out, and we didn't know any doctors in Madrid—and couldn't call any doctors. So we had to make a special trip to Euskadi, just to have my hand attended to."

"This happened in April," said Jon, "long before our September return to Madrid. We had bought our guns—small-bore pistols, pellet guns that use compressed air, gas guns, and so forth, and we had to go back to the store to buy more guns. On the way, we bumped into a police demonstration in the street—this is very rare for Madrid, for the police to demonstrate. This was right after the 'First of May'—during the demonstrations that year on the first of May, a policeman was killed, in Tirso de Molina. In reprisal, the police made a great many arrests, and people were tortured in ghoulish ways. The four of us had gotten together in the center of Madrid—we were planning to eat out, a paella—anyway, it was at a restaurant in the Gran Vía, next to Callao Street. The restaurant is on the second floor, and we could see the street from the windows, looking out over the Gran Vía. We were in the neighborhood of the Puerta del Sol," said Jon. "Suddenly, we heard odd noises from the street below—'Down with Garicano!' Garicano was the Minister of the Interior, so it seemed odd to hear someone yelling 'Down with Garicano!'" Jon paused. "But *this* time, it was the policemen *themselves* who were yelling! *They* were the ones demonstrating! They were carrying a coffin—the coffin of the dead policeman, the one killed in Tirso de Molina. There were three hundred policemen, all in plain clothes. They were from the 'Brigida Social' (the political police) and the criminal police. Their badges, pinned to their jackets, were clearly visible. They were yelling for the ultra, General Iniesta—Iniesta is a *crazy* ultra, like Blas Piñar. This happened during the same period Txabi hurt his wrist with the gun," concluded Jon.

"After the killing of that policeman during the May 1 demonstration," broke in Txabi, "there was a lot of talk about the 'violence of the masses.' This notion of armed masses was silly. It looked to me like the action of one military commando, and a commando who had with him only very rudimentary arms. The policeman was killed with a knife."

"There is a lot of confusion about the death of that policeman," Mikel added. "Also, most political opposition groups in Spain have no clear theory about revolutionary violence."

"But," broke in Txabi, "could you really call a spontaneous demonstration, a few people armed with sticks, chains, and knives —and that policeman was killed with a knife, as I said—'mass action?' I don't think so. What really makes a mass action?" mused Txabi. "What is the difference between that action and, say, an attack on the Official Syndicates by a small group from ETA? I think an action is revolutionary depending on the *results,* what effects it has, from what process it comes, its raison d'être—the question isn't one of arms or numbers of people." Txabi, who was writing a book on revolutionary theory, liked to speculate on the principles involved.

"We had a few more accidents while we were collecting our supply of arms," said Iker, who was anxious to get back to their own story. "All of them were due to our lack of familiarity with the way things are in Madrid. Like the heat. We had to walk around without jackets—only shirts. The heat was so terrible we couldn't even wear sweaters. It isn't like that in the Basque country. Here, even during the hot days, evenings are always cool, and it is natural to wear a sweater or to throw one over your shoulders. But in Madrid, it was so hot we felt like ripping off our own skins! All our problems managing the 'pieces' really came from the weather." Iker seemed to be obsessed with the Madrid heat.

"During the winter, as long as it was cold, it was okay if we carried the pieces in our belts or in our armpits. Well, each of us picked the place that seemed most comfortable. But we all found it uncomfortable to wear pistols. Then, suddenly the heat came— without any spring. The temperature rose to about 92° Fahrenheit. So, by that time we were only wearing T-shirts, which made it hard to hide the pieces. Also, we didn't carry small pistols, but huge Parabellums—9 caliber—and it is very difficult to hide the bulk of such a pistol. Our solution was to carry the Parabellums in small briefcases. We put the ammunition and cartridges for reloading inside the briefcases. But then we kept forgetting the briefcases everywhere we went—cafeterias, bars—it never became a serious problem, because we always found them. Each time we'd forget a briefcase and would be calmly walking along, suddenly one of us would remember: 'Coño! I've forgotten my piece!' —and he'd run back in a hurry to the cafeteria or bar—and there would be the briefcase, on a table or a chair. But once, a waiter must have realized what was in the briefcase . . ." said Jon, the natural storyteller. "It was Txabi———"

"Of course he saw it!" Txabi broke in. "A long time had elapsed before I realized that I had left the briefcase in the bar. When I went back it was gone. The waiter had put it out of sight. I was sure he had opened it and seen the pistol. He didn't say anything to me when he handed it over. I figured he must have thought we were from the police."

"Yes," Jon interrupted, "but that was the reason we decided it was a mistake to carry pieces. Even if you realize that you've forgotten the gun and don't go back to retrieve it, it would still have been serious for the 'commando,' because we are the only group to use the Parabellum. The Parabellum is the mark of ETA. They would have known *immediately* that the ETA was in Madrid!"

"That's one of the reasons that we needed other guns," explained Mikel. "We didn't want to always go with a Parabellum." He paused a moment, then repeated, "The Parabellum would have meant ETA was in Madrid."

[Parabellum 9 caliber is similar to a Luger, Astra and Smith and Wesson. Parabellum in Latin means "prepare for war."]

"But ETA was in Madrid," Mikel went on. "It was the 'big city' for us. When we weren't busy with Operation Ogro, we wanted to reconnoiter Madrid for ETA. We were learning new things— things that afterward could be useful to other militants. We obtained first-rate forgery materials, and, of course, the big thing was the arms. We filched them from the civil guard and from the army."

"This action—the armory holdup—was reported in the newspapers, although they didn't know that it was us, and they didn't say it was a political action, except for a vague reference," Jon explained. "Even though we left a few political tracts. In addition to the arms, we stole two damned good typewriters and a multi-copier. They're probably still wondering how that was done. Actually, we took them in such a casual way it even struck *us* as funny. We went through the main door, and the doorman himself —very accommodating—opened the door for us. We had printed the tracts because those weapons were very important for us, and we didn't want the police to know who took them. So we left the tracts to confuse them and signed the tracts 'FARE'—Fuerzas Armadas Revolucionarias Espãnolas—Revolutionary Spanish Armed Forces. Of course, 'FARE' was a figment of our imagination. We only made a few pamphlets—enough to leave in the store, since they were not meant for the general public, but only for the store clerks—just to leave the sort of clue that would mislead the police."

"Jon has enormous imagination—and when he dreamt up those pamphlets for the 'FARE'—shit, he really went to town! Once he takes off, there's no stopping him! In the text of the pamphlet, he said we were the most revolutionary group in Spain, that we were planning to swallow up the whole Spanish state—a whole bouillabaisse!" laughed Mikel.

"And even though the shop was shut down, only one local newspaper mentioned the whole story," Jon explained. "The robbery took place during the third week of September. At that time we already realized that the kidnapping was almost impossible—and our deadline was the beginning of October. We wanted to allow time for Carrero to go back to his old winter routine. But meanwhile, we pulled the armory stunt. Txabi wasn't with us at the time, and the three of us did it on our own."

"First," said Iker, "we had to find an armory that had favorable conditions for a successful robbery."

Then, with a sort of quick insouciance, Iker, Jon, and Mikel rapidly started to recount their exploits without their leader, Txabi.

Iker began. "It had to have few customers, an easy way in and out—we also needed a vantage point in order to spot people who might later recognize us. We took two armories into account, but the first one had a shitty exit—besides, we didn't think that armory had a lot of the stuff we wanted. So, we decided on the second armory. It's located on San Francisco de Sales Street, near Moncloa—where the university students hang out. We bought rubber gloves, so no fingerprints."

Jon: "This took time. We had to go there four or five times. But it wasn't too complicated. Everything was arranged within a week. There were only four points we had to consider: people entering and leaving, the time the store opened, and who was working there. Actually, there were one young boy, two men in their forties, one old man, and one woman."

Mikel: "We got our info sort of casually—we'd go into the store and buy buckshot—then we'd have a coffee or a beer at the cafe in front of the store. Sitting there, we could see every-thing . . ."

Jon: "So, sometimes we bought stuff in the store . . . other times, we watched from the cafe—all in all, it took us only three days. The owner, an old man, was almost never there. But his sons, a blond lady—I don't know if she was the owner's sister or his wife —a clerk in his forties, and a young guy were always in the store."

Mikel: "We 'borrowed' a car that was parked in Claudio Coello the night before we robbed the store. We found the car right after we finished our daily turn at the church."

Iker: "It was a Simca 1200—it belonged to an architect. Later, we read in the papers that the burglars in the armory case were seen leaving in a blue Seat 600 . . . which wasn't true. In a 600 you couldn't fit even one gun—that model would have been much too small. Anyway, we stole the car, changed the license plates, and got everything ready for the burglary. We thought the best time would be first thing in the morning, just when the store opened, or last thing at night, when they were ready to close up. We decided to do it in the morning, before customers started coming in. The night before our robbery, we left the car parked near the store. We parked another car—which we actually rented —in the same zone, near the university city. The getaway was to work as follows: We were going to put the stuff filched from the armory into the stolen car. Then we would drive up to the second car and make the changeover. The whole operation was to take a total of six minutes. We were going to switch the arms to the rented car and drive that car to a safe hiding place. When the coast was clear, we planned to transport the arms to Euskadi. It was very important to get the arms quickly out of Madrid and up to Euskadi. We had to do this *before* Operation Ogro—or we would have lost the arms."

Mikel started recounting the events. "The day of the action, we were at the store by 9:30. We were lucky. Instead of opening at 10, as usual, the store was already open—we didn't know why. But this worked to our advantage. Everybody was already in the store. We didn't have to wait. The blinds were rolled up halfway. The door to the street was open. So we just walked in."

"We managed to talk just the bare minimum—enough to give a few curt orders. We didn't want them to notice our accents," Iker said. " 'Everybody to the floor—hands up—do this—do that' —we didn't talk among ourselves except when absolutely necessary, and obviously, not in Basque. We carried different types of pistols, which we got in advance. One of them was stolen from a policeman, and the other was a 7.65," he said. "We didn't want them to know we were from ETA."

Jon continued the story. "We wore the rubber gloves. I remember I was the first one to enter the store. The counter was at the left. Guns were hanging from all the walls. I went straight to the back room. The owner's sons, the blond lady, and the clerk were all in there. The young guy was standing by the door. In passing, I said to him, 'Buenos días,' and proceeded with the pistol already in my hand."

Now Iker spoke. "While Jon went to the back of the store, Mikel and I discreetly pointed our guns at the young boy who had been standing in the doorway. We forced him to enter the store. This way, we had all five of them covered."

"When I entered the store," Jon continued, "the owner's son was talking on the telephone. I pointed the pistol directly at him. All five put up their hands. He asked us in a very nervous voice, 'What is this all about?' I didn't want to reply because he was holding the telephone in his hand. Then he said, 'Is this a holdup? —If this is a holdup, there is no cash in the cash register.' I realized that the person on the other end of the telephone could hear what was going on, so I took the telephone from him and hung it up. By this time, we had pushed everybody into the back room. We taped their wrists behind their backs—except for the young boy—and started to load up on the arms."

"We had locked the outside door," pointed out Mikel, "so that nobody could walk in unexpectedly. Also, it wasn't 10 o'clock yet, and the Persian blinds were halfway down. This meant the clerks weren't ready for customers."

"And we turned the sign in the doorway around—so it now read 'closed,' " said Jon.

Mikel continued, "While we were loading up on arms, the person who had been on the other end of the telephone called back. The same person from before. We gave the telephone to the proprietor's son. Jon had the pistol pointed at his chest. He spoke well. He was very pale and was perspiring, but managed to carry on a normal conversation about his work, and he indicated that nothing unusual was going on in the store."

"We decided to take all the small guns and all the automatics that we could lay our hands on. A couple of hunting rifles and all the ammunition we could manage. There was a lot of ammunition in the store—we couldn't possibly take all of it. The young boy showed us what was in the store, and we made our choices," Jon added.

"We specifically took some guns of the sort that the civil guard used some years back," Mikel went on. "In addition, all sorts of classes of rifles and guns. Also, quantities of documentation. Gun permits—guides indicating in what zones in Spain hunting is permitted—all sorts of papers. We didn't know it at the time, but one of those pieces of paper was going to be crucial in making Operation Ogro work."

"They wrapped the supplies in military cloth for us," Jon went on. "Then we put the supplies in the car and we left."

Then Iker spoke. "While we were in the store, taking the supplies, the proprietor's son asked us why we needed the arms. Did we plan more holdups? Jon told them no—he reminded them that shortly before our attack on the store a worker in San Adrián del Besos, on the outskirts of Barcelona, had been killed by the police. Jon said our holdup was meant to be an answer to the regime—assassins of the working class—and that the arms would be used for the people, against the regime, and against these assassins of the workers. He said the guns were necessary for an armed struggle. While Jon was inventing this explanation, he became very excited and emotional," Iker commented. "The man in the store replied that this was fair, but protested that he himself was also a poor man. Jon asked him how much all the supplies we were taking were worth. We had intended, if he had really been such a good man and so poor, to pay him back."

Mikel said, "As Jon kept getting more and more involved in his own long, political explanations with the man, which kept getting more and more involuted as he spoke, we gave him a sign with our hands—*finito!* Later on, we decided that the owner of the store was a piece of rotten fish. We saw, by what we took, that he himself had three pistols, a hunting guide, a permit for the use of heavy arms, and pistol permits. All that stuff in Spain is very difficult to get hold of—no ordinary citizen possessed those kinds of permits." Mikel paused. "He also had pistols from the civil guard. This meant that he repaired their arms in his shop."

"We had one other operation against the civil guard, but it was never reported in the newspapers, and it is the sort of operation we could repeat against them, so we can't give details now. But Iker can start filling in on the operation against the military headquarters. That was discovered by the police shortly after Operation Ogro," Jon said, and waited for Iker to speak.

"We stole a car from the military headquarters, and we later used the driver's papers from that car during Operation Ogro. Because we later used those same papers when we rented the Fiat 124 for Ogro, the police must have related the two events. They can't be *so* stupid—the assault on the military headquarters and Operation Ogro obviously were connected. Until Carrero was executed, though, they had no idea ETA was involved in the action on the military headquarters. Until Ogro took place, the police always assumed that ETA never operated out of the Basque country," concluded Iker.

"The action against the military headquarters," said Jon, "took place one week after the arsenal holdup. Txabi had come back to Madrid. Now we were four. We employed the same system as with the arsenal. We took a car, changed the license plates, and so forth. The action was prepared in advance, but also it was planned in only a few days. The building that was our target was the general headquarters—hombre!—the very heart of the military, more important than an ordinary barracks. One day we passed by what looked like an ordinary military barracks. It was very poorly guarded and badly kept up. We suddenly realized that this was the general headquarters, and we saw possibilities in it. We started to study the plan, very quickly, very quickly, in two or three days."

Mikel continued, "Jon, of course, started up again with his business of being a pamphleteer—the same business as with the FARE. He wanted to proselytize among the soldiers, to tell them what a shitty whore's life they were leading, and why we were doing that kind of action. But in the end we didn't use any propaganda."

Jon took up the account. "The escape maneuver was rapid. There was only a short distance between the place we abandoned the first car and the place where the second car was waiting for us, but we still had to rush between the two cars—you'll see why in a moment. The action was to take place on a very narrow street, which had a sharp drop down to Segovia Street. One of the building's entrances faces onto this little street. One of us had to wait in the second car. The other two had to be walking up the street, looking like they were engaged in ordinary conversation. Practically parallel to them, going up the hill very slowly, would be one of us, driving the first car. Then, when the two men walking up the hill reached the military headquarters, they would pull a gun on the sentinel there, disarm him and make him lie flat on the ground. We then would get into the first car, which would be coming alongside us. Then all three of us, after a short ride, would abandon the first car and, running down the stairs leading to Segovia Street, get into the second car and disappear. But what *actually* happened to us was extremely odd, because the negligence of the guards made things more difficult." Jon paused, then resumed the story. "The action had to take place at 9 P.M., but it wasn't possible at that time, so we just went there to see how things were. Two sentinels were at the corner of the street instead of standing guard by the doors. They weren't paying much attention to what was going on, and they weren't behaving that much as guards. They were spending so much time speaking to each other that we decided we might as well go ahead and attack the two of them and get two guns instead of just one. We rushed out to look for Iker and Mikel, who were in a cafe not very far from there . . . but when we came back, the sentinels were no longer at the corner. The guard of the lateral door was now in the *other* doorway, sitting on the floor and chatting with the second guard. Then they started to flirt with some girls who were passing by—I wouldn't have imagined such recklessness in a military barracks." Jon stopped a moment, bemused, —"but they were right! I would do the same thing . . . We walked up and down the streets, waiting for things to normalize. But then the *sereno* came—the man who carries the keys to the buildings in Madrid—and to complicate things, three kids who were passing by started to heckle the *sereno*—and he was already looking at *us*. The three kids teased him—then hid. Finally, all three kids went with the *sereno* for a drink."

"In all," Jon went on, "we kept waiting and waiting—and until 1 in the morning, there wasn't any chance of action. At 1 A.M., when the guards changed, we went ahead. We had been watching the headquarters since 9 that night!"

"Serrano Street runs two ways," interjected Iker. "There is a traffic light on the corner. When the taxis come in from Segovia and turn by the traffic light to go up the narrow street, the cars pass right in front of the doors of the military headquarters. This makes it dangerous," he explained. "We had to wait until the traffic light turned green before we started our action. We had to complete the action in less than one minute, by which time taxis, stopped by the light at Serrano, would be coming up the street."

"Slowly we walked up to the sentinel," said Mikel. "We pointed a gun straight at him and disarmed him. The soldier didn't make a sound—although he did try a little resistance. He tried to hold onto the machine-gun belt strapped over his shoulder, but we got it off him immediately. He wanted to yell something, but the words didn't form in his mouth. We told him not to be scared. Nothing was going to happen to him. We made him lie flat on the ground . . . he stayed quiet. It wasn't until we got into our car that we saw him trying to get up off the ground," Mikel added.

"It was very quick," said Iker. "When we changed cars, into the second car, ready for the escape, the light turned."

"It was very strange," said Jon, taking up the story again, "because several days later, when we walked by the military headquarters, their whole method of security had changed. The sentry boxes, which previously had been on the street, had now been placed on a first-floor balcony. The main sentry box had been removed to inside the courtyard of the headquarters. Now the guards stayed inside the sentry boxes, looking out on the street through the narrow slits in the wooden fronts of the sentry boxes."

"All of the actions and operations we carried out prior to Operation Ogro were for the purpose of a trial run," Txabi broke in. "If we came away with arms and supplies as loot, well, so much the better."

"It was an experience for us—an experiment to see how people in Madrid responded . . . because in Euskadi, of course, it was different. People supported us there. Whenever we rob a bank in Euskadi, the people are behind us—they often join us!—and we have proof of this," Jon said. "Sometimes they are a little scared, but they know nothing will happen to them, and they sympathize with us. They know that the money is to be used to fight the same oppressors that cause them equal suffering. But Madrid was an unknown for us—we had to find out the mood of the city, how people would respond to actions of this sort. In addition, we had to investigate good escape routes. We didn't want to be trapped like fish in a bowl of water, struggling to get out of Madrid. In Euskadi, the escape routes are country roads. In Madrid, one is dealing with a crowded city—an entirely different operation," Jon concluded.

"The traffic of Madrid could have worked for us or against us," explained Iker. "The city is a sort of jungle, easy to lose oneself within. On the other hand, there are blocked streets, one-way traffic, traffic jams—any of those could have also meant a fatal trap for us. One advantage was the subway—we could quickly run down the stairs. But all these pluses and minuses meant that we had to learn the feel of the city by practicing small actions."

"We noticed," said Jon, "in these small actions, that Madrid's police acted pretty much the same as those in Euskadi. We noticed that, if the action took place in a private organization, say, a bank or a store, they had no choice—they would have to report it to the newspapers. But when the police or the military were directly attacked, such as the case with the military headquarters, they maintained a rigorous silence—there were no releases to the press. For the regime, it's a hard blow to admit that they are vulnerable."

Mikel broke in, saying, "Do you remember, Txabi, how you felt during that action? You had just come back from Euskadi. You were exhausted. You didn't want to come with us. We had to pull you along, and you were half dead. Txabi had just brought us very concrete news from the direction—ETA."

"ETA direction," added Txabi, "said that if there was too much vigilance of the Ogro, too many bodyguards and so forth, making the action difficult, we should abandon the kidnapping project and think in terms of his execution. They told us to take our time . . . to study the problem carefully—all the risks—to be very careful and methodical in our approach . . . nothing was to be rushed."

"By now we had spent nearly a year in Madrid," Jon went on. "We moved around the city with a certain security, but we weren't exactly the most secure fish in our own freshwater pond of Madrid—we still were strangers. Mikel was always insisting that in order to do an action you have to be sure of your own terrain—he was always making cracks about being a fish out of water, or about Madrid being a big pond. He drove us *nuts* with his jokes on the subject—he was obsessed about our not being from Madrid. Txabi's news from Euskadi depressed us, too. We had everything prepared—we knew the streets, the zones, the subways. We knew we couldn't keep on with the idea of the kidnapping, but the effect of having to abandon a plan we had worked on for almost a year—we had rehearsed it a thousand times—everything so prepared, so studied—made us enormously depressed." Jon paused, recalling the emotions—he was always the one to recall such details and their emotional impact. He went on. "We were so sad at having to give up the possibility of freeing the prisoners. We had worked so hard toward this end!—and now we saw it simply was not possible. He was so carefully watched by now—Carrero—that kidnapping would have been nuttiness. We had to give up our plan once and for all. It weighed on us . . ." Jon stopped speaking a moment, then repeated himself. "It weighed on us . . . but we began work immediately on Operation Ogro. We continued to call it Operation Ogro—but *this* time, the goal was the execution. Naturally, when we began planning for this new phase, we were no longer virgins . . ."

CHAPTER SIX

Plans for the Execution
Two Domestic Tragedies
One Decision Made in Action
Now Let's Work
The Problem of the Date
Reasons for the Action

"Clearly," Txabi began, in his usual even, analytical style of narration, "we weren't starting out from zero. The information about the neighborhood, about the habits of Carrero—all this was going to be useful. What we had to do now was to study the way of doing the execution. Even though this might have appeared to have been an easier sort of operation, this actually was not the case. It carried with it all sorts of new complications. Even though it's true we didn't have to use a great part of our original plan—the apartments and so forth—which simplified Operation Ogro, we still had the problem of accomplishing the execution without leaving victims. If we had intended to execute Carrero without worrying about additional victims, we wouldn't have had any problems . . . we simply could have driven along Serrano and machine-gunned him from the moving car. Or we could have used two cars with explosives, left the car in that narrow street we discussed before—the street Carrero used—and, as soon as he walked by the cars, we could have dynamited him. We also thought of setting off a bomb that would have blown off the roof—the dome of the church. All sorts of solutions could have been found. Our problem was—how were we going to keep innocent bystanders from getting hurt?"

"We got *headaches* over this thing," said Iker. "You begin to think of the people involved. We wanted to make sure there were no innocent victims. We wanted a 'clean' operation—one directed at Carrero, who was the real enemy—at *him*—and no one else. We wanted to do this for the good of the people—and if you hurt somebody innocent? It just wouldn't work. We were very worried about this. We had tons of ideas. We rejected all of them for the same reason—they didn't offer enough guarantees of safety for innocent people," Iker said firmly.

"An action like this carries the risk of backfiring," said Jon, backing up Iker. "If it turns out badly, it can boomerang against you. To a large degree, the success of Operation Ogro was dependent on how the execution of Carrero was carried out—how clean an operation it was. We weren't afraid of risks to our own lives—we were afraid of anything that would risk the success of ETA's long-term struggle. We had to be sure of what we did. If you end up killing innocent people, for whatever reason—a mishap, an ill-thought-out plan—you are creating enormous problems for yourself. Even though it's also true that sometimes, if the consequences are important enough, certain risks are worth taking," he added. "But it is always better not to kill anybody. I know that in all the actions of ETA in which I participated this preoccupation for the safety of others was a constant worry. At the last moment, say, after you have carefully planned an action, a man suddenly crosses the street and gets in your way—at any rate, some little detail always could go wrong. This sort of risk constantly worries ETA. We're not worried about the real enemy, the Spanish state—they will *always* think we are assassins. What worries us is the average person. We want him to understand our struggle, and not to see us, falsely, as killers—which ETA has not been. It hasn't been a band of killers." Jon paused.

"When the actions are successful," said Txabi, "a lot of people think 'What luck!'—Well, perhaps—sometimes—but 99 percent of our success is not luck, but the result of hard, meticulous work, with small details carefully planned out—good, scientific analysis. We made a scientific study of our work in connection with Operation Ogro because we thought it would serve as an interesting document, an example for the future. We have showed the Spanish people, with Operation Ogro, that the most difficult goals—if people try hard enough—*can* be obtained. The very heart of the regime was *not* invincible. The police were *not* invincible. We proved all this with Operation Ogro. We were showing that revolutionary struggle—armed struggle—opened new possibilities to the people," concluded Txabi, always interested in commenting on revolutionary theory.

"A new action of this sort cheers people up," added Mikel. "After every successful action, we have seen new militants and new sympathizers join up with ETA. It's a matter of esprit de corps. That's why it was so important that Operation Ogro worked *well*. If not, it would have been a *negative* example—and then we would have had all those 'theoretical types' who are against armed struggle on principle explaining what was wrong with ETA! The theoreticians would say, 'You see, that is no way to plan an action . . . that is not the way of the future . . .' All that paralyzes ETA's struggle, holds us back," Mikel said. "What we want to show is that our way is one of *many* ways to attack the regime. We want to amplify the struggle—instead of using limited means, we want to be part of a varied struggle, with varied techniques—ETA is *one* of many ways."

Now Txabi took up the narrative again. "After we had eliminated all the possibilities that had occurred to us, and when we were very depressed and discouraged, we noticed one day that there was construction under way right next to the Jesuits' building, at the corner of Claudio Coello and Diego de León. We thought perhaps we could build a tunnel, about 7 meters long, from that construction site up to the center of the street. We wanted to make the tunnel during the night . . . so that it could be exploded the following morning. We immediately realized that this was crazy. Nobody could build a tunnel that quickly. We abandoned the project. Still . . . we liked the idea of a tunnel . . ."

Iker interrupted him. "Remember the apartments we had rented for the kidnapping? Actually, once we dropped the original kidnap plan they were very easy to dispose of. During the first fortnight of November, while we were studying possibilities for the execution, we went around to our various apartments and discreetly canceled our leases. We were actually quite lucky—everyone who had rented the apartments to us acted extremely graciously. With the exception of the widow who had rented us the refuge—the 'cage'—and who didn't return us the two months' deposit. All the others accepted our explanations and acted friendly toward us. They gave us back the money, and our relations stayed peaceful."

"We kept only two apartments," Mikel went on. "One was the one we lived in regularly, and the other was the marquise's. We kept that one just in case we might have some need of it at the very last moment."

"Yes," broke in Iker, "we saw it was a good idea to have a second apartment. I had an accident with my gun, and we had to switch apartments in a hurry. One day," he continued, "around the end of October, I was looking over a long 'Star'—one of the pistols we had taken from the arsenal shop. I knew that if the pistol was in the shop, some repair work was being done on it, so I wanted to check out the condition of the pistol myself. While I was remounting it, and had already reloaded the chamber, the gun suddenly went off."

"Fuck it!—you say the gun *suddenly went off?*" exploded Mikel. "What you *mean* is that you accidentally *shot* the gun, which is *not* the same thing! It was a real miracle that the bullet didn't kill me! It spun right past my eyes!"

"We thought we had been fucked for good!" agreed Iker. "That gun—the 'Star'—made a tremendous noise when it went off. We stood still a few seconds—none of us was able to respond. The bullet—Christ!—it hit the floor—bounced off the wall—then up to the ceiling—and once more to the floor, right *into* it. Now we had three bullet holes—the one in the floor was quite big— so were those in the wall. In that split second, while that fucking bullet was whistling through the air and ricocheting around Mikel—our balls turned blue—we were scared shitless! But we reacted quickly. We ran out of the apartment, to the staircase, yelling 'What happened?' We behaved as though we didn't know anything—acting very surprised by all the noise. Even though there were no repercussions from the incident, we became a little afraid. We had been living in that apartment for a long time, and everybody in the building knew we were Basques. We decided to move to the other apartment, and we removed all our belongings. We didn't give up the old one—sometimes we returned there to talk with the doorman. We told him we were traveling on business . . . but we were on guard."

"And just a few days later," Mikel said, "we had another accident. It was peculiar—two accidents so close together."

"Yes, we had a run of bad luck during that time," said Iker.

"We installed ourselves in the new apartment. But I felt jittery. I was suffering from some sort of complex about having let the gun go off accidentally—I was beginning to have misgivings. Then one day I went out. When I returned home, I saw Mikel and Txabi looking quite serious. Jon, laughing, said to me, 'Do you know what happened to me? Look—look—' and he showed me a big hole in the wall! Accidentally, he, too, had shot off a gun," said Iker.

"And *I* was the one who told him off for not being careful, for playing with guns in the apartment," interrupted Jon. "And then, well, I did the same thing."

"Then, when it went off, and it made a loud noise, we used the same story as before," said Mikel. "After those first few seconds of being taken by surprise, you are at a loss. But again, we acted immediately. We opened the door and asked—casually—'Qué hay?'—'What happened? What was that noise?' Our neighbor, the marquise, was there, too. Worried, she also asked 'What could that noise have been?' "

Iker spoke again. "We were lucky that the building was old and had very thick walls. That was real luck. Otherwise, the bullet would have hit the marquise in the head! But the bullet was stopped by the wall. This time the bullet didn't travel in a zig-zag trajectory like mine—when the 'Star' went off—instead, it went straight into the wall, bounced, and fell onto the floor. But the impact on the wall made a huge noise right near the headboard of the marquise's bed in the adjoining apartment. She must have felt something bouncing near her head, but the bullet didn't get through to her room because of the air chamber inside the wall, between the apartments."

"It was still early. It wasn't more than 8:30—in Madrid, this is late afternoon," Jon explained. "Unfortunately," he went on, "the marquise had gone to bed early. She acted very scared when she spoke—after all, it sounded like a real explosion. When the bullet from the gun—a Parabellum—bounced against the wall, it went —*BOOM!* Parabellums are very loud. But the marquise didn't suspect anything. What we *couldn't* do was move to another house, because we had already left all the other apartments; we hadn't kept any of the extra apartments, as now we had made an entirely different plan."

"We were going to release an ETA communiqué," Jon went on, "taking the responsibility for the execution of Carrero, several hours after his death. During those first few hours, there would be enough confusion to allow us to get away."

"In the new plan, we planned to escape from Madrid immediately after his execution," Mikel explained. "We would have been out of the Spanish state by the time ETA claimed responsibility—but our escape involved a long, long trip; and we can't explain where we went after Ogro."

"Long—and also complicated," Txabi added. "The first part of the trip, which took place within the Spanish state, we had well planned—maximum safety. Because at the last moment we also had the help of a militant—one who was with the information service of ETA, who was going to monitor the movements of the police for us. He was going to keep us informed as to the measures that the military and the police were going to take. That way, we would know precisely where the police were and what was going on. All that would permit us to employ techniques for our own safety that we'd used in the past and that were foolproof."

"During early November we were looking for a way to execute Carrero," said Jon. "It was during this period that we bought a car. We found out at that time that the police were controlling rented cars, so because of that, we decided to buy a second-hand Austin—1300—cream-colored. It's a very powerful car."

"We bought it at a Madrid Seat agency with false papers. The car was in bad condition. It had poor brakes, a hole in the gasoline pipe, and there was a leak in the oil valve. In the end, it would have been cheaper for us to have bought a new car—this one was a mess," Iker sighed.

"Now that we had the car, we studied the neighborhood carefully. We noticed that there were two basement apartments for rent in Claudio Coello—also, several furnished apartments. In that neighborhood," Mikel went on, "which is the Barrio de Salamanca, there are many apartments for rent, especially in some of the grander, older homes—it's an elegant, old neighborhood—you could see there were many vacancies. Clearly, the owners of some of the older buildings had gone to live in newer parts of Madrid. We decided to rent the basement apartment at 104 Claudio Coello. We picked Iker to handle the landlord." Mikel paused. "Iker—you tell it. It's your story."

Iker began, "By November 10 or 11, we were clear in our minds as to the next step. We *had* to build a tunnel. We needed the Claudio Coello apartment for this. I had my 'profession' carefully planned when I went to see the landlord. I was going to be a sculptor—the perfect profession for legitimately making a lot of noise without arousing suspicion. I went over to the Claudio Coello apartment and spoke to the super. He showed me around the apartment—it was a semibasement apartment, about 7 meters long by 4 meters wide. It had a kitchen, bathroom, and main room. There was a large, old-fashioned wooden chest for clothes, which was supported by a rectangular table pushed against the wall. That chest was *filthy* inside. Odd bits and old bottles of medicines, an enema, four out-of-date Paul Anka records. In the main room were two beds—one big one and a smaller one. Hombre . . . what a pigsty! Dirty, no taste—but for our needs and plans, it was perfect. The super told me it was for rent. He wanted 4500 pesetas per month [about $100]. When he told me this, I made a face, indicating that it was too expensive. I made a gesture with my hands that meant—'Well, I'll think about it.' I asked for the owner's address. Then I made an appointment with him," said Iker, pausing a moment in his story.

"I went to see him alone, because, according to our new plan, I was to live alone in the apartment. Sculpting. Our idea was to set off the explosion with an electric cable. One of us was supposed to be in charge of the apartment. The other two were going to be disguised as employees of the electric company—in charge of 'fixing the cable.' Theoretically, they had no connection with me, the 'sculptor' who would be living in the apartment. The fourth man would remain in the background—and, if some need or emergency arose, he would be on hand, ready to help. Therefore, it wasn't a good idea for either the owner or the super to see us together.

"I went to see the landlord," continued Iker. "Legally, his official residence was in the apartment just above the basement apartment at 104 Claudio Coello—but in fact he lived in another part of Madrid. He told me right away that the basement apartment was for rent—but he asked for 5500 pesetas. I told him it was out of the question—the super had told me 1000 pesetas less —and that it was too much money for me. I complained. I tried to bargain with him. But, on the other hand, I couldn't let the apartment slip through my fingers, and I could see that the man was determined. Then, during the same conversation, he started to mutter that he wasn't sure he wanted to rent it at only 5500 pesetas—that the day before he had been offered 6500. Suddenly, he wasn't going to let it go for less than that—and he started to bargain with me, to see how far he could up the ante. In my gut, I was raging! But I knew that the deal could be snafued, so I said, Bueno—it strikes me as excessive rent—but as I need the place for my sculpting—okay, I'll accept your conditions.' Naturally, when I accepted the deal, I thought I was making an arrangement with a normal type of person. The way we make business arrangements ourselves, in the Basque country, is with a slip of paper—each declaring his intentions, two signatures, a handshake—and, *finito*, done, over. But *this* bastard wanted to do everything with lawyers. In addition, he wanted to have me sign one of those contracts involving the future sale of the apartment to me! Now it wasn't only 6500 pesetas, but on top of that—*key money!*—80,000 pesetas in advance!—and all of this to be done in a lawyer's office. After six years, the mortgage on the apartment would have been amortized, and, with another payment, I would have owned it. *Then*, the greedy bastard said to me, 'Then . . . all this will be yours . . .'—as if he were talking about a fucking *castle* instead of this shit-filled hole in the wall! I knew this was high-class robbery—he was a real crook—but I put up—and shut up.

"Then he started to give me his life story—a real sob story, lamenting everything, like he was the victim, and at the same time trying to play a paternal role with me. He must have felt guilty, because he rationalized his greedy behavior by moaning to me that now that he was an old man, he needed some security, which this would give him, as he didn't want to have any financial problems in his age. The reason he wouldn't rent the apartment to me straight out, he said, for 6500 pesetas, was that then he'd have had the Internal Revenue on his neck. Legally, he was only supposed to rent the basement for 900 per month. So he got around that by making this crazy contract for the sale of the apartment. That's what they do in Madrid." Iker paused a moment, then went on. "The crook told me that in the end *he* was doing *me* a favor . . . that in the long run, I had a bargain. And so it went. I was raging, but I controlled myself. I was on

the spot. I had to pay whatever he asked—and he took advantage
of the situation. So, while this crook kept talking to me, I was
thinking, 'Just you wait, you prick . . . if our action goes off as
planned, are *you* going to have trouble with this apartment you've
sold me!'—Look, I just can't forget that scene—how that fucking
crook kept making me fork over more and more money.

"Finally, we signed the contract. Then the two of us met with
his lawyer—three times! But it didn't end there. The crook also
wanted to stick me with the bill for his lawyers! But when he
saw the expression on my face—by this time, I was in a real rage
—I couldn't stomach any more of his thievery!—so he didn't quite
dare. He paid the 6000 pesetas for the lawyer's consultation fee,
telling the lawyer he was paying the bill as a personal favor to
me. Naturally, if he had made me pay the lawyer myself, in the
end I would have had to, because we needed the apartment—but
I didn't want to—because the crook would have noticed something strange. He would have thought—it's too easy, creaming
money from this guy—what gives? I had to be very careful. Because, during our negotiations, he kept asking me—where did I
live?—where did I work?—did I have any friends or a bank that
could guarantee my economic solvency?—questions like that. I
sensed that he didn't have much confidence in me—he knew I
was young. I told him that I had just finished my career as an
industrial designer, and I earned my living now by making plans
for the Ministry of Industry, which gave me enough to live on.
I said that in my free time I worked as a sculptor. Finally, we
signed the contract, and the man relaxed a little. When he asked
for my address, I gave him the address of the apartment in the
working-class neighborhood that we already had. He asked who
could give me personal recommendation, and I told him the
super at the other apartment. When he heard that, he relaxed.
When he finally had the money in his hands, he never even went
to the other apartment to check up on me. He had no further
interest in who I was—he was in it for the money."

"Can you imagine—later, the police wanted to take credit for
their brilliant quick discovery of our other apartment," added
Mikel. "That didn't take brains. The landlord had the address in
his papers. We had *wanted* the police to find the other address.
We knew this would only confuse them further. Otherwise, we
wouldn't have given the old address to the landlord at Claudio

Coello. During that whole period, after the execution, the police were completely disoriented, hitting out in every crazy direction like blind men. They didn't know who or what they were looking for. We have proof of this from our 'information service.'"

Txabi commented, "Everything they published on the case immediately following the execution was completely false. They dragged out photographs of other militants that the police had in their archives. They invented their own 'commando' group from an assortment of miscellaneous photographs. They picked up isolated clues we had left—false identification papers, the contract for the apartment, physical descriptions of us. But these were appearances that we'd invented for ourselves—our phony disguises. For Christ's sake, none of the police even discovered the dynamite we had left in the trunk compartment of the car we had left parked next to the church! They didn't even realize that there was dynamite in that car—we were scared shitless about that because the dynamite was meant to explode the car at the very moment when Carrero was executed. When we realized that the police hadn't found the dynamite and that there could be a terrible accident, we were really worried. So, when we gave our press conference in France, we pointed out that there was still unexploded dynamite in the car. Clearly, in this case, one couldn't have called the Spanish police very effective," Txabi commented in his usual cool, even tones.

"Tell about your disguise, Iker," Mikel teased.

"Well, I wasn't exactly disguised—but I made some changes in my appearance. With my face, it isn't hard. There are plenty around that look like me—so, with the addition of a moustache . . ."

"Moustache and *eyebrows*—go on, tell about it!" Mikel kept at him.

"Yeah—that was some number you pulled on me, with that false-eyebrow bit," Iker went on. "During November, I was always pasting on those damned false eyebrows. The first day I went to see the landlord, I wore a suit that I had made especially for the occasion. Basques don't ordinarily wear suits with jackets. So, I had one made for myself—very elegant—and I wore a tie. That was when I went to sign the contract for the apartment. So they could see I was a serious type."

Jon broke in, "That suit must have been discovered later by

the police. Iker wore it only twice," said Jon, pausing. "You might call it our special gift to the police. Just think—some police commissioner now, no doubt, is wearing Iker's fancy suit!"

"After paying the landlord," Iker continued, "he and I went to see the super. He was an okay type. I could have never guessed that he was really a grise. I chatted with him for a while. His wife was also very pleasant and tried to be helpful—right off she made me feel at home. She said whatever I needed, the two of them were there and would be of help. The super saw only me—not the others—and I tried to arrange it so that he didn't even see me too frequently, or close up, because of the moustache and false eyebrows. If he had looked closely, he might have noticed that they were false."

"Nobody ever saw the rest of us," said Jon. "We only entered the basement at very safe hours—for example, at 7 in the morning, or around 10:20 in the evening, when the super had already left his cubicle, and the *sereno* hadn't yet arrived. There were always a few minutes when nobody was on guard; that's when we entered the apartment. When we wanted to go out, Iker would leave first," Jon explained. "He would go up the stairs to the front door and check to see if the super was around. If the coast was clear, the three of us followed him. When we came into the apartment, we followed the same routine. Iker would go to check things out—if it was clear, he'd make a signal, and then we'd follow him."

"We actually had a great deal of liberty and freedom of action," continued Txabi. "Also money—because of the nature of the work we were doing. With the apartment rented, we decided to go back to Euskadi to talk things over with ETA direction. We were going to explain our new plans. We were going to dig a tunnel between the basement and the church and fill it with explosives. These would be set to explode the moment that Carrero left the church and was standing in the street. We had to find out whether we should start digging the tunnel right away, or leave it for later. There was no point in digging a tunnel unless it was for immediate use. Otherwise it would be too dangerous because it could be discovered immediately. The direction gave us the go-ahead. They wanted us to have everything ready, and then wait for just the right moment. This time we were fairly precise in our dates. The meetings of the workers' legal syndicates—which gave them their small benefits—were scheduled for January. We weren't sure whether the execution of Carrero should take place before or after these meetings. We came back to Madrid. Four days later, the direction sent us their reply. After analyzing the situation, they decided that the execution should take place *before* the labor agreements in January."

[ETA never moves impulsively. Part of ETA's method is to plan each step guided by political analysis. Jon suddenly decided to give a long example of ETA thought processes.]

"By the end of 1963," said Jon, "there were the beginnings of a world crisis in the capitalist countries. This crisis is continuous and has become the norm in most countries. This will be sharpened by pressure from the Arab countries against the capitalist nations. European countries will be hit hardest, due to their dependence on the Arab oil supply. With the high rate of inflation and high prices, the workers' demands will be augmented. The workers must put up a strong fight during the January meetings to get their demands met. Should Carrero be executed *before* or *after* these workers' battles? In Spain," Jon went on, "a struggle by the workers always produces immediate repression. If, during the period of repression, Carrero was executed, the workers would have seen this as an answer to the regime's repression, and they would be less discouraged. If our action occurred *before* the workers had massed for their own action, an armed struggle, using revolutionary force could frighten the workers. Their opposition style is pacific—and this could have caused them to 'brake' their own movement before it got started. We discussed all the pros and cons, and we brought up the case of the Huarte kidnapping. After the kidnapping there was a huge general workers' strike in Pamplona. This was a tremendously powerful strike—I don't think it would have been that successful if the kidnapping hadn't taken place. On the other hand, other groups who aren't in agreement with ETA sometimes are interested only in meeting the workers' immediate financial demands. They are perfectly content, otherwise, to work within the system. They aren't interested in any real social change in Spain. Armed struggle gives strength to a real struggle. That is what we believe. But an over-

ROUTE TAKEN BY THE OGRO

A. Home of the Ogro
---- Ogro's route to the church
B. The Church of San Francisco de Borja
-·-·- Ogro's route for returning home
→ Arrows showing traffic directions

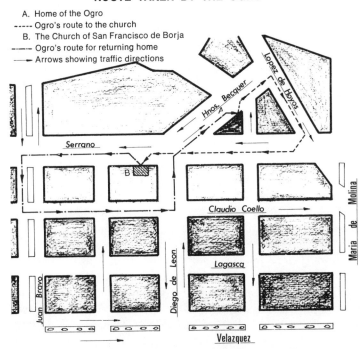

THE PREMISES AS THEY LOOKED AT THE TIME OF RENTING 104 CLAUDIO COELLO

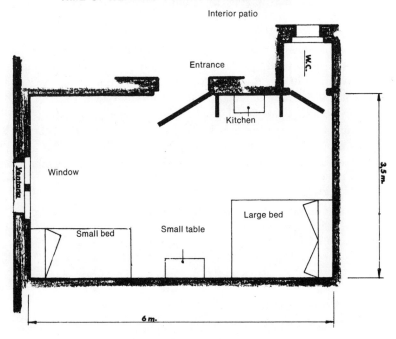

all struggle must have some cohesion among its different elements and diverse techniques. But let me explain why, despite this, we finally decided to kill Carrero *before* the January labor meetings," said Jon, pausing a moment in his account. "If Carrero was killed, it would produce an immediate governmental crisis—and a change of ministers. All sorts of tensions within the regime, between ultras and the middle-of-the-road groups, which Carrero had kept under control, would surface. Then the labor meetings would take place in January—smack in the middle of a tremendous government crisis. The workers, in the midst of this political crisis, would themselves be forced to discuss more than possible salary raises. With Carrero dead, their own political future would also be at stake. The post-Franco era would have begun."

"In the end," Mikel began, "we decided to go ahead with the execution before January, and, as soon as we got the reply from the direction, we immediately started to work on the tunnel. During those November days we had everything planned out in our imagination. We had to dig a tunnel 21 feet long, which would reach the middle of the street. This tunnel was to be T-shaped. The explosives were to be placed where the 'T' crossed the long part of the tunnel. One in the center, the other two explosives on either side of the transverse.

"We planned to start the tunnel. It had to be very narrow, in order to avoid falling debris. We needed to dig as deep into the ground as possible to prevent gas from escaping, and sewage disposal from leaking, and so forth. We needed very little equipment —pickaxes to dig through the ground and plenty of bags for disposing of the dirt that we were taking out of the tunnel and collecting in the basement. These were all plastic garbage bags— we bought them in a local hardware store. In addition, we also used three bags we had bought in the Rastro—the Madrid flea market—the previous summer. Before building the tunnel, we had used them to move machines from one site to another. These three bags were very dirty, very old. 'USA' was stamped on them in big block letters. That's where the press must have gotten hold of the crazy rumor that the CIA was involved in the execution— and also some other nutty ideas . . ."

CHAPTER SEVEN

We Make a Tunnel Under Unfavorable Conditions
We Plan a Date That Has to Be Changed
A Small Episode in the Calle Hermanos Bécquer

"The work in the basement was started on December 7. We had no previous experience in building tunnels," Iker began.

"None of us! Can you imagine—and me, with my claustrophobia on top of everything else. For me to put myself in a closed place makes me gasp for breath. I become asphyxiated," Jon complained.

"We brought some pickaxes from Euskadi," Iker added, "which turned out to be too large for that type of work, and, in the end, we couldn't use them. We had to buy chisels and other instruments of that sort."

Now Mikel spoke up. "The first part of the work consisted of making a hole that somebody could enter to get underneath the sidewalk. But in order to do this, we had to bore a hole through the foundations of the cellar apartment—this was hell!"

"Actually, it was a semibasement apartment," Jon broke in. "On the top part of the wall there was a window that faced the street. The bottom of the window, which was on a level with the sidewalk outside, was more or less at my height—my head touched the window. The apartment was about 5 feet 6 inches below the ground. We began to dig away at the wall just where it reached the floor of the apartment. We made a hole of about 18 inches," said Jon.

"The hole wasn't level with the floor," interrupted Mikel. "It was about 5 inches higher than the floor of the apartment."

"Later," Jon went on, "once the wall was broken, we had to dig deeper."

Txabi now spoke, with his usual calm precision. "The hole began 5 inches above the floor. It was about 20 inches high. We began picking away with a chisel and a mallet, because the wall was very solid and there wasn't enough room to use picks. Each time we penetrated farther along into the tunnel, we had to buy longer chisels."

"The hardest part was this first part," said Iker. "We felt we would never see the end of it—the first day, we didn't even get beyond the wall to the earth. The whole time was used in picking away at the wall. We became more and more discouraged," Iker remembered. "We'd no sooner get rid of one piece of brick than, right behind it, would be *more* brick! As time went on, we became more and more exhausted, and the work seemed harder. In the beginning, we were only able to penetrate the *wall*—at first, only 9 inches at a time—then that went on—more bricks—finally, we were maybe 15 inches deep . . ."

"The construction bricks were very tightly packed, with no air holes," added Txabi. "Very hard to work with."

"And the concrete mortar was damned hard!" interrupted Jon. "I remember that first night—we went back to our own apartment extremely depressed. We weren't used to that type of hard work—digging with chisels—and we hadn't worn gloves, but had worked with our bare hands. Our hands became completely blistered in our struggles with the concrete."

"That first day," said Txabi, "we worked from 9 in the morning until very late that night, locked in that apartment. We didn't lift up our heads during the whole day—except to eat a few sandwiches. This also was a mistake, because we hadn't calculated well the time it would take us to dig a tunnel. We had started out very revved up. We had thought we'd work in teams of two, taking shifts, several hours for each shift. Our original plan was to tear through the wall during the morning and to work during the rest of the afternoon and night in the tunnel itself. We planned to be finished with the tunnel in two days," Txabi explained. "But we immediately realized this was absurd—it was impossible."

"It was heavy going—chiseling through that wall. Took us one solid day. We worked in relays, taking twenty-minute shifts—more than that was impossible. We hadn't even hit dirt by night-

fall! The following morning we came back. By noon the second
day we perforated the wall," Jon said.

"But just barely," Iker added. "We could just manage to get one
arm through the hole and start digging dirt out with the other
hand. We worked all day on enlarging that hole—and by that
night, one person could crawl into the space. We picked the
skinniest man in the group for that job—he'd take up the least
space. Now, with this much space at our disposal, we were able
to make better work plans for the following day. We kept working
in shifts. Each three-quarters of an hour, we'd rotate. It was
impossible for a two-man team to take more than four turns per
day—too exhausting. We would have ended up sick. Not so much
because of the work itself, but because of the conditions in which
we had to work." Iker paused a moment, then continued. "The
stink was atrocious! As soon as we hit earth, it began to reek of
escaping gas. There wasn't a large gas leak—but the earth was
impregnated with gas. It was soft, greasy, humid earth. When I
touched it, I could see and feel that it had been impregnated by
gas. And every time we pulled the toilet chain in the water-closet
—hombre!—there was a stench that just about knocked us out.
When we dug through the sewage, we must have opened one
of the conduits to the toilet disposal. It was impossible to with-
stand that stink."

"There were small leaks throughout the earth. Nothing big, but
still, leaks everywhere—old pipes, sewage, filth. It was a bouillabaisse of the world's garbage!" remembered Jon.

"But we didn't run into any *real* obstacles—like gas pipes, electrical wiring, things of that sort," Mikel explained. "We could see
the gas pipe, and we worked beneath it. We started digging 5
inches above the floor of the basement apartment, so when we
started digging into the earth, we realized that the height of our
own ceiling was on a level with the gas pipe—so we worked a
little lower. Once into the earth, we planned our work better. We
had five or six of those plastic garbage bags ready, and we began
filling them with debris."

"In the beginning, it was easy," Iker went on. "When we had
just started to penetrate the tunnel, the same person who was
chiseling away could fill his sack and hand it over to the man
behind him. That man—the second man—stayed in the entry way
to the tunnel—in the wall we had just penetrated. The first man—

shoveling the dirt, using an old-fashioned shovel of the kind used for coal—could fill a sack and pass it underneath his legs to the second man, behind him. But when the hole became larger, we needed one man to shovel, a second man behind him to take the sacks of debris, and a *third* man in the hole in the wall at the entrance to the tunnel. The first man passed a sack of debris to the second man, who then passed the sack to the third man, waiting in the hole between the apartment and the tunnel, just at the entrance. The third man then brought each sack of debris back into the apartment. Now, while this operation was going on, the fourth man rested—on one of the beds in the apartment. And that's how we dug out the first few feet."

Jon interrupted Iker, to elaborate on the tunnel-digging story. "Because the plastic bags tore easily, we bought a basket similar to those used in church to collect alms for charities. We nailed two boards to the bottom of the big basket, for support, so that the basket couldn't disintegrate with use. We then tied a length of rope to either side of the basket—one for the man shoveling, one for pulling the basket back into the apartment. Now, whoever was shoveling kept the end of one rope tied around his waist and kept the basket underneath him as he worked. When he had a plastic bag filled with debris, he signaled the second man, behind him. The second man pulled the basket backwards and signaled the third man, waiting at the entrance, at the hole in the wall. The third man, using the rope tied on *his* side of the basket, pulled the basket back into the apartment. He'd then take the plastic bag full of debris out of the basket and hand it over to the fourth man. By now, all four of us were working on the tunnel at the same time—taking a great deal of care to make sure the plastic bag didn't rip. Then the fourth man carefully piled up the bags and put an empty plastic bag into the basket. The first man, shoveling, would then pull on his rope, dragging the basket and fresh bag back to his end of the tunnel. And he kept on digging. It was a very rudimentary procedure—but it worked!"

Iker was good at recalling this sort of detail. "We had moments of real panic. When we were 4 or 5 meters inside the tunnel, there was a small landslide. A lot of asphalt, rocks, and dirt suddenly started to fall into the tunnel. We were scared shitless!— Our balls were in our throats! After that, we decided to take our pistols with us while we worked in the tunnel—in case of an accident. Mikel and I wanted those guns with us, because if something happened inside that tunnel, we didn't want to die of asphyxiation. Better to use the pistol. Working in the tunnel was very frightening—aside from the feelings of asphyxiation, we heard everything that was going on above us in the street. What made far more noise than the passing cars was the sound of women walking—clack-clack—in their high heels on the sidewalk just above us."

"That was a very critical moment," agreed Mikel. "When we had gotten so *far,* had worked so *hard* on our plans, inside the tunnel—to think that at any moment, we could be killed by a landslide—or that the sidewalk could cave in and our whole show be discovered. Fuck! We sure were scared shitless."

"That was a real worry for us," Txabi went on, calmly, but solemnly. "We stopped at that point, and talked over our plans for the tunnel. We now had no choice, no exit. The tunnel was well under way. We *had* to continue it, but it was now getting more dangerous. We had to finish that tunnel as quickly as possible. At any moment the super or the landlord—who was no bargain and a bit of a crook as well—could have come snooping around the apartment. The only real solution was to get a technical engineer, who could advise us about the construction of the tunnel. Someone to tell us how to proceed, what the dangers were. But we didn't *have* a technical advisor—nor was there any time to go to Euskadi to find one—so the four of us decided that we had to keep on going. This is when Mikel came up with a new solution."

"I thought we should consult a technical book on the construction of mines," said Mikel. "It would at least give us some idea of what we should be doing. We'd feel a little less disoriented and have a little information to go on. We had to try everything! That's when I told the others I would go over to 'Casa del Libro' —I think that's what it's called—a large bookstore in the Gran Vía. They knew me in that bookstore. I had already purchased all sorts of books there. There was a very *simpático* salesman there. I knew he'd let me browse among the books on my own. Other times, when I'd gone there to get information on graphic arts, he let me take notes from books I didn't even buy. So, we decided that Jon and I would visit the bookstore.

"Because it was already around 5 in the afternoon, Txabi and

Iker were going to take a nap and then go home. Iker reconnoitered the situation—when the coast was clear, he signaled the rest of us, and we all left the apartment. By then, it was miserable —freezing Madrid winter weather. We got into a taxi and shut the windows—as soon as we did, a stench from the tunnel filled the cab. We'd become so used to that stench we didn't realize we carried it with us. But all our clothes were permeated with the smell—we *stank*. The fresh air from the street seemed to make the stink even worse. The cab driver looked at us in his front mirror; he must have been thinking—these men are either excavating sewers—or they walk in shit. We arrived at the bookstore —we must have looked—and smelled—terrible. Two walking disasters! When you're living in tense circumstances, you don't always think of things like that.

"Inside the bookstore, I spoke to the salesman I knew. I told him I wanted to look at some books on mine construction. We had a friend, I explained, to whom we had to give a present. The book had to be on mines—his specialty—but we didn't know which of the books to choose. He was extremely courteous. He took us over to one of the book stands, showed us where the books on mines were—and then he let us browse. There were several books. One two-volume set looked good. One chapter in this set explained how to prop up tunnel walls. We read that chapter, and Jon took notes. It didn't seem to be a difficult procedure to follow—but for the sort of tunnel we were constructing, the information wasn't applicable."

Mikel sat back, and Jon took up the story. "We read that the easiest way of propping up tunnel walls was to put a wooden pole in the center of the tunnel with two wooden planks—one supporting the pole on the bottom, the other supporting it at the top. But this technique was for much larger excavations! In our passageway, which was so tiny, it was hard to make room for even one human body—there was no room for a wooden column and two supporting planks in the middle! A second method we read about was equally impractical—we would have had to put boards across the ceiling of the tunnel and along either wall. But our tunnel was too small—it would have been filled with boards! So, the only solution was to keep our pistols with us, and put up with all the difficulties," Jon said, and paused. "We just had to hope things worked out for us . . ."

Mikel spoke once more. "I told the others what we had found out by reading the books on mining in the bookstore. But for some reason, the panic we'd felt about building that tunnel had quieted down. I relaxed a little, once I understood that the complicated interior propping up of tunnels—building an interior structure—was meant for much larger tunnels. Clearly, *our* tunnel, because of its small size, presented less of a risk. In height, it was no more than 24 inches—and in width, no more than 20," Mikel concluded.

"The next day we made more progress," Iker went on. "Our working conditions were really fucked up! Now the problem wasn't landslides—it was that the earth inside the tunnel was completely impregnated with gas. And the deeper we dug, the worse the gas leaks became. There were many times we became dizzy . . . and a couple of times, I passed out."

"We couldn't stay inside the tunnel more than a quarter of an hour at a time," added Txabi. "By the time we'd gotten about 25 feet in, which was when we started to construct the arms of the 'T'—digging lateral holes to the left and to the right—the air became completely unbreathable. Putrid. We couldn't last in that hole even ten minutes—air too foul," Txabi commented.

"The problem wasn't only that the tunnel was longer now—and we had to go farther in—but that we were now working in teams of three, which meant that there was less oxygen for each of us," explained Mikel.

"In the final stages," Jon broke in, "one man would be positioned in the extreme end of one arm of the 'T'—for example, in the left arm of the 'T'—while another man would be at the point where the two lines of the 'T' crossed. The third man stayed in the long part of the 'T'—in the part of the tunnel leading from the apartment to the arms of the 'T.' During this stage of the dig, there were always two of us who were in the far depths of the tunnel. The man positioned at the very end of an arm of the 'T' now had to work under extremely adverse conditions. The hole was so small he couldn't stand up—or even *sit* up! He had to lie flat in the dirt, stretched out on his stomach, and dig from a prone position. The small amount of oxygen in the tunnel was now completely contaminated with gas." Jon paused a moment in his account, then went on. "I've already mentioned that I'm claustrophobic—I panicked . . . felt I was choking in that unbreathable mess. But . . . when you have to do a job, it has to be done . . . and that's that. There are worse things in life than digging a tunnel," he concluded quietly.

"Many times I'd come out of that stinking tunnel half asphyxiated," said Iker. "And I had such terribly violent headaches I thought my head was exploding. We were all suffering from the severe aftereffects of being continuously intoxicated by the gas fumes," he added.

"And we couldn't open the windows of the apartment to ventilate it," said Jon, "because the air in the room smelled. With the windows open, people walking along the street would have noticed the fumes. And the entire floor of the apartment was covered with dirt—the putrid stench of that dirt also contaminated the room. By this time, there was the same stench in the basement as in the tunnel. We couldn't open the apartment door, either, because the smell instantly escaped into the hallway and up the staircase leading to the first floor. We had to seal up the door frames, so that none of the smell would escape into the outer hall," Jon concluded.

"In the beginning," Txabi recalled, "we tried to ventilate the apartment. One night, before going back to our own apartment, we left the window open. We just couldn't take being in that basement any longer without airing out the place. When we came back the next morning, the whole street was permeated with a horrible stink. I don't know why the *sereno* didn't sense that something was wrong; the smell of the escaping gas fumes was overwhelming. After that, we decided that it was safer to put up with the sealed apartment—and the fumes. If the neighbors or the super thought there was a gas leak—and reported it—well, this could have been very dangerous for us."

"If you could have seen us then—we were really a sad crew," Jon sighed. "After four or five days of working in the tunnel, our skin was ashy-green and had a greasy texture. We had deep shadows beneath our eyes. At night we would go out for a quick sandwich and a beer. That basement apartment didn't even have decent enough sanitary conditions for us to wash ourselves. So we were pooped out—exhausted—and dirty. The only thing we wanted to do was to lie down and stretch out on the bed—but we had to go to the café first and get something to eat and drink. In the café, the clientele moved away from us. We *stank*—our hair, our clothes, our skin—you could smell us several feet away. Even now, as I try to describe it, the stench comes back to me, like a bad dream."

"It actually took us about eight days to build the tunnel," Iker said. "We started it around the seventh of December, and worked until the fifteenth. By the thirteenth, we realized that we had to do the execution as quickly as possible. That was when Txabi went to get the explosives."

"No," broke in Txabi, "I got the explosives later—when the tunnel was already completed. I remember that I had an appointment scheduled for December 15, and we had planned by then to give very exact measurements of the tunnel—and what was needed in the way of explosives. That was when Iker bought the tapemeasure."

"Yes, that's right—you gave me a hard time about that tape-measure! Me, I did exactly what was necessary. I went out, bought the tapemeasure, and came right back to the apartment," said Iker.

"Yeah, but they managed to sell you the most expensive tape-measure in all of Madrid," Jon teased. "You'd think it was made of gold—hombre, you got creamed! You paid 400 pesetas [about $7] and all we needed was a simple measuring stick, to use *once*, to measure the length and width of the tunnel."

"Iker said I got the explosives on the thirteenth," Txabi interrupted. "Actually, he was incorrect. I didn't work with the other three men on the thirteenth, because I had to go to the post office—indeed, several post offices—we had many postal boxes— and I had to get our mail. Then I had to write out a report for the direction and send it on to them. Plus take care of some other errands. Actually, it was on the thirteenth that ETA direction decided we should set the action for the eighteenth. By the twelfth of December, it was clear that there wasn't going to be any mass demonstration by the workers for the December 20 trial of the Carabanchel Ten."

"We were worried about the trial of the Carabanchel Ten," explained Mikel, "but when the twelfth of December came and went and nothing happened, we decided to go ahead with our plan. Jon pointed out that, as the workers hadn't held any mass demonstrations, our action in December would be a good thing— and a further support of the workers."

"Yes," corroborated Jon, "the best thing, of course, would have been a general strike—but the workers hadn't organized themselves, so at least *our* action would be some form of protest.

[The Carabanchel Ten is the nickname for the ten members of the illegal workers' commissions who had been held in Carabanchel prison, near Madrid, for fourteen months, and who were being prosecuted for "illegal assembly" in a monastery at Pozuelo. The Spanish center-left had wanted the case of the Ten to be their great show trial, dramatizing the immediate and crucial issue: whether a modern, industrialized Spain would legalize trade unions. The workers were represented by prominent lawyers including Gil Robles, the former head of the conservative Catholic CEDA during the Civil War, and Ruiz Gíminez, Franco's former Minister of Education. Though the heaviest support for the workers' commissions comes from communists, liberal Christian Democrats and socialists also maintain loose relations with the commissions. Hundreds of members of the workers' commissions have been arrested, jailed, beaten, and tortured. Still, some officials in Franco's regime as well as some factory owners have dealt with the commissions as though they were semilegal. The mass worker support for the trial of the Carabanchel Ten did not get under way as effectively as people had expected. The general strikes called for before the trial didn't come off. This is what Txabi, Iker, Jon, and Mikel are referring to when they say they were waiting to see what happened in Madrid.

The actual trial shocked foreign observers by its brevity and its almost complete lack of legal procedure. Cardinal Enrique y Tarancón—later called the "red Bishop" during Carrero Blanco's funeral by the ultra rightists—was not permitted to act as a character witness for Father García Salve, the worker priest who got a nineteen-year sentence. The journalist Nicolas Satorius, son of El Condé de San Luis, one of Spain's richest, most aristocratic families, also got nineteen years. Marcelino Camacho, the acknowledged leader of the commissions, got twenty years. The defense built their case around the fact that the men involved denied ever having had a meeting in the Pozuelo monastery. Unlike Burgos, they did not put the regime itself on trial. This is what Jon, Mikel, Iker, and Txabi are discussing. In March 1975, a shaky, uncertain regime reduced, in an appeal, the sentences of the Carabanchel Ten to five and six years apiece.]

"We have to separate out two things—what went on in Spain prior to the trial and the trial itself," Txabi explained. "We, of course, could have nothing to do with the trial itself. Once we knew the date of the trial, we were very concerned with how to proceed in the period prior to it. We were worried that if we executed Carrero early on, this might brake a possible workers' demonstration for the Carabanchel 10 . . . because this was a trial against the workers—they had to give their own reply, with workers' demonstrations and strikes—or a general strike, such as there was in Euskadi during the Burgos trials. It was up to the masses to react. We didn't have too much confidence— there seemed to be little movement in the direction of a protest. Still, we waited, as the direction wanted us to, until the twelfth (which was to be the day of demonstrations) to see if any general movement would get going. Nothing happened. So our problem, with a choice of days, was the period prior to the trial. As for the trial itself, that didn't worry us as much. It was very clear that the execution of Carrero wasn't going to influence one way or another the sentences given to the Carabanchel 10. The sentences were terribly severe—brutal. But, they would have gotten the same sentences even if nothing had happened to the Ogro. A fascist state like Spain, which is based on force and terror, won't permit the visible heads of movements such as the workers' commissions to remain unscathed and unpunished. They needed to make an example of the heads of the workers' commissions in order to terrorize the people. They needed to suppress any protest. Look at the way they garroted that young student, Puig Antich!"

"Yes," Jon corroborated, "the best thing of course would have been a general strike—but the workers didn't organize themselves, so at least our action would be some form of protest. But the date—December 20—turned out to be pure coincidence— indeed, a pure necessity."

"I don't understand what kind of defense the lawyers and the Carabanchel 10 put up," Mikel mused. "I still don't understand that case. The people expected something stronger . . . more positive statements, something that would have inspired the workers' struggle, who had their eyes fixed on their spokesman, on the trial in Madrid. Fuck it—on trial were the principal *leaders* of the workers' commission . . . for them to say nothing . . . Balls . . . what the hell sort of leaders are these?"

Iker interrupted, "Mikel is right. I was surprised by the trial. Think of the Burgos trial . . . and compare the two. Their slogan was 'Like Burgos—But *more* than Burgos.' People were waiting for the leaders of the workers' commission to denounce the oppression of the workers, the lack of liberty and freedom, the lack of legal workers' unions in Spain . . . the same way that ETA denounced the Spanish oppression of the Basque country, and the oppression of the factory workers in the Basque country. They used the Burgos trial well. They turned the trial around. Instead of letting themselves be the accused, they became the accusers of the regime, and put the regime on trial. This is the meaning of a true political trial, no? And in Burgos, the death sentences were being asked, and they still went ahead, they still put the regime on trial."

"As soon as we sensed there was no 'ambiente' in Madrid on December 12—no protest action—Txabi gave the go-ahead for December 19," said Mikel. "We calculated that we'd be ready.

"On December 15 we went to get the explosives," said Txabi, taking over the narrative. "Our rendezvous was a halfway point between Madrid and Euskadi. The meeting went off without incident. The men who brought us the explosives didn't run into any problems along the way. They used the same precautions as on previous occasions. They weren't stopped en route—they had no problems with police controls, or things of that sort. They arrived at the meeting place exactly as planned. We transferred the explosives into my car. The men who delivered the explosives didn't know about Operation Ogro. They merely knew they had to bring a certain quantity of explosives to a certain agreed-upon destination—this they did. After the transfer, they followed me for several miles as a support convoy, in case of trouble. As soon as they were sure I was in no danger, they drove off. They went back to Euskadi. I went on to Madrid."

There was a long pause. Txabi seemed to be thinking. "The explosives fit very easily into the trunk compartment. They weighed a lot, though . . . around 80 kilos. We had asked for more explosives . . . but they sent us 80 kilos." He paused a moment, then continued. "Transporting the dynamite wasn't too dangerous. When dynamite is well protected, well wrapped, it's not very likely that there will be an accident. A detonator is needed to set it off. Without a detonator connected to the dynamite, an accident is unlikely. While the detonator—the system for setting it off—and the explosives are kept separated, it is almost impossible for the dynamite to explode. Naturally, something could always go wrong. In order for an explosion to occur, you'd have to have an accumulation of great density of heat in one spot. This could happen, say, if two automobiles collided— but the possibility of this happening is very small, provided, of course, that the explosives are extremely well wrapped." Txabi paused thoughtfully, then went on. "We also transported two rolls of cord for the detonator, each 100 meters long—also, a dozen detonators. We had both electric detonators and ordinary ones. We needed both kinds because, in order to insure maximum force during the explosion, we'd place the ordinary detonators around the electric ones. It was very easy for us to get the explosives into the basement apartment. Around 10:30 in the evening, which was the time we generally left the apartment, neither the super nor the *sereno* was guarding the building. This was the hour we picked for slipping in the explosives. Our car was parked near the apartment. We took out our suitcases, much in the manner of people returning from a trip."

"There were two huge bags and two suitcases," Jon recalled. "We moved like lightning. Nobody had a chance to realize what we were up to."

"The explosives were 'Goma Two'—these explosives were taken from the Hernani Powder Magazine—which has a big warehouse of explosives. More than 3000 kilos of explosives had been stolen from Hernani. Later, the police were able to trace and get back only 1000 kilos. Of all the industrial explosives, the strongest is pure Goma—virgin Goma. The strength of explosives is judged from the starting point of pure Goma—all are made in Río Tinto. There are all sorts and classes of Goma. We used Goma Two, because that's what we were given, and we had the guarantee that this was an explosive with sufficient force to explode the tunnel upward. As a matter of fact, not all of our explosives were Goma Two. We had 50 kilos of Goma Two—the rest was a variety of weaker explosives. But those sausages of Goma Two were stupendous! Just like sausages from Pamplona. *Huge!* Each sausage weighed over a kilo. Also, they were extremely well packaged. Each one came wrapped in heavy plastic to protect the explosives against any premature damage," concluded Txabi.

"They weighed a lot of milk. Those sausages—nearly killed me —getting them packed into the tunnel!" Iker burst out.

"But that was also due to the cramped position we were in. The tunnel was so narrow that you had to move about in an awkward way. When the time came to actually put the dynamite inside the tunnel, it was very difficult—and awkward," Mikel added.

Jon began speaking, taking over the explanation of the explosive system that the commando used. "Now that we'd finished the T-shaped tunnel, our plan was to distribute three packages of explosives—20 kilos each—two in either extreme of the arms of the 'T'—the third, in the middle, where the 'T' crossed. Therefore, all three packages had to be placed in a straight, horizontal line [see diagram]. This line of explosives was 7 meters long, just below the street in the place where Carrero's car had to pass. The three packages of dynamite were joined by a detonator cord, which also ran the length of the tunnel, back into the apartment. Actually, there were three detonator cords, one for each package of explosives. The three detonator cords and three electric wires from the detonator cable were joined inside the apartment. In the middle of all the explosives we put an electric detonator with several ordinary detonators around it, to make sure of even greater explosive power. All these cords and wires were wrapped together with heavy-duty rubber tape. The ends of the electric detonator cable were joined to an electric cable. This electric cable was drawn through the window, then it continued the length of the whole street—Claudio Coello—alongside the electric telephone wires. It stretched the length of Claudio Coello up to Diego de León. There, it dropped to the street. At street level, we put the end of this cable inside an 'electric box' hidden inside a briefcase. Naturally, the cable inside the electric box was split into two wires—negative and positive. There was a battery inside the box, too—and the cable was joined to the battery." Jon

PLAN FOR THE POSITIONING OF
EXPLOSIVE CHARGES

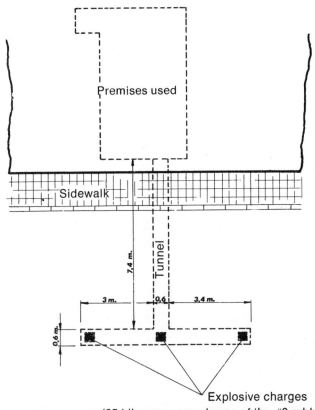

Explosive charges
(25 kilograms per charge of the #2 rubber type explosive)

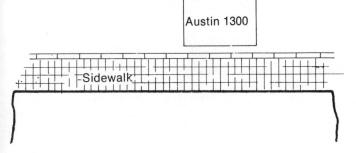

Calle C L A U D I O   C O E L L O

THE PREMISES AFTER
COMPLETION OF THE TUNNEL

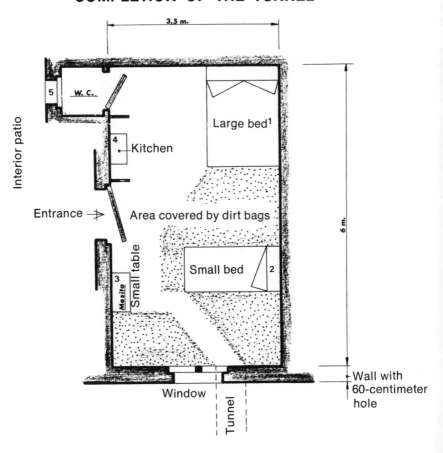

Calle CLAUDIO COELLO

1. Double bed
2. Old bed with tattered mattress
3. Small cabinet with odds and ends in it. Here are found all sorts of things, from an enema syringe to records, pills, etc.
4. Double burner camping stove.
5. Bathroom window facing the inside patio.
6. Window facing Claudio Coello

paused a moment, then continued. "The battery had a switch.
The switch turned on the current—and set off the explosion.
Therefore, one of us had to be at the corner of Diego de León—
Claudio Coello isn't visible from this vantage point. He would be
carrying the briefcase with the electric box containing the battery. Then—with his hand inside the briefcase, on the switch—he
would wait until one of the other men gave him the signal. One
of us would be stationed on the same corner—but watching to
see when Carrero's car passed just over the tunnel."

Txabi broke in, pointing out that none of the men was a specialist in explosives. "But we did have some rudimentary knowledge," he went on, "even more than rudimentary knowledge about
how explosives worked. *All* militants of ETA do. This operation
didn't demand any extensive or complicated knowledge of explosives. The only real problem was to make sure that the explosion didn't go *horizontally* through the tunnel—we needed *verti-
cal* force—straight up through the street! We figured out how to
manage such an explosion—and we did it."

"We were worried about the foundations of nearby houses,"
added Iker. "There could have been a lot of damage. We studied
rather carefully how to set off the explosives in order not to overdo
the force and cause damage to the other houses on the street."

"We carefully calculated a way to place the explosives so that
all the force would go upward," Mikel continued. He paused,
then said, "It's true, though—none of us had any real experience
with explosives before Operation Ogro."

"All those speculations in the newspapers—that we were technical experts—were ridiculous," said Jon. "Everything that was
reported on this subject was a lie—and absurd! It was even
rumored that there was an expert in optic lenses—an electrical
engineer—a mining engineer—ridiculous! People were trying to
appear smarter than they really were about how the execution
was done. Also, the Government had to deny what had happened
—that in reality it could have been so *simple* to kill Carrero
Blanco—the head of the Government. They had to show the
people that the forces that destroyed Carrero had some tremendous, omnipotent power. The regime intimated that it was an
international conspiracy—international Communists, united with

Swedes—elements of the IRA, helped by the OAS—the CIA—and all the rest of the crazy rumors printed in the press," commented Jon impatiently.

"As for all those scenarios," interjected Txabi, "they didn't believe a word of it themselves. Fuck . . . the Government isn't that naive . . . what happened is, they couldn't accept the simple truth. 'They killed our Carrero Blanco? Hombre! Then the greatest technical skills of the world must have been used in this conspiracy . . .' "

Mikel commented, "If the military thought that this was an operation that demanded a great technique, as they kept saying—all it meant is that they were actually in the dark as to what took place. They didn't have one fucking idea what happened! What they called 'tank mines' in the press were ordinary packages of dynamite that had been stolen nearly a year before. Which meant that the dynamite we used had already lost about half its strength —quite a bit *more* than half its strength. The essential ingredient, what was absolutely necessary—and about this they wouldn't have had the slightest comprehension—was the *reason* for our struggle. Our *belief* was the true dynamite that gave us strength . . . our *real* secret power for finding solutions to the problems that came up. Clearly, from what we've said, Operation Ogro wasn't easy . . ." Mikel suddenly allowed himself to become emotional. He continued. "We had to overcome many difficulties. We were often discouraged. We won't deny that. But we overcame everything. And we will overcome future problems, and be victorious in even more difficult undertakings. Many of us will die along the road . . . but new members will join us, and each time we will grow bigger. And we will strike back even harder."

Iker joined him. "I want to underscore that the reason we did Operation Ogro wasn't that *technically* we were well prepared for it—but because of the necessity of doing it. We understood that Operation Ogro had to be—and then, we found the way to go about it. If you see the justice of doing an action—that it is for the good of the people—well, then, you simply *do* it. *Hay que hacer lo*—that's Jon's phrase. When you have clear objectives, the difficulties along the way can be overcome."

"Remember, when we first came to Madrid, in our guts most of us felt the action would be impossible to accomplish," said Jon, echoing the feelings of Iker and Mikel. "As time passed, though,

little by little we learned to overcome each obstacles in our way
—and that was how we finally got to Operation Ogro."

"To say the contrary would be to negate the potential revolutionary power of the people," added Txabi, more calmly. "They
have to be awakened—to see the necessity of liberating themselves, of organizing for the struggle."

"In respect to this action, I realized something very concrete—
the way the bourgeoisie is able, through the media, to manipulate
the thinking of the general mass of people," said Jon—he always
came back to his disgust with the press. "For example, fifteen
days ago, two militants of ours were killed. Two young boys,
carrying a bomb, which exploded in their arms and killed them.
Result: In the newspaper, it was reported that they were two
very young boys who didn't know anything about bombs, and,
because of their inexperience, the bombs exploded. This is what
the people were taught to believe. But it is not what happened.
Those two boys were both technically well trained in explosives.
One of them was the best technical expert the organization had.
On the other hand, in describing Operation Ogro—the press
depicted us as 'exceptional.' It was so well done, they said—it
couldn't have been ETA. It was the work of technical experts—
geniuses! They made the general public believe this. The truth
of it is that our group of militants had very little technical experience or training in explosives. But this is how the media manipulate the thinking of the general public, by making them believe
all the time the exact opposite of what is really going on," concluded Jon.

"They want to keep the general public in ignorance," Mikel
said. "On the pretext of giving information, they confuse and
slant the truth. Operation Ogro—and how it was treated in the
press—all their misconceptions—taught us a lot about mass
media. Even other anti-Francquist groups mixed up the information, gave out the wrong data. Fuck! It was disgusting, their
performance," Mikel added angrily.

"It was an aberration on their part to think that an operation
so well thought out couldn't have come from the left. That indicates a lack of belief in the people and their struggle that is
unpardonable," Jon added.

"In brief," he continued, "it doesn't take a mining engineer
to make a tunnel! Nor an expert in explosives to dynamite the

tunnel. Nor does one have to be a specialist in optics to have a car well placed, signaling the exact spot to be dynamited. Nor is it impossible to have a man standing nearby, ready to give the go-ahead signal. All that myth must be eliminated. Nobody is a god—nor is a god needed. This was the work of normal men."

"After we unloaded the dynamite that first night," said Iker, coming back to the main chain of events, "we left everything wrapped, without taking the explosives out of the suitcases. We now had very little to do—except to place the dynamite, which we didn't plan to do until the very last moment. So, we left the basement apartment, and started back home."

"Yes—home. But before we got there, we had that quarrel with the man who owned the Seat 600—it was all Jon's fault—the way Jon had given him a look," Txabi commented.

"With Jon, we always had a lot of trouble," interjected Mikel. "It was the way he *looked* at people. We would be in a bar or a cafeteria, sitting down, drinking or having something to eat, and Jon would stare at some man or woman—with a glassy-eyed stare —never removing his eyes from that person. We'd ask him, 'What are you *staring* at?' And he'd reply, 'Who, *me?* I'm not staring at anyone . . . I'm just thinking.'" Mikel paused. "That guy—he has a *unique* way of thinking! That night, his 'thinking' got us into trouble."

"It was around 11 at night," continued Txabi. "After leaving the dynamite in the basement apartment, we drove down Hermanos Bécquer in the direction of the Castellana. Iker was driving, and Jon was sitting next to him. I don't know exactly how it all happened, but a Seat 600 came alongside us—one man and two girls. I saw that the car was coming to a full stop, right next to us. I stopped our car. The man got out. He came running toward us. In a fury, he yanked open our car door and screamed at Jon—'Chulo! Pimp! You bastard!'"

"No!" protested Jon, the fair-haired innocent, "it all happened a little differently. First of all, while the man was still inside his car, he started to make gestures at me. I guess I *was* staring—I was distracted and didn't realize that I'd been staring. When I saw the man making those angry gestures at us, I thought that maybe Iker had been driving too close to the man's car. So *I* made a gesture—as if to say '*Qué pasa?*—what gives?' That's when he parked his car and came running over. He ran right across the street—and it was *me* who opened the car door."

"But all this took place right in front of the Ogro's residence!" exclaimed Mikel. "That was all the fucking trouble we needed! We needed *that* kind of trouble like a hole in the head! To be stopped in front of the Ogro's house—with all those grises just a few feet away from us, standing in his doorway!"

"So I opened the car door," continued Jon stubbornly, "and he said, 'Oye, niño—hey, boy—you're some prick, aren't you? Do you think you can stare at people that way? That was some fresh stare you gave! You have no education—one of these days you're going to get your head smashed in!' Then Iker said *he* was going to get out of our car and smash in the man's face! He said we should pull the car up a little farther—he was getting out. And I said to Iker, 'Come off it! Come off it! Drop it!' Finally, we kept on going. We crossed the Castellana—but Iker kept on muttering, 'I want to stop the car here. I'm going to wait for that guy.' But Mikel calmed Iker down—and we kept on driving."

"We lost a good chance to give that prick a few swift blows," said Iker regretfully. "It was one of those moments—you're tense, you put up with things, put up, put up, put up—then comes a moment when you want to let it all out. Even though you know you shouldn't. The slightest thing can make you jump. You *have* to let off steam . . . but then you've got to grind your teeth, and keep your cool. For me, that's rough. It doesn't gò with my nature."

"That guy was a showoff," added Txabi. "He had two girls with him, and he wanted to show what a big cocksman he was. He'd had a few, and he was ready to mess with someone. The crazy thing was that it happened to us in Hermanos Bécquer—just in front of the Ogro's house."

"It wasn't the first time we nearly got into a fight in Madrid," Iker recalled. Things of that sort happened to us a couple of times. Some provocation in a bar—or even something more serious. You see some injustice, something inhuman—and you can't help wanting to stop it. But we couldn't afford that luxury—we couldn't get into any fights. You just had to keep your cool and avoid the situation—like some sort of shitty bastard."

"Also," Txabi pointed out, "we were living under constant

tension. By the end, the work was choking us. And when you live the way we did—four lonely bastards—so many months away from home—without being able to speak to another soul, without family, without our friends, without our own environment—there comes a moment when such close living among a small group of militants . . . Shit! Even though you don't want it to be that way —it becomes difficult."

"This is a life you can't take for too long," Jon sighed. "Nobody can endure too much time like that. Sometimes you feel it inside. You start thinking—you are young . . . you'd like to see some girls . . . but you can't. Immediately, it would be—'What do you do? Where do you work?' And if you're not just looking for a casual pickup, you can't lie. It becomes—like I said in the beginning—a monk's life," said Jon, sighing again.

"Don't pay too much attention to Jon," Txabi said. "He complains—but in the end, he is the strongest one of us all. Everything we did seemed to Jon to be 'excesses.' He is the austere member of the commando." Txabi paused—then changed his tone, and became serious once again. "A technical difficulty came up, so that we couldn't do the action on the eighteenth—December 18. We decided to go ahead, instead, on the nineteenth. Then Kissinger came to Madrid—and we felt that day would be wrong, because of the extra guards that would be in the neighborhood for the occasion. So we decided to do it on the twentieth."

The private residence of the President of the Government, Admiral Luis Carrero Blanco.

The Church of San Francisco de Borja, where Don Luis Carrero Blanco attended mass daily.

Number 1 Calle Mirlo. Apartment 12-C was the residence of Commando Txikia in Madrid.

Number 30 Calle Mediterraneo. One of the apartments used by Commando Txikia in Madrid.

View of Calle Claudio Coello from Diego de Leon. A. Place where the electric circuit was closed in order to set off the explosion. B. Street position of the guard. From here he gave the "go" signal for Operation Ogro. C. Position of third militant on the corner of the street. He was the back-up in case first guard ran into trouble.

104 Calle Claudio Coello. A. Basement window

Calle Claudio Coello A. Recently renovated cornice. B. Exact site of the explosion. Please note recent renovation. C. Door of 104 Calle Claudio Coello.

Car belonging to Prime Minister Luis Carrero Blanco after the explosion. Witnesses said the Prime Minister's car was hurled against the edge of the roof of the church, bounced over it and landed on the second floor terrace on the other side of the building. (UPI)

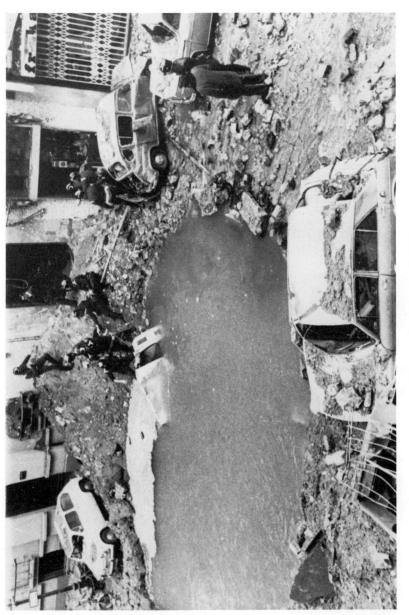

The explosion site. (UPI)

Commando Txikia and colleagues in a press conference with the international press sometime after the incident.

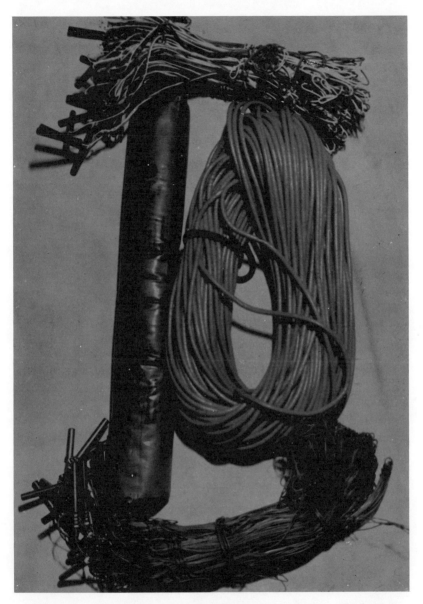

Detonators, fuse and explosives belonging to the kit which Operation Ogro used to set off the charges in the tunnel. These materials came from "The Riotinto Explosive Union S.A."

This material was part of the ammunition taken in Hernani by the Commando Txikia. Contrary to what the Spanish press published, the Spanish police actually informed the Portuguese police (P.I.D.E.) concerning the exact origin of the explosives.

CHAPTER EIGHT

The Last Three Days
Unforeseen Incidents with a Ladder
Kissinger Is Not Invulnerable
The Twentieth of December—
The Decisive Date
Some Hydroelectric
Employees Get Wet
Our Bed Breaks Down
The Complicated Optical
System Says "Now!"

"On Monday morning, December 17, we packed all our belongings," began Iker, "in order for Txabi and Mikel to take our things to the militants they were meeting in Aranda de Duero, near Burgos. The militants planned to get our belongings back to Euskadi for safekeeping. We started wrapping our books. We looked carefully in every corner: but we didn't take everything. We left many things there—my new suit jacket, the gymnastic equipment and dumbbells, and a lot of bed linen. We put in the car only the most indispensable items. Then Txabi and Mikel went to Aranda de Duero. We were supposed to pay our rent on the twentieth." Iker paused. "Listen, now I remember . . . we never paid it . . ."

"Should we apologize from here?" Jon asked, amused.

"No—no apology," Mikel rejoined, "we left our landlord two months' advance deposit—he ended up with more than enough."

"We noticed that the super wasn't greeting us—we hadn't tipped him. We didn't remember to do it because we were working hard on the tunnel," Iker went on. "Before, we used to look for some excuse to give him good tips. For instance, we asked him for some 'churros'—doughnuts—or to do some other invented errand. But, just before 'Ogro,' we didn't have a free moment—we didn't ask for churros or anything else, and he was rather unpleasant. When he saw us on the morning of the seventeenth, taking out the suitcases and putting them into the car, he got mad. 'These gentlemen are going away—they're taking out their belongings!' he yelled at his wife. She rushed over to us—I thought she was going to grab us by the neck!—and command, 'You have to pay the rent!' I was preparing an alibi for her—we were going to pay next week, and so forth. Instead, she brought us a Christmas card. We gave her 400 pesetas [about $7] and the next two days—the eighteenth and the nineteenth—they were all smiles and kindness."

"While Txabi and Mikel went to get the luggage, Iker and I went to rent the car," Jon added.

Iker continued, "I filled out all the papers in a car rental office in the Plaza de España—the office was next to a self-service cafeteria. I took out my money. I had only about 4500 pesetas [about $80] on me. They asked me for 5000. I was short 500 pesetas. We wanted to leave as little deposit money as we could get away with—we didn't want to lose money unnecessarily. But this seemed okay to everybody. They asked me for my driving permit. I was a little antsy, because my driving permit actually belonged to a man 28 years old. By this time my hair was cut short. I had had a shave, too—not with an electric razor—but with a sharp razor, by a professional barber—so now I looked like a clean-shaven bourgeois. This face of mine makes me look even younger than I am, so I still felt a little uncertain about the permit's saying I was 28. But the panic was momentary. They told me, in the car rental office, to go to their garage on Alcántara Street—where the company's rental cars were stored. That took me an additional twenty minutes or half hour. During the negotiations, I was still scared that the main office might notice something odd about my papers, investigate, and telephone ahead to the garage. Jon and I were both worried about this. So, just in case, I went into the garage alone, and Jon waited outside for me.

Anyway, I had taken certain precautions. When they had asked me for my driver's license, instead of simply handing it to them, I included my identification papers. It's easy to forge a driver's license—but everybody knows that it's hard to fiddle with identification papers. This plastic covering makes it very difficult to tamper with them. On my phony identification card, my name was José M. Casas Blanco. That also made me nervous. We had stolen the card from a man who actually lived in Madrid. By some crazy coincidence, maybe I was renting a car at *his* garage! Those were the wild thoughts that were going through my head. The man in the garage who drove the car out for me asked to see my driver's license. I gave him the same wallet I'd given the man in the rental office—with both the false identification papers and license inside. The man—the one who drove out the car—was looking at a list he had. I was thinking that if the man whose driver's license we'd filched had reported it—and his name was on that list—we were snafued . . . lost. But then I figured out that the list was a list of those people who owed the company money. After a few minutes, this man returned my papers. He gave me the car keys. It was a white Seat 124. I don't remember the license number. It was a new car—had about 4000 kilometers on it."

"With the car at our disposal, we made a trial run of the action on the eighteenth," said Jon. "We precision-timed the operation. First, we picked the safest place to leave the car during the action. Then we practiced the escape and the changeover of cars. At first we thought we would leave the car in Diego de León, right near the corner of Claudio Coello. But we decided it was too near the church. There was a lot of traffic in this neighborhood—and we could run into problems. We finally chose Lagasca. We would go down toward Juan Bravo, take that street, pass next to the electric car race game, then to the Plaza de Ruben Darío, crossing by Miguel Angel, and, finally, stop in front of the Police Training Academy, where we'd swap cars. We planned to park our getaway car there—something the police would never in a million years imagine that we'd do! We made our trial run at 9:30 in the morning—the same time the actual action would take place. And we saw that, if everything worked well, the entire maneuver would take us three minutes."

"But," explained Iker, "there was the problem of one traffic light. If we hit the traffic light during a stop period, we had to figure on taking more than three minutes. It's the traffic light in the street where Juan Bravo and Serrano cross. When it's red, it takes a long time to change to green, because of traffic. If we hit red, it would be dangerous for us, because we would be stopped at a point very near the locale of the action itself. We couldn't race through the light—that would call too much attention to us and be even more dangerous. In spite of the problems with the traffic light, in the end, we decided that this was the best escape route at our disposal."

"By 10 o'clock, we had finished our trial run," added Mikel. "With that done, we then went through the city to buy everything that we still needed for the action." He paused a moment, then began to enumerate the items: "electricians' uniforms . . . electricians' tools . . . overalls . . . a metal box . . . a ladder . . ."

"We lost a whole morning running around Madrid in search of equipment," Jon broke in. "Electricians' tools, screwdrivers, scissors, pliers, cable cord, insulating tape, plus an assortment of extra tools, just for effect. We knew that electricians always carry a lot of stuff with them. We bought most of the supplies quickly at a hardware store in Magdalena Street, next to the Tirso de Molina subway stop. We also bought electric light bulbs for testing the current. But we couldn't find cable cord in that neighborhood. We were told we could buy cable on Mayor Street, and we found some in a store there. We needed very thick cable, for outdoor use—we bought 150 meters. We didn't want a new-looking briefcase—the briefcase for hiding the electric box—so we went to the Rastro—the flea market—to pick up a second-hand one. Couldn't find one in the Rastro, so we bought a new one. We picked a dark one that wasn't very conspicuous. We didn't want to call anyone's attention to it. During those last few days, we spent all our time racing around Madrid on errands. We had a problem with the ladder because at first we couldn't find one!"

Txabi broke into Jon's long monologue to make a quick explanation. "The ladders electricians use are constructed of two parts—you pull a cord and the second part extends upward. We could now write an encyclopedia on the subject of special ladders! On that wintry December day in Madrid we got a complete 'ladders' education."

"The sort of ladder we needed," Jon went on, "is owned *only* by official service companies—the electric company, the telephone company. Big ladders of this sort are difficult to transport, and the service companies carry them in trucks. The driver deposits them on the street where the construction is going on. The ladders are locked with chains and have the name of the service company stamped on them. We needed a very tall ladder—one that would look like one of the service ladders—but it had to fit into a car or taxi. We couldn't find one that was both large enough for our use and small enough so that we could transport it ourselves. The stores didn't have any. We stopped workmen who were using them in the street and asked them where they'd obtained their ladders. But the workers were just salaried day workers—they had no idea where the ladders came from. The workmen seemed surprised at our questions. They did try to answer us. They gave us all sorts of addresses. We zigzagged back and forth across Madrid—but we couldn't find our ladder! We were getting nervous. This was beginning to be a major problem. Finally, someone told us that in Calle del Pez there was a carpenter who made ladders. We went right over. At last—we had found a ladder in two parts—*perfect* for what we had in mind."

"I remember that Jon and I had a long conversation as to whether the ladder would be tall enough for stringing up the electric cable," said Txabi. "There was a cable that was strung just beneath the balcony of the house opposite the carpenter's house. The cable was attached to the corner street sign. When the carpenter heard us discussing the height of the ladder we'd need, he took the ladder out into the street, placed it against the house to the height of the street sign, and told us to try it out. He urged Jon to climb up—that way, we could make sure that the ladder was what we wanted."

"I didn't have any choice! I had to climb up—and it was a very narrow ladder," said Jon, taking up the story. "It seemed *endless* to me. Also, the street was very steep—we were in the high part of the street, near the corner. The ladder couldn't be placed on level terrain, and it kept wiggling. But, I was supposed to be a professional, so I couldn't stop climbing—I had to go to the top. So, with one hand gripping the ladder and the other hand using the wall of the building as additional support, I climbed to the top. I yelled down to the carpenter, 'Yes, the ladder's fine! Just what we need!' We hailed a taxi and tied our ladder to the luggage rack on the roof, then brought it over to the basement apartment. This was at 1 o'clock, just before the lunch hour. We still had to paint the ladder. We planned to stain it walnut—we were going to try to make the wood look old, well used. We got to work immediately. By late afternoon, the ladder was dry. Our big problem was that everything we had was *new*—briefcase, tools, overalls—and even though we rubbed all the equipment against the floor and stamped all over everything with our feet and even used water to wet the equipment, we couldn't get the brand-new look off what we'd bought. True, by the time we'd finished, everything looked *dirty*—but it still looked *new!*"

"By then," Txabi explained, "we were able to enter the basement apartment without hiding ourselves—as though we were normal electricians, doing our regular work. Iker had told the super that several electricians would be coming to the apartment to make an electric installation. He told him to give the electricians the keys to the apartment—and told him not to bother them—it was all right for the workmen to go straight in. *We* were the 'electricians'—and we went in and out of the apartment as though it was normal for us."

"I made sure I was never seen with the others," Iker explained, "so they couldn't connect the 'sculptor' with the 'electricians.' I purposely disappeared on the day they came to the apartment."

Jon remembered the super's wife (people always made a strong impression on him). "She was very *simpática*. When we arrived I said to her, 'We are electricians—we are running an electric line from Diego de León into the basement apartment. The sculptor in the basement apartment has ordered additional voltage for his work.' We gave her some other complicated explanations which I no longer remember."

"Then we went out to eat," Txabi continued. "Sitting in one of the local taverns, we saw quite a panorama . . . all of Madrid suddenly seemed to be under military guard. We realized that the heavy military guard in the streets was because of Kissinger's visit that week. Christ! We had everything prepared—everything ready—and now *Kissinger* fell on our heads!"

"Of course, we had known that Kissinger was coming to Madrid and that he'd visit the American Embassy. But we never imagined that there would be that much military protection during his visit," Iker explained. "We thought there would be some surveillance—to prevent demonstrations, protests, things of that sort—but nothing more than that. We never imagined that all the roofs and subway entrances would be manned by grises with machine guns. In every corner there was a pair of grises. Soldiers were patrolling the streets of Madrid in army jeeps. There was a jeep stationed on the corner of Diego de León and Serrano. There was too much police and military vigilance. During our lunch, we decided to delay the action."

"It's impossible to describe how crowded that quarter of Madrid was—because of Kissinger. We ourselves saw crowds of people. Also, it's very probable that the place was saturated with plainclothesmen," said Jon. He paused, then added, "That day, it felt as though all of Madrid was on the street."

"If we had been sure that Kissinger was going to go to mass the following day with the Ogro, we would have run the risk, because it was worth it—even if just to show our solidarity with the Palestinians. But we had no certainty of what conditions would be with Kissinger in Madrid, and no really compelling reason for doing the action on the nineteenth, so it didn't seem worth our while to take any additional risks," continued Iker. "We decided to postpone 'Ogro' until the twentieth, when we would be operating under safer conditions."

Mikel took up the narrative. "Later that afternoon—well, it was practically night by then—we drove back to the basement apartment. The ladder was dry by then. It was ready for use. The rest of the equipment was in order, too. We packed the piles of dirt in the apartment more tightly. By this time, most of the floor was covered with piles of dirt, and the wall connecting the basement apartment to the super's apartment was completely lined with dirt. It was one of those strange moments in life—when it all seems *endless*. You know that zero hour is getting near. You are scared that new difficulties will crop up at any moment. We talked a little bit among ourselves, about how we felt. We were becoming restless. We couldn't wait for the next day to come. We knew we couldn't delay 'Ogro' any longer—with the dirt piled up in the apartment, it was getting dangerous. At any moment the super could walk in. In fact—the three of us were sitting on the bed when suddenly the doorbell rang!"

Iker, interrupting Mikel, began speaking. "The super was just outside the door—he wanted to come in! For a second, we were all paralyzed. What could we do? The place, by this time, smelled *putrid*. We had emptied a bottle of room deodorizer to improve things—but the mixture of the deodorizer and the other smells had made an even worse stink! The apartment was foul. We were sure this was why the super was knocking on the door. We stared at each other. One of us answered, 'Who is it?'

'It's the super . . . I have a message for you.'

We all kept staring at each other in absolute silence.

'Look . . . I'm working now . . . I *can't* come to the door,' I said.

'But it's only for a minute,' he persisted.

'I kept saying '*No!*'

Finally, he said, 'Bueno .. . I'll try to slip it under the door . . . let me see if I can push it through . . .'

'Bueno, Bueno,' I muttered.

The super pushed the slip of paper under the door and replied, 'Adiós! Good night!' and left. I read the message on the slip of paper. It was a message from the tenants' committee! The following day, there was to be a tenants' meeting on the sixth floor to discuss—of all crazy coincidences—problems concerning *the walls of the building!*"

Iker paused a moment, shaking his head. Then he continued. "Just at the moment we were reading the tenants' committee message—in fact, the moment we'd opened it—the *bed* suddenly collapsed! The combined weight of the three of us had been too much for it. When that bed collapsed, it scared the shit out of us! —the super was still standing just outside the door! I suddenly had a marvelous inspiration. I made believe I was with a girl. I started yelling—'Don't make so much noise, baby! Don't move around so much! Shit—All you broads are alike!' The super must have thought: 'So . . . he didn't open the door because he was with a girl . . . typical artist!' "

"So the next day," Iker went on, "using the pretext of the tenants' committee meeting, I asked the super's wife where her husband was. She told me he had gone out. 'First of all,' I said to her, 'I'd like to apologize to your husband. Yesterday, when he knocked at my door, I'm afraid I might have seemed rude . . . but just at that moment . . . I was occupied . . . I couldn't go to the door . . .' 'Nada, nada—don't worry,' she answered. 'Those are the normal happenings in life. We want you to feel right at home here!' Then I also told her that I couldn't go to the tenants' meeting. Christ! If I'd gone to that meeting, I'd be introduced to at least another dozen tenants who could get a good look at my false eyebrows and moustache. I told her that I had been in the building only a month and was new, and I still didn't understand much of what was going on in the building, and what the problems were, so it would be better if I came to one of the meetings later on. She kept insisting that I should join in—it would be good for me. But I told her I had too much work during December, and she dropped the subject. They were good people. Actually, I didn't see the super much. I had my first real conversation with him when I went to make excuses about the noise we'd made—that was on the ninth of December, when we perforated the wall. The noise was awful—the whole building shook! Well, on that day, I saw him, and I apologized. I was going to say that I had to make a lot of noise in my work as a sculptor—I had some excuses ready. He interrupted me as soon as I started—'Bueno . . . it's normal, all that noise. You must be doing some repair work in the apartment. Go right ahead, it's *your* apartment—don't worry about it.' So I answered, 'Bueno, gracias. But if by any chance the neighbors complain, you'll let me know, and I'll try to keep the noise down.' After the night the super slipped the tenants' committee note under the door, I didn't really have any further conversation with him. Only one time, when we crossed each other rapidly in the hall. A quick 'Adiós'—'Adiós'—I didn't have much contact with the super, but he was always very pleasant with me."

"Our Iker has a certain weakness for that super," Mikel teased. "He always talks about him; he always remembers him."

"We didn't have anything to do that night," Txabi went on, "so we took advantage of having some free time and went to see *The Day of the Jackal*. It got very good reviews," he added. "After the execution of Carrero, people identified us with the Jackal. I don't remember where I read it, but according to some report, ETA had contacted 'the Jackal' to help us kill Carrero. Later, the press reported that, according to well-informed sources, it was *known* that the Jackal had participated in the action. The Jackal also, no doubt, slept with the Virgin Mary! Fuck! What bullshit! And then

—before that one—there was another newspaper report that said we'd hired a Légionnaire, had promised him Christ knows how many millions of pesetas, and then, *after* the action, kicked him in the ass and dropped him without paying—there was all sorts of garbage in the press," Txabi concluded.

"After leaving the movie theater, we went home. We kept on talking about the Ogro until late into the night. We couldn't go to sleep. We smoked cigars," remembered Mikel. "Jon told me that the whole operation was very important for him personally. A series of myths he had lived with had been destroyed, and this gave him greater confidence in himself."

"I never would have imagined that a person as important as Carrero would have been so *available,* so easy to take," Jon broke in. "One of the last times I saw Carrero was during the Fiesta of San Francisco de Borja. I don't remember the exact date. In Carrero's church it is the custom, on that day, to kiss the relics of San Francisco. When Carrero went up to kiss the relics, I went up right behind him—my chest was practically touching his back. I had him right in front of me, even though, by this time, because he was President, he was now surrounded by many guards." Jon paused a moment, then continued. "Experiences of this sort change a person, and his view of how things actually work. I lost my preconceived notions and ideas of what is possible. You realize that you're stronger than you think! Frequently, you don't go ahead with 'actions' because it all seems so impossible, so unattainable."

"During that long night, listening to Jon, I knew he was right," continued Mikel. "I had the same emotions. The entire operation had been a tremendous experience for me. I was learning a new form of reality. There was one thing about the Ogro that made a deep impression on me. It was seeing him *looking* just like a normal person. He looked like a decent person, who took his communion regularly, each morning. He had a daughter who always smiled at his grandson. The family looked the very picture of normal respectability," he said. "And then, to think, this man in reality was a killer—that, during most of his lifetime, he left church, went home for his breakfast, and then went to the Pardo —or someplace like that—and gave his support—indeed, *pushed* —for many death sentences. *He* was the man who signed those death sentences. The enormous contrast between Carrero the family man and Carrero the assassin . . . Hombre!" Mikel paused.

"I felt that same mixture of emotions," he went on, "the first time I was arrested by the police. First, they beat you—they destroy you—*then* they take you in to see someone who does the soft pedaling—'You poor thing.' They try to butter you up. I was with the good torturer when he got called to the telephone in the next room. I could hear that he was talking with one of his daughters . . . and he was saying, 'Adiós, Bonita . . . Adiós . . .' Just as though he were a normal man! Fuck it! There you are, *knowing* that he is a torturer. *Those* are the things that eat at your guts. We talked, that night, for hours. We finally went to sleep at 3 in the morning. The following day was the nineteenth."

"We got up early," said Iker. "We did our gymnastics. It was the last time we were going to use those dumbbells and weights. We had breakfast. And by 9 we were in the basement apartment. We made the last trial run. The next day would be the twentieth —the day of the action. Once again, we went through an entire trial run with the car. This time, the 'electricians' wore their overalls to test how long it would take to get out of them—we wanted everything timed *exactly*. The 'electricians' peeled off their overalls even before we'd reached Juan Bravo in the car. We also carefully observed the people passing by us in the street—this was something that had worried us. We saw that hardly anybody passed by. Several people could be seen wandering in the distance —but nobody came directly into the zone of our explosives. We also saw that the jeep with the grises—because of Kissinger— was still parked at the corner. But right after that, Kissinger left Madrid," Iker concluded.

"It was a very cloudy day," added Jon. "Very cold, too. Later, in the afternoon, it started to rain. After eating lunch, we waited for several hours before returning to the basement apartment. Toward the end of the day, we went out to work in the street. We went out to set up the wires, as 'electricians.' Because our overalls, even though we'd managed to make them look dirty, still looked new, we picked an hour when there wasn't much light. We didn't want people to get a good look at our overalls —or our faces. Actually, it was almost nighttime when we took our ladder and tool chest out into the street," Jon remembered. "We were fairly well disguised. I don't believe that anybody

who knew me would have recognized me. The same for Txabi—
he was well disguised, too. And we didn't want to leave any clues.
We knew that afterwards the police would go to that street and
ask questions. It was important that any information people
could give would be inaccurate."

"We placed the ladder," continued Txabi, "and I climbed to
the top. My balls were in my throat every step of the way. I wasn't
afraid of the police—I was terrified of falling from that height.
Once I got to the top of the ladder, I twisted my feet around the
top rung. I held on to that ladder with my legs, gripping it as
tightly as I could without losing my balance. I needed to keep
both hands free. Later—near the end—I became more used to
the ladder. But in the beginning . . . Fuck! I had to keep swallowing my balls! On the day of the action, I was still stiff from being
on the ladder. Everything ached—my legs, my back, my kidneys."
Txabi paused. "I started to hang the cable, laying it along the
telephone line; we didn't want to run the cable through the basement window yet. Too early for *that* maneuver. So, we left the
cable just outside the basement window, with the loose end discreetly rolled up. As I said, we followed the telephone line with
the cable. At first, we tried to attach the cable with electrician's
nails, both to the telephone line and to the wall of the building.
But at that height, nearly all the apartment houses on that street
had marble facades. The pronged nails wouldn't work. Finally,
we used insulating tape to attach the cable to the telephone wires
and to the facades of the apartment buildings."

"While they worked," broke in Iker, "Mikel and I—each of us
stationed on a different corner—maintained our vigilance of the
street. I was at the far corner—some distance away from my
basement apartment window—in a place where people wouldn't
recognize who I was. The grises were still parked in the street, in
their jeep. Kissinger had already left; there were no more police
on the rooftops. But the police in jeeps and the police on the street
were still patrolling the area. They weren't paying too much
attention—but they were still present in the neighborhood. Our
function was to intervene if the 'electricians' ran into any trouble,"
added Iker. "To cover them if they had to make a quick getaway."

"While we were attaching the cable," Jon broke in, "*all* the
supers from the neighborhood came out into the street and asked
us why we were putting up the cable. *I* was the one at the

bottom of the ladder—so *I* had to do all the talking!" Jon, who always liked being inventive, paused a moment before telling his story. "I told them all we were from the hydroelectric company. We were bringing in a new line of electric current from Diego de León for the sculptor who had his studio in number 104 Claudio Coello. They asked me, 'But what's going on? Doesn't he have electricity? What's the problem?' So I told them, yes, of *course* he had electricity, but he needed a more powerful line for the sort of work he was doing. 'He has one of those machines,' I said, 'a huge drilling machine, one of those machines sculptors use.' I was vague—well, I couldn't explain exactly what type of machine he was using, because I don't have a clue about what sculptors use! So I had to be vague, inventive. But, I figured the supers wouldn't know anymore about sculpting than *I* did, so I elaborated on my story. 'He has one of those modern machines that sculptors—*modern* sculptors—use now. Because it isn't like the old days. Sculptors don't use chisels much anymore. Now, it's all done by machine.' I explained to them that this machine was used for working with stone, and high-intensity electric current was needed. *Then* they asked—those supers!—'But why aren't you taking the current from Claudio Coello or from Maldonado, which is much nearer?' I was very firm in my reply: 'No. The type of current this sculptor needs only runs through Diego de León.' I had to invent a whole script for them! 'But, anyway, you shouldn't worry—there will be no problem. We will take our equipment away very quickly. This is only temporary. Our problem is that that crazy sculptor has taken it into his head that he must start work tomorrow. So, we have to be finished by the end of the day. If he'd been willing to wait three or four more days, we'd have been able to install the *real* cable, the one that will stay permanently. Imagine, taking the current from the Jesuits! But he *insisted* on tomorrow. He must be a real big shot, must have pull, that guy. Anyway, our orders are to finish the job *today*. Well, that's life . . . this sort of thing is always happening to us—and in this weather!' " Jon sat back a moment after spinning out his story, and continued. "And December 19 was unusually cold—it was raining hard, and our overalls were soaked. So, with all the explanations, the neighbors—the supers—relaxed. As soon as we gave them some sort of excuse, they didn't question us any further. All they wanted was some sort of explanation—

any sort would have done. Without having an explanation handed
to them, naturally, they'd have realized something was fishy."

"None of them knew the first thing about electricity," added
Mikel, "so they accepted whatever we told them as the truth."

"When we got the cable as far as 106 and 108 on Claudio
Coello, there was a garage. A car pulled up—a black, chauffeur-
driven Mercedes—with a lady in the back seat. When the lady
went inside the building, the chauffeur stayed in the doorway of
the garage. He asked us what we were doing—what sort of work
—the usual questions," said Jon. He continued, relishing another
anecdote. "We grumbled about the weather. I looked up at Txabi,
and kept on complaining about the weather and the work. 'I don't
want to work this late—the *hell* with that fucking sculptor bastard
who wants his work done yesterday. *Today,* of all days— in this
freezing weather! When we could have been working inside, well
protected. The *boss* doesn't give a shit if it's raining! That sculptor must have real pull!' I remember the chauffeur commiserating
with us, 'With me, it's the same thing. That señora I work for . . .
with this terrible weather . . . I can't see anything, driving on a
day like this . . . raining . . . the streets muddy . . . the car could
skid in a second, and *bang,* you've had it! But we have to go out
. . . a whim of the señora's aunt . . .' "

"If we reported in *Operation Ogro* everything that the chauffeur told us about his fancy employer, that chauffeur would be
out of work," Txabi commented wryly.

"Actually," Mikel broke in, "the whole neighborhood is filled
with Mercedeses—and all chauffeur-driven. That's the most common car seen in the Barrio de Salamanca," he added.

Jon went on, "There was a balcony above the cable line on the
last building on the street—number 110, I think—so Txabi, who
was working on the cable beneath the balcony, was protected
from the rain. But as I was out further on the street, at the foot
of the ladder, I got soaked! I asked the janitor at 110 if I could
go inside his building to dry off. The guy gave me a dirty look,
but finally he let me go inside to warm up. Later, I gave him the
same scenario, about that bastard the sculptor, and he became
very sympathetic."

"Number 110 is the corner building on Claudio Coello. We
had to then carry the cable past the corner, up to Diego de León.
We needed to continue along Diego de León until we reached

the middle of the street—that's where we planned to drop the lines," said Txabi. "We didn't want anybody in the Ogro's car to see electricians working on that corner," he went on. "But, because the electric wires are much higher in Diego de León— Claudio Coello is 4 meters, Diego de León 6 meters—we couldn't get up high enough with the ladder we had. So, finally, we had to drop the line in Claudio Coello. We followed the outline of the doorway of the building. On the ground floor there was a store with a ledge, about 2 feet wide, which projected out onto the street. We hid the end of the cable behind the ledge in such a way that it was unobtrusive. We left it ready for the following morning." Txabi paused a moment, then went on. "After placing the explosives in the tunnel as planned, we would come back to the corner of Claudio Coello, take out the rolled end of the cable, and then—at the last possible moment—connect the cable to the battery."

"Right after the assassination," Iker broke in, "the newspapers printed many reports of a kind of signal—a paint mark near the doorway of 104." He paused. "That paint mark had nothing to do with our action! It had been there before. Some kid must have scrawled on the wall. Our signal was our car. Two or three days before the action, we became concerned about some of the fine points. In order to press the button at *exactly* the right moment, to explode the dynamite directly beneath Carrero's car, we needed to know *precisely* the very second his car would pass over the explosives. We planned to abandon our first car—we weren't going to use it for our getaway—so we got the idea of leaving some additional explosives packed inside it. That way, the car could be destroyed—exploded—so it couldn't be used. At the same time, the explosion would serve as our signal," concluded Iker.

"The car would serve two purposes," Txabi went on. "First, as a landmark to indicate the precise position of the explosives in the tunnel beneath it. Second, and almost more important, if the car were double-parked it would act as an obstacle to force the Ogro's car to veer slightly to the right at that point in the street —his car would pass directly over our explosives."

Now Jon took up the story once more. "We mentioned earlier that some of the dynamite didn't explode. That was the dynamite we had packed in the car. A few days after the action, we saw the newspaper photos of the explosion. When we realized that the car hadn't exploded, we were alarmed. We were afraid the dynamite inside it could explode haphazardly, causing random damage. That's why, as soon as we got to France, the first thing we mentioned at our press conference was the problem of the unexploded dynamite in the car we had left behind. When we were in Portugal—before we got to France—we thought of sending a telegram to the Spanish, but decided it was too risky—remember, this was about four months before Portugal's revolution," Jon explained.

"It would have been funny if the car had exploded on the day of the funeral," said Txabi, "during the oration of the Warriors of Christ the King in front of the church! After the official burial, Blas Piñar, the nutty leader of those ultra-right-wing fanatics, and several of his followers went to the hole in the church where Carrero's car had been dynamited. Blas Piñar gave a long oration. It was funny, because during his oration, a police helicopter circled just above him, and nobody could hear a word he said! So we were told. *Bueno!* He gave his speech, and, right after that, they all started to sing 'Cara al Sol,' the hymn of the Falange. Then everybody gave the Fascist salute. Blas Piñar and his group still worship Hitler—they are so crazy." Txabi paused a moment, then continued, "Mikel said that it would have been great if, during all that ardor and emotion, the unexploded dynamite in the car—upon hearing so much emotion—*por simpática*—had burst forth, sending the whole crew directly to hell," Txabi added mildly.

"Considering all the crazy rumors after Carrero's death," said Mikel, "hombre! What if *then* the car had exploded with Blas Piñar! In Madrid, they would have said it was the work of the Chinese . . . or somebody in league with the devil."

"Getting back to the story," interrupted Iker, "that night we finished our work. We felt good. We were filled with joy. The thing to do was to have a great dinner."

"Yes," said Jon. "We had been surviving on an endless stream of sandwiches. We'd been eating badly during the whole time we were digging the tunnel. We'd been half-intoxicated by the gas fumes, and this had taken away some of our appetite. So, that night, the night of the nineteenth, we decided to have a first-class dinner."

"We didn't know if it was going to be our last dinner for a long time," added Iker, "so we decided that this dinner should be super."

"Iker was obsessed with the idea of eating a dish of baby eels as a celebration," said Mikel. "But Jon said no—that the baby eels were for afterward—if the operation went well—*not* before. Our pal Iker disagreed. 'Look,' he said, '*after* the operation—that means if it's a success—but if it's not? No, I think it's more practical to eat the baby eels *before*.' The two of them argued about those baby eels. In the end, we went to a good restaurant, and Iker had his plate of baby eels," said Mikel, deadpan.

"For days Iker had talked about the baby eels, and, in the end, he ate them," remembered Jon, speaking very seriously. "I remember that, when we left the restaurant, when it was getting close to zero hour, I began to think—Fuck! Christ only knows if we'll ever get out of here! And I remember that I said to Iker, 'You did well in eating the baby eels. Now, I am sad that I didn't ask for them, too.'"

"A wave of depression overcame Jon," said Iker, "and he invited us all for a whiskey—something he *never* does . . . Jon never takes more than a swig of wine. He is more austere than the holy wafer itself. So, that night, Jon invited us for a whiskey. We went to a bar, drank a whiskey, and went home. Almost in silence. Very different from the night before, when we'd stayed up until 3, talking. This night, we went straight to bed," Iker concluded.

"We got up very early on the twentieth," said Jon, switching the subject away from his depression the night before. "We went to the basement apartment. We still had to put the dynamite into the tunnel; we made sure it was well-wrapped before we started. This was the final installation. We checked everything out. We had to be ready for zero hour—nine or ten minutes past 9."

"Our last visit to the apartment at 104 was very normal," said Iker. "Nobody saw us enter. It was still dark outside."

"But we began to notice things that were sort of bizarre," interjected Txabi. "Until the moment of the action, everything on that last morning, the morning of the twentieth, suddenly struck us as odd. But that's a normal reaction under such circumstances."

He paused. "First, when we arrived, we saw a car parked at the corner of Maldonado and Claudio Coello—a man was sitting inside it. That immediately struck us as peculiar. We were startled. We didn't say anything to one another, but we *all* noticed that car, and we all had our private fantasies about it. Later, when we went out to pack the dynamite in the trunk of our car, we saw that he had moved his car. Now it was in front of our door. That bothered us even more. It was very early in the morning. Not the normal time for somebody to be reparking a car on that street. But right after that, a girl came out of one of the buildings and jumped into the car. The two of them drove off. We all breathed a sigh of relief. They looked like a working-class couple. The man must have been waiting for her, to take her to work. At the time, none of us made any comment; it was only later, when we were remembering all the different stages of the action, that we admitted our fears to each other—that there had been something strange about that car. None of us wanted to bring it up at the time—we didn't want to panic. Then we packed the dynamite into the tunnel. The packages were tightly tied with cord, for a more effective explosion. We ran the deto-nator cord into the apartment. For the time being, we left the detonator cord loose inside the apartment. Then we filled up the hole to the tunnel with dirt, packing it down well."

"We packed the tunnel hole with dirt about 3½ feet deep into the tunnel," said Mikel. "With the tunnel sealed this way, the explosion would be much stronger. This meant that the explosion *had* to go straight up—the dynamite was prevented from ex-ploding horizontally and going back into the apartment. As we said before, we were very much worried that there might be an accident. We wanted to avoid that."

"Then Txabi and I went outside, dressed in our overalls," said Jon, "disguised as electricians. This was a little after 8 in the morning. Naturally, we had to appear to be working during nor-mal working hours. When we started to 'fix' the cable, which we had hidden near the doorway of 104—and just at the moment we had run the cable down, ready to bring it into the apartment through the basement window—a grise came out of our own building! He was young, around 30. We were startled. *Bizarre!* A *policeman*—living in such a high-rent building—with the low salary *he* got?" Jon paused a moment, then continued his story.

"Txabi and I didn't recognize him at the time, because only Iker had spoken to him, but that grise turned out to be our own super! Later, we read in the newspapers that the super at 104 was a member of the armed police!"

"We finished lowering the cable meant for 104," Txabi went on calmly, "and ran it through the basement window. Now there remained only the other end of the cable—which we had left rolled up, hidden behind the ledge at 110, the corner building. We went to 110, lowered the cable to the ground, and connected it to the battery in the 'electric box.' We had to make a final test to make sure that the cable worked—that there were no breaks at any point," commented Txabi, who always meticulously explained the scientific details of the operation. "We used one-and-a-half strength batteries. Actually, we used two batteries. We used a tester to check the current, to make sure it was live. Then we made the final connections. We attached the cable, which we had run through the basement window to the detonators. Then we left the apartment—*finished*. We left the window to the apartment slightly open, with just enough space for the cable. We closed the apartment door and, dressed as two electricians, we went out to the Diego de León." "It took us very little time—five or six minutes. We left the battery unconnected until the last possible moment—to avoid an accident. We had to wait until about 9:15—just before Carrero left the church—to come back and connect the battery."

"So, by 9:10," interrupted Jon, "Txabi and I—the two 'electricians'—were at the corner of Diego de León and Claudio Coello waiting, and we saw Mikel circling the corner across the street."

"My function was to protect them," explained Mikel. "I was on guard, just in case there should be a last-minute mishap. We thought that after the explosion Jon or Txabi might get dizzy, or fall down—we weren't sure just what would happen. This way, if one of them fell down, the other two of us could carry him to the car."

"Neither Txabi nor I was on top of the ladder," said Jon. "We left the ladder against the wall of the building after lowering the cable. But nobody climbed up it again. We thought that would be very dangerous. With the noise of the explosion, whoever was on top of the ladder could get dizzy and fall to the street. We were both down on the street. The ladder's function had terminated. But we were scared of a possible accident. We were stationed right next to a store with an enormous beveled-edged glass window—the sort of window that could shatter all over the two of us."

Mikel broke in, saying, "Earlier, around 8 in the morning, Iker and I had gone to have breakfast at the Cafeteria Chiquito while the 'electricians' were finishing connecting the cables. We bought *La Prensa*, ABC and YA. We leafed through the papers. Kissinger had already left Madrid. After that, we went over to the cars."

Iker now took up the narrative. "That was about 8:30," he said, and continued, "my mission was to leave the Austin well placed— double-parked—for the action. I parked the car as planned. I left the window slightly open, as though I were just leaving the car for a moment while running a quick errand—as though I'd be right back. But, to make it look natural, I left the door locked. And the window was sufficiently closed so that nobody could get his hand through the window—nobody would be able to move the car. Then Mikel and I went to warm up the 124. December 20 was one of those typical freezing Madrid winter days. The car— the 124—had been out on the street during the whole night, so it needed to be warmed up, ready for the getaway. First, we drove it around a little to warm it up. At 9 we drove past Carrero's house—to make sure he was going to mass that morning. After three months of following his routine, it might have worked out that—just *that* day—he didn't go to church. But we saw him leave his house."

"Seeing him in the flesh made a strong impression on me," said Iker. "The last time you see a person . . . when you know that right after . . . you are going to send him flying . . . Hombre! Mikel and I talked about that. Mikel said he'd got the same queasy feeling when he had observed the Ogro in church. We talked for a while, about that. Then Mikel said to me, 'When they assassinate our brothers—the workers—those who are in the struggle—they don't stop a minute—and they don't *think* anything.'"

"We saw Carrero get into his car," Iker went on. "We followed him up to the church. We continued to Juan Bravo. We turned into Claudio Coello—and passed over the tunnel. We made certain everything was *perfect*—and that there was no danger of an accident. When we passed by the corner—at Diego de León and Claudio Coello—we gave a signal to the 'electricians'—a smile— that meant that the Ogro was in church—and he would be passing over the tunnel. About a yard further down the street, I dropped Mikel off so that he could take his position. Then I drove to the corner of Lagasca and Diego de León. Then something very peculiar happened to me. Remember, at the beginning of 'Ogro' we mentioned that everybody in this quarter parked very badly—and there was never any free space?" Iker paused a moment before continuing. "During those final minutes—between 9:15 and the moment of the action—strange things started to happen. In the entryway of a garage on the corner of those two streets—Lagasca and Diego de León—there was a four-door 1600—half-in and half-out of the entryway. Then, when I pulled up, the man at the wheel of the 1600 drove his car out, letting me take his place, and he double-parked. He kept the windows closed, and stayed inside the car. That made me a little suspicious. But I didn't think it was too important. That was at 9:20. Right after that, a small truck drove up—and parked just behind the 1600. This meant that, during the getaway, I was going to have to steer our car around both the 1600 and the truck. This would certainly slow down our escape." Iker paused.

"This was *minutes* before the action. I was nervous. I had to quickly maneuver the car slightly farther out into the street to facilitate our escape. I began to feel that the place was filled with guards—that *everybody* was watching me. It also struck me that all sorts of odd things were going on around me. Then there was another mishap. A man—he looked like a worker—pulled up and parked his Citroen 4L in front of the 1600. Nervously, he kept looking at his watch—his car was also double-parked. During those last seconds, I thought: Fuck! Something is going on here! These guys are getting ready for something! I opened all four car windows. In case of a gunfight, it would be easier for me to shoot. Unobtrusively, I unlatched three of the car doors—for Mikel, Txabi and Jon. It was already zero hour. It couldn't happen any later. For me, those last few moments were an eternity." Iker paused once more.

"Then, at exactly 9:36 according to my watch, I heard a sharp explosion. Not too loud an explosion. Nothing shook. I heard hardly any noise. It seemed strange. I'd been revved up for the sound. Then I was surprised—the sound was so muffled."

Iker continued the account. "Where were my pals? I looked down the street, anxiously. They were only a few seconds late— but for me, it felt like hours. For a moment, I thought they weren't going to make it. Finally, I saw them coming quickly down the street. Txabi got in front, next to me. Jon opened one of the rear doors and climbed in. Mikel, the last one, entered the other rear door. I saw it all—and I saw nothing. Just before the three of them got into the car—at the very moment of the explo- sion—the worker, who was standing by his Citroen 4L, looked at his watch, jumped into his car and started the motor. There were several suspenseful seconds. But I saw in the rear-view mirror that he was racing to take the parking space I'd just vacated! I breathed a sigh of relief. We drove out of there rapidly —with Mikel, Jon and Txabi all safely inside the car—making an unspectacular escape."

"We made a right turn on Juan Bravo," Iker continued, "and then, when we crossed Claudio Coello, we saw a cloud of smoke and people gathering in the distance. It was our bad luck, just at that moment, that the traffic light turned red. We waited for the light to change—our car was alongside a black police car. They looked at us. We looked back. There were other cars, but nobody seemed to notice that anything had happened. In spite of being in the vicinity of the explosion, clearly, nobody had realized what had happened. We could see that the people were going about their business half-asleep. The Madrileños were on their way to work—they still weren't fully awake. That red light took a long time to change—but there was nothing alarming in the mood of the people around us. We saw a grise coming from the direction of the American Embassy. He walked over to the six policemen in the car alongside us. But we realized he was just following his usual routine. We sensed that, in those first two minutes, nobody had realized what had happened. The light finally changed. We drove fairly rapidly—but not so quickly as to call attention to our car. By this time, Jon and Txabi had taken off their overalls. We got to the Plaza Reuben Darío. I turned right, continuing along Miguel Angel. I stopped directly in front of the military school. Our third car was parked there, ready for us to make our final escape."

DETONATION AND WITHDRAWAL

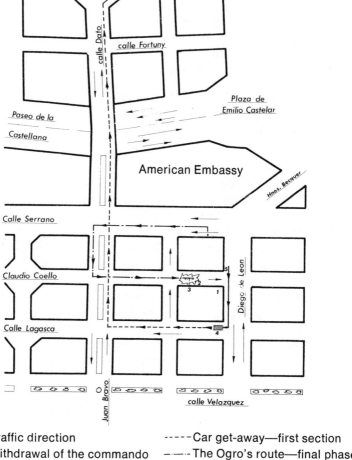

Plaza de
Ruben Dario

calle Dato

calle Fortuny

Plaza de
Emilio Castelar

Paseo de la

Castellana

American Embassy

Hnos. Becquer

Calle Serrano

Claudio Coello

Diego de Leon

Calle Lagasca

Juan Bravo

calle Velazquez

— Traffic direction

—— Withdrawal of the commando on foot

- - - - Car get-away—first section

— · — · The Ogro's route—final phase

1. Site where the two "electricians" carried out the detonation.
2. The double parked Austin 1300. It served to:
   1) signal the closing of the circuit which produced the explosion at the moment the Ogro's vehicle arrived;
   2) to force the Ogro's vehicle directly over the explosive charge.
3. The direction of the tunnel's construction and the charges.
4. Parked automobile for the first part of the get-away; the chauffeur was inside and the engine was running.
5. Location of the fourth man who, in order to prevent any accidents, covered commandos who carried out the detonation.

After Iker completed his account, the other three backtracked to tell what they were doing for the last half hour, while he was in the car.

Jon began. "When Txabi and I saw Iker driving past us, smiling, signaling that the Ogro was in church, we immediately went on alert. That was when I joined Txabi, and the two of us went back into the basement apartment for the last time, so that he could connect the battery."

"Jon came over to me and whispered, 'I would have preferred it if Carrero *hadn't* come,'" said Txabi.

"Yes," Jon admitted, "that's true. I did say that. When we went back to the corner of Diego de León and Claudio Coello, we *also* began to notice odd things in the atmosphere around us. There were a lot of guards. We realized that we could be seen by the men in the jeep in front of the American Embassy. The grises were all inside the jeep, but they still had a perfect view of us from Serrano. There was one of those street vendors—cigarettes and matches—on Diego de León. He *also* had a clear view of what we were doing. Then, at 9:15, a man pulled up in a car. He parked the car just at the corner. He kept looking at us, sort of pensively. The guy seemed to be thinking about something. He was staring at us with a steady, fixed gaze. Then he looked away from us. He started his car, advanced a short distance, then stopped again. He put his car in reverse and backed into the same precise place from where he'd started! He started to stare at us again. Then he looked away again. He looked at something he had in the car. He picked up something. He got out of the car. He kept on staring at us and closed the car door. Then, he walked toward us, going in the direction of Claudio Coello. He turned around again. He went back, another time, to the car. He opened the car door and sat down inside the car again still another time. Then he looked at us again. He fiddled around some more. He got out of the car still another time. This time out, he locked the car door. He walked over to where we were standing—stared at us—looked over toward Claudio Coello. He sure was busy thinking about *something*. Sounds crazy, but—still another time back to his car! He sat down in the car again—looked inside the car for something—got out and locked it again. I think he had a tapemeasure in his hand, and some papers. He came over to where we were standing, looked at us again . . . and then kept on walking. He'd kept up this back-and-forth routine for at least three or four minutes. We were tense . . . waiting . . . I saw Mikel across the street, looking at us nervously. I thought I could hear Txabi whispering to me, 'They're watching us . . . They've surrounded us . . . What's going on around us?' "

"Remember," Iker broke in, "we'd seen the grise leaving 104 shortly before. You start adding up incidents, and you get nervous."

"On an ordinary day, you don't pay attention to what's going on around you," Txabi added, "but on a day like that—*everything* takes on a different aura."

"Yes, but that man, he kept staring at a fixed point—and *we* were the fixed point!" said Jon, the one in the group who was always teased about his staring.

"About 9:25, a boy passed by," continued Txabi, "a kid around 16 years old, tall, skinny. He asked me for a light. Hombre! I had my hand in the briefcase, the batteries were connected—and the kid asks me for a light! I didn't even know where my matches were . . . nothing . . . but I also didn't want to ignore the kid. I found my matches and gave them to him. Two minutes later, another kid, but slightly younger, around 14—the same thing! He wanted a light! Finally, the second kid left." Txabi paused a moment. "Then I saw that Jon was staring fixedly toward the end of the street, and I waited for his signal."

"That's when I saw Carrero's car coming along Juan Bravo," Jon broke in. "I saw the two cars coming—his car and the guard car following him. They had to stop at Juan Bravo. His car was in the far right lane, and they had to wait for the cars passing in the opposite direction—going toward Serrano—before his car could make the left turn onto Claudio Coello. The other cars, in the opposite lane, passed him . . . and his car came up Claudio Coello slowly . . . slowly . . . slowly . . . When his car reached Maldonado a woman with a child was crossing the street. So his car stopped there again. After the woman and child had crossed, the car came slowly . . . slowly . . . slowly . . . up Claudio Coello. The car reached the place . . . in the end . . . in the end, what a person feels at a moment like that is something one can't even begin to imagine. His car reached our Austin . . . and I said to

Txabi . . . 'Now.' I didn't see the car . . . but I saw that it went
up into the sky. The explosion made a muffled sound. There was
a moment . . . it was when Txabi pressed the button . . . I had
already said 'now,' and I imagined that he had pressed the button.
I didn't know, because I couldn't see. There was a moment when
it seemed that nothing had happened. Those are the particles of
a second that feel like years. That's the way it seemed—that
nothing had happened. And then, suddenly, I saw—almost without any noise—it had made a noise, but very gentle, very soft—I
saw the street suddenly open up! The street went upward . . . and
a black cloud of smoke went up as high as the rooftops. We
began to cry, 'Gas! Gas!' We had decided beforehand to create
the impression that there had been an explosion of gas."

Txabi picked up the story. "In those last seconds, while we
were waiting for Jon's signal—I was thinking only of one thing—
Josu. I couldn't get him out of my mind. I imagined his body,
riddled with bullet holes . . . that's the way they killed Josu," said
Txabi quietly. "More than one hundred and fifty policemen surrounded the house. They ripped off his neck by firing at him—
one bullet after another—I felt that *he* gave me courage—and I
remember whispering to Jon in a low voice . . . when I pressed
the button, I didn't see anything. It was impossible, from where
I was. It also took me several particles of a second to hear the
explosion. But Jon was already running. I saw Mikel, across the
street, coming toward us. I dropped the briefcase with the batteries. I started to run."

"We all ran," Jon continued. "In the middle of the street, there
was construction going on—in Diego de León—on the right—
between Claudio Coello and Lagasca. A man from the construction site, a construction worker, stared at us and asked, 'What is
it? What happened?' And while I was running . . . bueno . . . we
weren't really running—we were walking rapidly—between
walking and running, I said to him, 'It's a gas explosion, a gas
explosion.' Iker later said that we *thought* we screamed 'Gas explosion!'—but in reality, we said it very softly, almost without
any voice."

"It's true," Iker broke in, "they did say 'Gas . . . Gas . . .' but
in voices filled with emotion, mere threads. But they didn't attract
any attention to themselves. I could tell that while they were
walking toward our car," Iker explained. "It looked very natural

to the people watching—to see that somebody had been frightened by the explosion. They got into the car, and there was a short exchange among us. While I was driving the car away, I asked, 'Did it all go off all right?' Then they answered me. Jon said it had been terrible. He *meant* that it had been a big explosion, but he *said* 'terrible.' I asked him if the car had kept on going. They told me, no, they hadn't seen anything. I remember that Jon said only two things to me . . . 'hit in the middle' and 'it was terrible.' He didn't say anything more. And Txabi, he only kept saying . . . 'Josu is avenged . . . Josu is avenged . . .' and 'Josu gave me courage . . . Josu give me strength . . .' Mikel was silent. But when we crossed Claudio Coello, and we saw the smoke, he grabbed me tightly by my shoulders, and he said, very emotionally: 'We overcame everything. We have won.' I gently pressed the accelerator and, until we changed cars, we didn't say anything more."

Basques Protest Political Prisoners

Some 200,000 workers and students deserted their factories and classrooms today in three Basque provinces of northern Spain in support of political prisoners now being held in Spanish jails and of political freedom in general.

The action called by leftist labor and political groups and by Basque nationalists was estimated to be the biggest political strike in Spain in 26 years. It was an impressive show of force by a part of the Spanish population that has traditionally been treated as subversive by the present Government and that will consequently be kept out of the legal play of political forces under the plan announced last week to allow limited freedom of political association.

Of the 450 persons estimated to be held in Spanish jails for crimes with political motives, 89 per cent are connected with the Basque nationalist group E.T.A. The Basque initials stand for Basque Nation and Freedom. About a third of the total have been on a hunger strike over the last two weeks to back their demands for amnesty.

Today's walkout in the provinces of Guipuzcoa, Vizcaya and Navarra was all the more impressive because political strikes are rare in Spain and this one took place just before the Christmas holidays when workers try to earn as much as possible.

The Basque area centering on the cities of San Sebastian, Bilbao and Pamplona has a long history of nationalist and labor militancy. In 1948 thousands of workers struck at the call of the Basque Nationalist party to support the area's freedom. And in December, 1970, at least 150,000 came out in support of 15 Basque nationalists who were on trial in Burgos.

Despite a big deployment of security forces, there were several Basque demonstrations. In Hernani, near San Sebastian, a youth was wounded by gunfire from civil guards.

The police were reinforced with riot contingents from Madrid and Logroño.

Tonight, while a cold steady rain beat down on San Sebastian, the police were out in force to stop threatened demonstrations. Early in the day, 10 persons were reported to have been arrested.

Tracts scattered along downtown streets denounced "the crimes of the dictatorship," demanded freedom for political prisoners and self-determination for the Basque provinces. The high cost of living was cited as another reason for the demonstration but the predominant note was political.

THE NEW YORK TIMES, December 12, 1974

Basque Political Prisoners, October 1974

This is a list of 245 Basque prisoners in Franco's prisons, as of October 1974. These are their names, the names of the prisons in Spain and the number of years the prisoners are serving. When no figure is given, either the prisoners have not yet been brought to trial or information about the length of their sentence is not available. The defendants of the Burgos trials are in Cartagena, Cordoba and Caceres. "Tupa" and "Tanka" are listed as being in Basauri prison. They have since been transferred to Carabanchel, near Madrid. 146 of these Basque prisoners, including Basque priests, were on the hunger strikes in November and December 1974 carried out in at least nine Spanish prisons.

Cartagena

GOROSTIDI ARTOLA Jokin. Deba (Gipuzkoa) (96 urtera kondenatua)
LARENA MARTINEZ Xabier. Santurde (Bizkaia) (63 u.k.)

Cordoba

DOR RONSORO ZEBERIO Jose M. Ataun (Gipuzkoa) (67 u.k.)
IZKO DE LA IGLESIA Xabier. Berango (Bizkaia) (110 u.k.)
SANTOYO GUTIERREZ Dionisio. Lazkano (Gipuzkoa) (48 u.k.)

Caceres

ONAINDIA NATXIONDO Mario. Eibar (Gipuzkoa) (81 u.k.)
URIARTE ROMERO Eduardo. Gazteiz (Araba) (90 u.k.)
ZALBIDE SALABERRIA Jose Luis. Bilbo (Bizkaia) (20 u.k.)

Palencia

BARENKA Andoni. Sestao (Bizkaia)
CHACON Mikel. Santurde. (Bizkaia)
ISASI SAGASTIZABAL Jon. Basauri (Bizkaia) (16 u.k.)
MIMEN ZAMOIA Patxi. Orozko. (Bizkaia) (16 u.k.)

Santander

APRAIZ EGILEOR Sabin. Amorebieta. (Bizkaia) (15 u.k.)
ASUA
GAZTELUMENDI Manuel. Elizondo (Nafarroa)

GURRUTXAGA ERRASTI Jose M. Lezo. (Gipuzkoa)
URETA Ramon. San Salvador del Valle (Bizkaia)

Alcala de Henares (Madrid)

AREVALO LARREA Maite. Sestao (Bizkaia) (25 u.k.)
ARANBURU Arantza. Oñate (Gipuzkoa)
AIZPURUA EGAÑA Itziar. Deba (gipuzkoa) (15 u.k.)
DIEGO DEL ALAMO M. Angeles. Bilbo (Bizkaia)
DOR RONSORO ZEBERIO Jone. Legazpia (gipuzkoa) (50 u.k.)
LAMARIANO IRIONDO Itziar. Gazteiz (Araba)
ODRIOZOLA Miren. Azpeitia. (Gipuzkoa)
SAN PEDRO LAYUNO Arantza. Bermeo (Bizkaia) (3 u.k.)
TELLETXEA Clara. Bermeo (Bizkaia) (3 u.k.)

Carabanchel (Madrid)

ARANBURU ARALUZE J. Antonio. Bilbo (Bizkaia)
AGIRRE ARTOLA Xabier. Ondarrabia (Gipuzkoa) (3 u.k.)
GARCIA FERNANDEZ DE LUCO Patxi. Gazteiz (Araba) (7 u.k.)
IRAETA KINTELA Juan Ramon. Azkoitia (Gipuzkoa) (2 u.k.)

Jaen

ARMENDARIZ TAITA Xabier. Iruña (Nafarroa)
ARRAZURIA ORKOIEN Alejandro. Iruña (Nafarroa)
ARZUAGA AGIRRE Iñaki. Durango (Bizkaia)
BARRIOLA Jose. Legazpia (Gipuzkoa)
CARCOBA CANO Jose Koldo. Basauri (Bizkaia)
GOIKOETXEA Jose Manuel. Andoain (Gipuzkoa)
SARASOLA Juan Jose. Lazkano (Gipuzkoa) (12 u.k.)
SEIJO Juan Manuel. Lekeitio (Bizkaia)
GOIKOETXEA Joseba. Hernani (Gipuzkoa)
ZUMETA Jose Mikel. Lasarte (Gipuzkoa) (4 u.k.)

Soria

ABRISKETA KORTA Jose. Miravalles (Bizkaia) (80 u.k.)
AIZPURUA BERASATEGI Koldo. Eibar (Gipuzkoa) (30 u.k.)
BEGIRISTAIN ARANZASTI Jose. Lazkano (Gipuzkoa) (48 u.k.)
EGIA LIZASO Lorenzo. Lasarte (Gipuzkoa) (100 u.k.)
ETXEBARRIA LULOAGA Venancio. Isasondo (Gipuzkoa) (65 u.k.)
FERNANDEZ TRINCADO Pedro. Bilbo (Bizkaia) (60 u.k.)
GESALAGA Enrique. Eibar (Gipuzkoa)
IBARGUTXI SAN PEDRO Josu. Eibar (Gipuzkoa) (30 u.k.)

IMAZ GARAI Joseba. Bakio (Bizkaia) (17 u.k.)
ISASA ITURRIOZ Manuel. Añorga (Gipuzkoa) (30 u.k.)
IZAGIRRE ESNAL Felipe. Hernani (Gipuzkoa) (10 u.k.)
LASKURAIN MANTILLA Mikel. Lasarte (Gipuzkoa) (70 u.k.)
LOPEZ IRASUEGI Gregorio. Bilbo. (Bizkaia) (40 u.k.)
ORBETA BERRIATUA Iñaki. Bilbo (Bizkaia) (34 u.k.)
SOLAGUREN URRUTXURTU Luken. Amorebieta (Bizkaia) (21 u.k.)
UNANUE Iñaki. Donostia (Gipuzkoa)
URGIZA ARRASATE Koldo. Andarroa (Bizkaia)
ZABALO BILBO Koldo. Basauri (Bizkaia) (45 u.k.)
ZUMALDE ROMERO Benito. Amorebieta (Bizkaia) (21 u.k.)
ZIRIZA ARMENDARIZ Koldo. Iruña (Nafarroa)

San Sebastian

ALBIZU Guillermo. Urnieta (Gipuzkoa)
ALKAIN DOMINGUEZ Iñaki. Donostia (Gipuzkoa)
ALVAREZ MAIZ Emilio. Ordizia. (Gipuzkoa)
APALATEGI MINTEGI Vicente. Beasain (Gipuzkoa) (15 u.k.)
APAOLAZA BERAZA Jose Mikel. Hernani (Gipuzkoa)
ARANZABAL BALZATEGI Victor. Mondragon (Gipuzkoa)
ARAKISTAIN Juan Victor. Donostia (Gipuzkoa)
ARRIETA ARRIETA Jose Ramon. Donostia (Gipuzkoa)
AIESTARAN REZOLA Rafael. Zaldibia (Gipuzkoa)
BEIZAMA LARRARTE Carlos. Zarauz (Gipuzkoa)
CALVO ANSA Jesus M. Ordizia. (Gipuzkoa)
ETXEBARRIA SUKIA Iñaki. Zaldibia. (Gipuzkoa) (15 u.k.)
FERNANDEZ PALACIO Roberto. Bilbo (Bizkaia) (15 u.k.)
GARMENDIA Iñaki. Loiola-Donostia (Gipuzkoa)
GOIKOETXEA JAUREGI Jose. Zumarraga (Gipuzkoa)
GUERRA MUXIKA Victor. Beasain (Gipuzkoa)
HERCESPINA Miguel Angel. Zumarraga (Gipuzkoa)
INURRIETA GALDOS Jose Koldo. Mondragon (Gipuzkoa)
IRASTORZA GORROTXATEGI Pedro. Ordizia (Gipuzkoa)
IRAZO Ramon. Andoain (Gipuzkoa)
IRURETA ZUBIA Jose Andoni. Zarauz (Gipuzkoa)
ITURRIA ISASTI Andoni. Zarauz (Gipuzkoa)
IZAGIRRE Koldo. Pasai (Gipuzkoa)
IZAGIRRE ZUBIARRAIN Marcos. Lezo (Gipuzkoa)
JAUREGI Mateo. Pasai (Gipuzkoa)
LABORDETA Juan M. Lezo (Gipuzkoa)
LARREA GARMENDIA Arantza. Lezo (Gipuzkoa)
LASA LIZARRAGA Jon. Donostia (Gipuzkoa)
LIZAUR Jose M. Donostia (Gipuzkoa)

MARTICORENA Andoni. Usurbil (Gipuzkoa)
MENDIZABAL Iñaki. Zaldibia (Gipuzkoa) (15 u.k.)
OLANO GOENAGA Iñaki. Zaldibia (Gipuzkoa)
SATRUSTEGI Xabier. Herrera-Donostia (Gipuzkoa)
URDANPILETA Kepa. Azpeitia (Gipuzkoa)
URRETABIZKAIA Jose Koldo. Renteria (gipuzkoa)
VALVERDE LAMFUS Carlos. Donostia (Gipuzkoa)
ZUBIMENDI Juan M. Usurbil (Gipuzkoa)

Zaragoza

ARTABE BILBO Narciso. Lejona (Bizkaia)
AURTENETXE MARKO Jon. Bilbo (Bizkaia)
CARDENAL IOLDI Iñaki. Bilbo (Bizkaia)
GERRIKABEITIA. Bilbo (Bizkaia)
IRIONDO Andres. Lasarte (Gipuzkoa)
LASARTE ZENIKAZELAIA J. Barakaldo (Bizkaia)
ROLDAN SARRIA J. Ramon. Bilbo (Bizkaia)
SANTA COLOMA ALEZAGA Felix. Barakaldo (Bizkaia)

Lerida

CUEVAS Iñaki. Sestao (Bizkaia)

Logroño

OLANO Jose Manuel. Hernani (Gipuzkoa)
ZUBILLAGA Jose M. Hernani (Gipuzkoa)

Pontevedra

GARCIA ARREGI
GRACIA Alejandro. Errenderi (Gipuzkoa)
IRIONDO Esteban. Amerebieta (Bizkaia)
LAKKAR Jose. Santesteban (Nafarroa)
MENDIBURU
MUXIKA Emilio. Amorebieta (Bizkaia)
OLABARRIA Kepa. Durango (Bizkaia)
ROLDAN Patxi. Donostia (Gipuzkoa)
URRUTIA J.M. Bilbo (Bizkaia)

Iruña

IZTUETA IRRISARRI Koldo. Ordizia (Gipuzkoa)

Segovia

AMIGO QUINCOCES Angel. Iruña (Nafarroa) (15 u.k.)
ARANBERRI Jose M. Eibar (Gipuzkoa)
ARANA BILBO Victor. Bilbo (Bizkaia)
ARANA BILBO Sabino. Sestao (Bizkaia) (32 u.k.)
ARRIZABALAGA BASTERRA Andoni. Ondarroa (Bizkaia) (20 u.k.)
ARTETXE OREJON Jose Koldo. Basauri (Bizkaia) (17 u.k.)
AURTENETXE MARCO Ramon. Bilbo (Bizkaia) (14 u.k.)
BEDIALAUNETA LAKA Andoni. Ondarroa (Bizkaia) (25 u.k.)
BEGOÑA MOLINERO Jesus. Bermeo (Bizkaia)
BILBO COS Josu. Bilbo (Bizkaia) (12 u.k.)
EGILUZ SAGASTIZABAL Iñaki. Arrakundiaga (Bizkaia) (5 u.k.)
EGILUZ SAGASTIZABAL Txomin. Arrakundiaga (Bizkaia) (5 u.k.)
EGIREUN TOTORIKA Jose Luis. Galdakano (Bizkaia)
EIZAGIRRE FERNANDEZ Felipe. Lasarte (Gipuzkoa)
GARCIA ARAMBARRI Iñaki. Ondarroa (Bizkaia) (25 u.k.)
GARITAONAINDIA GARNATXO Carmelo. Bilbo (Bizkaia) (37 u.k.)
IBAÑEZ ORTUZAR Xabier. Bilbo (Bizkaia) (15 u.k.)
ISASA Gotzon Lasarte (Gipuzkoa)
ITURBE TOTORIKA Juan Ignacio. Basauri (Bizkaia)
IZAGIRRE IZAGIRRE Fernando. Lasarte (Gipuzkoa) (50 u.k.)
JAKA Patxi. Berastegi (Gipuzkoa) (25 u.k.)
CARRERA Antton. Amezketa (Gipuzkoa) (12 u.k.)
LARRAZABAL Gregorio. Santurze (Bizkaia)
LORONO ETXEBARRIA Josu. Basauri (Bizkaia) (12 u.k.)
ZUBIAGA ORTIZ ANDA Jose Maria. Mondragon (Gipuzkoa)
  (14 u.k.)
MALAXETXEBARRIA Juan Angel. (2 u.k.)
MANAROS AGINAGALDE Iñaki. Deusto (Bizkaia) (4 u.k.)
MUNOA GALARRAGA Josu. Donostia (Gipuzkoa) (40 u.k.)
ORDORIKA GOIRIENA Juan Antonio. Bakio (Bizkaia) (12 u.k.)
RODRIGUEZ GONZALEZ Dario. Bilbo (Bizkaia) (12 u.k.)
URKIZU SARASUA. (5 u.k.)
VIAR ETXEBARRIA Iñaki. Bilbo (Bizkaia) (25 u.k.)
IARZA ETXENIKE Jose Ma. Lasarte (Gipuzkoa) (160 u.k.)
ZABALA LEGARRA Manu. Bilbo (Bizkaia) (12 u.k.)
ZILOAGA ARRATE Txomin. Bilbo (Bizkaia) (15 u.k.)
ZUBIKARAI OSA Jesus Ma. Ondarroa (Bizkaia)
ZUGADI RAMIREZ Pedro. Bilbo (Bizkaia) (12 u.k.)

Oviedo

BADIOLA Francisco. Lazkano (Gipuzkoa)

Zamora (clerical)

AMURIZA ZARRAONAINDIA Xabier. Amorebieta (Bizkaia)
ETXABE GARITAZELAIA Jon. Elgoibar (Gipuzkoa) (50 u.k.)
GABIKAGOGEASKOA Alberto. (12 u.k.)
KALZADA Julen. (22 u.k.)
NABERAN Josu. (12 u.k.)
TELLERIA Nikole. (10 u.k.)

Almeria

ARAMAIO AGIRRE Jose Koldo. Ondarroa (Bizkaia)

Bilboa

ARANA ARRIZABALAGA Patxi. Ondarroa (Bizkaia)
ARREGI AZPEITIA Jon. Amezketa (Gipuzkoa)
CUÑADO LANDA Jon. Guetxo (Bizkaia)
DURALDE LEJARDA Nerea. Eibar (Gipuzkoa)
GABIÑA ITURRIAGA Mikel. Bilbo (Bizkaia)
GOENAGA Iñaki. Ondarroa (Bizkaia)
GOENAGA Xabier. Lazkano (Gipuzkoa)
GISASOLA ARANZABAL Genaro. Donostia (Gipuzkoa)
LANDA AROZENA Jesus M. Azpeitia (Gipuzkoa)
LANDA GEREKITZ Gernika (Bizkaia)
LOPEZ Antton. Berango (Bizkaia)
MADARIAGA Lazkano (Gipuzkoa)
MENDIOLA Juan Jose. Lutxana (Bizkaia)
MENDIZABAL GARCIA Jon. Santurde (Bizkaia)
MEÑAKA GANKOITI Jesus. Plencia (Bizkaia)
MEÑACA ESUNZA Jose Iñaki. Bilbo (Bizkaia)
MITXELENA Manuel. Errenderia (Gipuzkoa) (30 u.k.)
OBACE URIA Eusebio. Donostia (Gipuzkoa)
ORTUZAR URIBE Xabier. Gernika (Bizkaia)
ORUBE ETXEBESTE J. Agustin. Bilbo (Bizkaia)
OTSOANTESANA ETXABURU J. Ondarroa (Bizkaia)
PUENTE BILBO Josefina. Algorta (Bizkaia)
SALAN IZTUETA Jose M. Eibar (Gipuzkoa)
URRUTIKOETXEA BARONA Gorka. Bilbo (Bizkaia)
ZABARTE ARREGI Jesus M. Mondragon (Gipuzkoa) (100 u.k.)

RECENTLY IMPRISONED

GARMENDIA Jose Antonio. Albazisketa. (Tupa)

ARRUABARRENA Jose Maria. (Tanka)
SERRANO IZKKO Vicente. Iruña
FOREST TARAT. Madrid
DURAN VELASCO Antonio. Madrid
ANTONIO BAYO Eliseo. Madrid
FALCON O' NEILL Lidia. Madrid
SANZ DE LA PEÑA Vicente. Madrid
BALLESTEROS GILABERT Maria Paz. Madrid
VADELL CARRERAS Bernardo. Madrid
NADAL BERTARD Maria Del Carmen. Madrid
GURRUTXAGA EZENARRO. Plazenzia de las Armas. (Gipuzkoa)
APALATEGI Jose Maria. Beasain (Gipuzkoa)
LABURU BENGOETXEA Juan. Llodio (Araba)
IBARROLA UDAETA Jose Luis. Llodio (Araba)
ALDAITURRIAGA ZORROZUA Norberto. Llodio (Araba)
MENDIZABAL MENDIOLA Maria Pilar
GARMENDIA LASA Julia Maria Ignacia
ELORRIETA ZABALA Diego
ELORRIETA AMUNDARAIN Juana Amagoia
GISASOLA LARRINAGA Agustin
ETXEBERRI ELORDUI Jesus
AGUIRRE Jose Antonio
MUGIKA Xabier Santos. Plazenzia de las Armas. (Gipuzkoa)
ETXEBARRIA GENETXEA Xabier. Amorebieta (Bizkaia)
GONZALEZ ZELARAIN Maria Isabel. Villafranca (Gipuzkoa)
AIZPURU Maria Ester. Gadakano (Bizkaia)
INSAUSTEGI ELIZONDO Jose Jokin. Lazkano (Gipuzkoa)
BAZKARAN Iñaki Xabier. Plazenzia de las Armas (Gipuzkoa)
ARRIBILLAGA ASKASIBAR Jose Antonio. Elgoibar (Gipuzkoa)
OSORIO LOIOLA Jose Domingo. Elgoibar (Gipuzkoa)
ARANZABAL ZUBURRUTI Miguel Angel. Bergara (Gipuzkoa)
MARKINA Iñaki Xabier. Plazenzia de las Armas (Gipuzkoa)
VELEZ BEDIA. Donostia (Gipuzkoa)
ALCALDE IRURZUN Maria del Carmen. Donostia. (Gipuzkoa)
PAGOAGA GALLASTEGI Enrique. Mondragon (Gipuzkoa)
SASTRE Alfonso. Madrid
BILBATUA Miguel. Madrid
SAINZ Hermogenes. Madrid
GUERRERO Enrique. Madrid
OSO Angel. Madrid
ASTRAIN MURUA Carlos. Donostia (Gipuzkoa)
ARANGUREN LIZARRALDE Ramon. Anzuola (Gipuzkoa)
AZKARATE JAUREGI Juan Jose. Anzuola (Gipuzkoa)
AGIRRE URBETA Francisco Javier. Lezo (Gipuzkoa)

ZORROZUA Maria Begoña. Lezo (Gipuzkoa)
OTAEGI. Azpeitia (Gipuzkoa)
URBIÑA GREGORIO Luis Maria. Portugalete (Bizkaia)
ARGOITIA ZARRAGA Feliciano. Portugalete (Bizkaia)
UGARTE BIDAURRAGA Javier. Portugalete (Bizkaia)
URRUTIKOETXEA MORENO Angel. Portugalete (Bizkaia)
ALONSO FERNANDEZ Alberto. Bilbo (Bizkaia)
BUENO VASCO Manuel. Bilbo (Bizkaia)
VILLATE OLANO. Bilbo (Bizkaia)
UGALDE UGARRIZA Tomas. Zeberio (Bizkaia)
EGIGUREN SALZEDO Jose Luis. Miravalles (Bizkaia)
BORDE GAZTELUMENDI Antonio. Miravalles (Bizkaia)

The Four Communiques of E.T.A., December 1973

E.T.A. Communiqué Number One

The Basque Socialist Revolutionary Organization for National Liberation, Euskadi Ta Askatasuna (E.T.A.), assumes responsibility for the act which today, Thursday, December 20, 1973, has produced the death of Mr. Luis Carrero Blanco, President of the current Spanish Government.

Throughout the struggle, in Southern Euskadi and the rest of the Spanish state, the repression has clearly shown its fascist character by arresting, jailing, torturing and murdering those who struggle for the freedom of their people.

In a very short time span the criminal fascist forces at the command of the Spanish upper bourgeosie have murdered nine of our comrades —Txabi, Txapela, Xanki, Mikelon, Iharra, Txikia, Jon, Beltza, and Josu—and other Basque militants and patriots who were only defending their most basic rights.

The operation carried out by E.T.A. against the power structure of the Spanish oligarchy in the person of Luis Carrero Blanco, is the Basque people's and the working class's retaliation against the murders of our nine E.T.A. comrades and those who have struggled for a world totally liberated from all forms of exploitation and oppression. It must be interpreted as our justified revolutionary reply.

Luis Carrero Blanco—a "tough" man, violent in his repressive schemes—was the key factor that would have guaranteed the continuity and stability of Franco's system; with him out of the picture, it is certain that tension will be dangerously heightened among the different factions within the bosom of power who are addicted to General Franco's regime—Opus Dei, Falange, etc.

Thus, our action against the President of the Spanish Government constitutes a major step forward for socialism in Euskadi in our struggle against national oppression, as well as for the liberation of the exploited and oppressed in the Spanish state.

Today the workers and people of Euskadi, of Spain, Catalonia and Galicia, the democratic, revolutionary and antifascist people of the world, find ourselves liberated from an important enemy. The struggle continues.

Onward with national liberation and socialism!

GORA EUSKADI ASKATUTA!!

GORA EUSKADI SOZIALISTA!!

Euskadi Ta Askatasuna E.T.A.

E.T.A. *Communiqué Number Two*

Euskadi Ta Askatasuna reaffirms its total responsibility for the execution of Mr. Luis Carrero Blanco.

The commando "Txikia," author of the act, is at this moment safe and sound in a very secure place.

The execution of Mr. Luis Carrero Blanco constitutes the just reply to the wave of violence unleashed by his Government upon the Basque people which resulted in the death of nine E.T.A. militants.

We categorically deny the declarations made by entities or persons alien to E.T.A. (Mr. Leizaola, President of the Basque Government Plenum of the C. E. of the Spanish Communist Party) inasmuch as they deny our responsibility for the execution of Mr. Luis Carrero Blanco. Such an attitude, to our understanding, reflects a grave lack of political honesty that is incomprehensible in those who label themselves leaders of the opposition to Franco's regime.

We are firmly determined to continue the same line of action if the repression continues to prey upon our workers and our people. We shall strike again at the fascist power in the persons, places, and times that we consider most suitable.

GORA EUSKADI ASKATUTA!!

GORA EUSKADI SOZIALISTA!!

Euskadi, December 22, 1973

E.T.A.

(Euskadi Ta Askatasuna)

E.T.A. *Communiqué Number Three*

Several European sources of information have echoed the declarations of a supposed E.T.A. militant, according to whom, "If they as much as touch one strand of hair of a refugee, there will be in less than a month one thousand corpses in Madrid. We are ready to do anything. We'll even blow up the Metro if necessary."

Such a declaration, attributed to "a responsible militant of the move-ment," can come only from a provocateur or from some newspaper-man's irresponsible imagination. We deeply regret that some groups—self-appointed revolutionaries and antifascists—via channels of infor-mation at their disposal, have tried to take advantage of such an absurd declaration in order to discredit the cause of the Basque People, when they know very well what our ends and means are.

We are Basque revolutionaries, not terrorist-murderers; we know how to distinguish our friends from our enemies. The latter are solely comprised of the big Spanish capitalists with all their fascist power machine. In our struggle for Euskadi's Independence with Socialism, we consider the workers and the Spanish people as our allies.

We then consider that the aforementioned declarations and the attitude of those who echo them can do nothing but confuse the understanding among those who struggle against Franco's regime for the freedom of their people.

GORA EUSKADI ASKATUTA!!

GORA EUSKADI SOZIALISTA!!

Euskadi, December 26, 1973
E.T.A.
(Euskadi Ta Askatasuna)

E.T.A. Communiqué Number Four

The Spanish mass media, controlled by Franco's Government, have initiated a new propaganda campaign after Carrero Blanco's execution.

As on previous occasions, the Spanish state tries to mix our revolu-tionary activity—carried out in Southern Euskadi or in the rest of the Spanish territory—with the Basque refugees who benefit from political asylum in Northern Euskadi or in the rest of the French state.

According to certain official sources, Franco's Government tries to obtain the extradition of many Basque refugees by accusing them of being directly responsible for the execution of the "gray brain" of the regime, even when some refugees have proven beyond any doubt that they did not participate in the operation.

The possibility of extradition in such cases is very real: Everyone knows about the very close ties that exist between both states. On previous occasions, Paris has yielded to the repressive demands of the Spanish Government. For this reason, and although E.T.A. struggles for the freedom of the Basque people precisely against fascism, it is probable that Pompidou and his Government might give in to the pressures of Franco's regime. Even when it cannot be definitely stated that the requested extraditions shall be granted, it can be assured that the French state shall not remain insensitive to the Franco Government's demands; one can, then, foretell the expulsion of Basque refugees, be they of Northern Euskadi, the border sectors, or the entire French territory.

On the other hand, the refugees do not have any organization ties with E.T.A.; our activity and the study of the setting up and development of our operations are always done in Southern Euskadi or in the rest of the Spanish state. Up to the present, the French Administration has been unable to prove whether E.T.A. has "bases" in Northern Euskadi or at any other point of the French state. Much to the contrary, we affirm that such "bases" only exist in the imagination of the Spanish dictatorial power, which intends to cover up the inefficiency and incapacity of its secret services and to push the French Government to take punitive measures against the Basque political refugees.

We call upon all the democratic, antifascist and revolutionary people of the world, as well as international public opinion, to form a massive and active mobilization against the implementation of any reprisals against the Basque political refugees.

GORA EUSKADI ASKATUTA!!

GORA EUSKADI SOZIALISTA!!

Euskadi, December 28, 1973

E.T.A.

(Euskadi Ta Askatasuna)

APPENDIX II

The August 1973 Declaration

Here is the August Declaration, which was widely distributed not only throughout Euskadi, but also throughout the rest of the Spanish state by Commando Txikia.

To the Revolutionaries, Democrats, Anti-Fascists of Euskadi and of the Entire World

1. EUSKADI IS A PEOPLE STRUGGLING FOR THEIR NATIONAL AND SOCIAL LIBERATION.

If the Basque problem exists it is because a Basque People, different from their neighbors, exist; as such, it has the right to a different solution. Throughout their history, the Basque People have always reaffirmed their will to achieve national liberation.

The French Revolution (1789) and nineteenth-century Spanish liberalism created two centralized states, which were violent negators of the national minorities; our people were split in two by the imposition of the artificial boundry of the Bidasoa River (1841). Their own laws, juridical reflections of a precapitalist society, disappeared; the new legislation reflected only the dependence on the interests of the big Spanish and French capitalists.

The national oppression on the Basques began with the introduction of the capitalist modes of production.

The French bourgeoisie abolished the autonomy of the provinces of Benabarra, Laburdi, and Zuberoa (Northern Euskadi); with the country occupied militarily, the Northern Basques resisted submission to the centralism of incipient French capitalism. Northern Euskadi, isolated as a result of the economic evolution of the latter, suffers the consequences of such a system: The economic planning of the French state is done without regard to the needs of the people; it responds instead to those of the capitalists. As a result, the place granted to Northern Euskadi is that of "a green vacationland." The small agricultural enterprises do not have an outlet in the French market; corn becomes practically the sole crop, sold to monopolies that ruin the "baserri-tarras." The country becomes depopulated. Socially and economically segregated from the mainstream by the Parisian bourgeoisie, Northern Euskadi slowly agonizes.

Bourgeois liberalism implies the violent integration of Southern Euskadi (Gipuzkoa, Bizkaia, Nafarroa, Araba) into the political, economic, social, and cultural structures of the Spanish state since the armed victories of the Carlist Wars and the subsequent judicial abolition of Basque autonomy laws (Fueros). The Spanish state authorized the European capitalists (particularly the British) to exploit the Basque iron ore. A heavy industry developed as a result of this activity, first around Bilbao and later in the rest of Bizkaia and Gipuzkoa; this industry, with an antieconomic character and enormous technical regressions, was created by its bosses for the sole purpose of maximizing the profits within a Spanish market protected by the state.

Thus emerged the modern Basque upper bourgeoisie, which developed greatly at the beginning of the present century out of the hydroelectric enterprises, finance, and the naval industry. It interlocked with the Spanish land-owning class and the financiers, giving way to the present oppressive oligarchy. In relation to the Basque community, these oligarchs essentially behave as the declared enemies of the aspirations for national freedom, however small these may be.

The emergence of the Second Republic (1931) implied for Southern Euskadi the acquisition of the Statute of Autonomy (1936); although not representative of all the national aspirations of our People, the Statute at least confirmed the reality of the Basque existence.

In order to maintain its sway, the bourgeoisie needs a crushing military and repressive apparatus. When the risk of the revolution becomes more acute, this apparatus will be put in motion without hesitation; if the risk is imminent, the bourgeoisie will provoke a civil war and, if it triumphs, it will implant the most horrendous military tyranny. The military uprising of July 18, 1936 confronted landowners, financiers, and industrialists, supported by a handful of military aristocrats and by the Catholic hierarchy, with the democrats, antifascists and revolutionaries of the different peoples of the Spanish state. The defeat of the latter meant the implantation of the dictatorial regime of Franco fascism at the command of the Spanish upper bourgeoisie.

The fascist regime is extremely reactionary: Its only means of dialogue is brute force; it strikes with unwonted violence not only at the revolutionaries, but also at the most moderate democrats.

Nowadays, even the minimum liberties are denied. We the workers do not have the right to associate in order to mutually assist one another and to defend ourselves against capitalists; we do not have the right to our own press in our own separate locale in order to freely express ourselves; we do not have the right to strike, and our attempts to organize unions and our own political groups are penalized as acts of subversion. In declared social conflicts, the Official Unions, the Police, and the Civil Guard are always on the side of the bosses; when the press, radio, and television report on conflicts they always distort the truth; everything that is official and almost everything that is legal is used to make antiworker and antipeople politics. The entire state machinery is nothing but an impressive apparatus for repression at the service of the oligarchy.

The attitude of the ruling class is coherent: If on the economic and social levels it treats the Working People with repression and scorns their most elementary rights, on the level of the national character of the oppressed peoples it employs the same kind of politic; in our case, its behavior has been special.

From the express prohibition of the use of our language, Euskara, to its use of punishment geared to embarrass school girls and boys for not expressing themselves correctly in Spanish because they come from surroundings that are mostly Basque-speaking, the Spanish bourgeoisie has systematically combatted the language and culture of the Basque people. In the thirty years of Franco's regime, the Basque language has retreated more than in the almost one hundred years that elapsed between 1778 and 1863.

2. E.T.A. INTENDS TO ASSUME AND SOLVE THE DUAL PROBLEM OF THE BASQUE WORKING CLASS.

E.T.A. is a Basque socialist and revolutionary organization for national liberation. We are Basque socialists and nationalists. Our strategic objective is the creation of a Basque Socialist State headed by the working class of Euskadi, which will serve as the instrument for all our people in the creation of a classless Basque society. In such a state, the political, economic, social and cultural power should be exercised by the Basque people for the Basque people; we, then, see the Basque Socialist State as an entity growing out of the federation, in the area of Southern and Northern Euskadi, of the workers' committees and "batzarres" of towns and districts, which are to be understood as the means of revolutionary power created by our workers and our people during the process of our struggle.

Man is not an abstract entity that escapes from being molded by the pressures of reality; on the contrary, he is a very concrete being with very concrete interests and problems. WE ARE BASQUES, workers of Euskadi, from a very defined and determined national community; we are in a very specific situation of national oppression.

It is impossible either to forget or to disregard the national plane of our struggle as a Basque working class. Our liberation will not be possible unless it includes the total picture of our reality, unless it includes each and every one of our facets and the entirety of our complex human projections as workers and as Basques.

We are in favor of a socialist Basque culture, a liberating culture inasmuch as it is the negation of foreign and bourgeois cultures; inasmuch as it is the affirmation of our national class entity as proletarians of Euskadi.

We affirm that the Basque People's cultural problem will be definitely solved only through the total Euskerization of the People of Euskadi, starting from a situation of trilingualism that will achieve the desired objective if it is channeled in a revolutionary fashion. In Euskadi there are immigrant workers who have not seen the need to integrate fully with the Basque national reality; we must facilitate at all times such an integration. Those who legitimately choose not to integrate, those who wish to continue being Spaniards, Galicians, or Frenchmen, must have their rights guaranteed so as to avoid even the slightest speck of discrimination or inequality within the future Basque society.

The bourgeoisie is the principal enemy of the people's national rights. In fact, the national oppression arose as a result of the consolidation of the capitalist system. This implies that the solution to the national problem necessarily involves the destruction of bourgeois power. Class struggle and national problem, then, form a unit. We are socialists. Our struggle for liberation develops out of and is inscribed in a revolutionary class perspective.

Capitalism is a mode of production based on man's exploitation of man; there exists a basic contradiction between our interests as proletarians and those of the bourgeoisie. Such a contradition can be solved only by the Socialist Revolution.

Improvements elevate the standard of living and the security of the working class without thereby destroying the bourgeoisie's power. They are useful inasmuch as they allow millions of people to lead a less painful life. But they are unable to undermine the foundations of the system. We shall extirpate the roots of our exploitation; we shall destroy each and every one of the capitalist production relations. For this reason, in our struggle for emancipation our battles are geared to end wage-based labor and private ownership of the means of production, with the ultimate goal being the classless society.

We cannot conceive of a free Euskadi under the bourgeoisie. We are determined to be Basques in a society free from exploitation; we are, therefore, in favor of a Basque Socialist State.

WE ARE ADVOCATES OF INDEPENDENCE; we honestly be-
lieve that our problem as Basque workers, as an exploited class in a
context of a people nationally oppressed and divided, cannot be
solved within the French or Spanish scope. Certainly, our liberation as
a class would be viable within the framework of a socialist Spain or
France, But, in our opinion, only an independent power in our hands,
that is to say, only a Basque Socialist State, can guarantee the solution to the other side of the problem: our liberation as members of an
oppressed national community: Euskadi.

Naturally this independence takes on for us a socialist meaning: It
will be a separatist independence with respect to imperialism and the
capitalist states of Spain and France; it will be a unionist independence with respect to all of the peoples of the world and specially with
our immediate neighbors. Independence means the creation of a
Basque social system, totally controlled by our people, in which the
degree of commitment to unity with the neighboring peoples will be
a function of the historical moment. We shall advocate the abolition
of borders when the conditions for men exploiting men and countries
exploiting countries cease to exist. Our struggle for independence is
conceived of as being within the unity of the workers of the world
and functioning within the interests of the Socialist Revolution.

WE ADVOCATE ARMED STRUGGLE; E.T.A. intends to carry
forward an armed struggle aimed at the apparatus of the oppressor
states; this struggle shall function in our interest as a working class
and those of the rest of the Basque people.

The oligarchy will not yield its position or its privileges without
resistance. As a matter of fact, it spends greater and greater sums
of money in the maintenance and creation of highly specialized and
unscrupulous repressive units. Those who believe in change without
violence seem to forget what daily experience teaches us: The
oligarchy does not hesitate for one moment to throw the power of its
repressive apparatus upon the helpless workers and the people
whenever it deems it necessary.

Armed struggle is the supreme form of struggle of the working
class. Our liberation as a class and as a people will be possible
through an armed insurrection of the proletariat and the rest of the
people of Euskadi in a revolutionary tactical articulation with the rest
of the peoples who comprise the Spanish state. Precisely for that
reason we are putting forth an armed mechanism that will gradually
increase its size in accordance with the radicalization of the Basque
People's struggles, until it becomes a military apparatus capable of
offering a revolutionary power's alternative to the present oppressive
and exploiting regime.

Although favorable to the role of armed struggle, there are those who argue that its use at the present time is a reactionary practice because there aren't any conditions for its development; those who reason in this fashion seem to ignore two factors: that such revolutionary conditions already exist (the best proof of it is our own existence as E.T.A.) and that these conditions can be only created in struggle.

Although there is no doubt that the strengthening of the armed organization goes together with the growing politicization of the oppressed, it also cannot be doubted that armed struggle on a major scale will emerge only as a product of its constant practice. To try to expand and to increase it is, then, the imperative task of all revolutionaries.

Today our military struggle presents two aspects: On the tactical level, it's a matter of strengthening and supporting the mass dynamics that the working class and the rest of our people are developing; on the strategic level, it is a matter of setting up the foundations for the formation of an armed apparatus in the hands of the workers and of the Basque popular strata, which will be able to paralyze and topple the oligarchy's pillar of repression in Euskadi.

It is clear that the progress made in the struggle will bring along with it a great increase in repression. There exists the possibility that some groups will crack under such pressure, since they refuse to accept military strategy as valid. These groups are already looking for a theoretical justification of their revolutionary incapacity by using arguments such as the one that classifies military dynamics as "intrinsically petty bourgeois," "suicidal adventurism," or "Third World strategy." They will refuse to recognize the steady loss of their revolutionary character and they will intensify their criticism in the hope of regaining a revolutionary process—ours—that is already today slipping out of their grasp.

3. WHO ARE OUR ALLIES AS THE BASQUE WORKING CLASS?

The main contradiction of our revolutionary struggle is that which pits the Basque popular classes led by the industrial proletariat against the monopolistic Spanish and French bourgeoisies; there exists some objective uniting ties, some common class interests—not identical—that determine the popular and not merely proletarian character of the impending revolution in Euskadi.

In our case, such an affinity of revolutionary interests is strengthened by the existence of a national oppression common to the working class and to the other popular classes of the revolutionary social layers: *"arrantzales," "nekazaris,"* administrative workers, small proprietors, merchants and industrialists, students, intellectuals, and other wage-earning workers.

The Basque Popular Revolution constitutes the first phase in the construction of socialism in Euskadi; and implanted by it as a substitution for the present monopolistic relations, the Basque popular revolutionary power should completely destroy the oligarchy's power over the economic, political, social and cultural planes and begin to build the Basque Socialist Society.

A future society is inconceivable without the abolition of the oppressive political, economic, social, and cultural relations among peoples; that society is contained in the socialist character of the present struggles. If now the revolutionary struggle is carried out in such a manner that some groups within it employ oppressive relations against other groups, the triumph of the revolution is incompatible with such groups and their politics. For that reason, an indispensable condition for every internationalism is the respect for each people's particularity. In our case, we demand that the fact of the Basque people's liberation in itself, and therefore, our possession of a particular strategy and of our own movement be recognized as revolutionary realities that all of our allies should admit and respect.

For our part, at the same time that we demand the respect of our national particularity and our strategic independence, we the Basque workers are to labor intensively at getting the Spanish and French workers to understand that our struggle for independence is not directed against them. We therefore condemn those who wish the independence of a rich, strong, and heavily armed Euskadi, ready and able to oppress and exploit the immigrant workers who have no political or union rights, and to exploit intentionally an underdeveloped Spain. Our military strength will serve to eliminate oppression, never to exploit other peoples. Our economic potential shall serve to contribute to the creation of a society in which not only will men not exploit one another, but also in which no people will take advantage of the wealth that is theirs in order to neo-colonize another people.

Furthermore, the wealth that exists in Euskadi is to a great extent the product of the sweat and labor of thousands of immigrant workers. If for the Spanish and French workers the elimination of all cultural and national inequalities with respect to the Basque people is an internationalist obligation, for us, Basque workers, the obligation is to contribute to the development of a future socialist Spain and France.

Our condemnation of Basque national chauvinism goes together with our condemnation of the social imperialism of certain Spanish and French groups. To claim that the struggle for Basque national independence divides the working class is to perpetuate, in reality, a unitary feeling that is the work of the bourgeoisie. There is real unity only for us, the Basque workers and the Spanish and French workers, if one as well as the other abandons all chauvinism, if the latter truly understand and support our struggle for national liberation. We therefore condemn the covering up or the deliberate misrepresentation of this problem as counterrevolutionary attitudes.

Our national and social liberation as a Basque working class will be possible through the coordination—not the subordination—of the revolutionary efforts of all those oppressed and exploited in the Spanish and French states. We then understand—in the Spanish state—that the anti-Franco organizations who wish to ally themselves with the Basque revolutionaries cannot ask as a previous condition the abdication—even if temporary—of our struggle for national reunification and independence. Very much on the contrary, they should accept the reality that our combat does not contradict the anti-Franco unity and revolutionary action. The need for effective coordination and mutual suport should be based on this premise: The actions of the masses, the strikes, can broaden and become more effective by erupting at the same time and supporting themselves in the totality of the state.

E.T.A., which practices armed struggle and has the extension of it as a strategic principle, is particularly interested in the mutual support of all the groups that may employ armed struggle today or tomorrow. The coordination among the nuclei of armed struggle and the extension of it will be done in solidarity in order to be doubly effective, to prevent errors provoked by alienation and immaturity as well as those provoked by the concentration of repressive forces in one specific area.

The anti-Franco unity is formed principally in its base and its practice by the struggle of the masses and armed combat. We do not forget, however, the different options in terms of substituting the regime, and we support these in varying degrees.

As Basque revolutionaries, we struggle against all oppression: against national oppression and capitalist exploitation. For this reason, we are in favor of a Basque Socalist State. The only motive that drives us toward it is the full conviction that in no other way could we obtain the correct answer to the question posed by our existence as Basque workers who are expoited as a class and oppressed and divided as a people.

Commando "Txikia" of the E.T.A. Organization
(Euskadi Ta Askatasuna)

APPENDIX III

On the Reactions of Other Oppositionists

A Document Written by Commando "Txikia" at the Time of the Interview with Julen Agirre

I could not end this document without first reexamining (even if in a brief and incomplete fashion) the positions, in the face of Carrero Blanco's execution, taken by some personalities and some political parties of the opposition who carry out their activity in the Spanish state.

1. In the first place we see the position taken by Luis María Leizaola, President of the Basque Government in Exile since the death of its former President, José Antonio Aguirre. Leizaola is a distinguished elder member of the Basque National Party.

Immediately after E.T.A.'s first communique became public, where our organization affirmed its responsibility for the execution of Carrero Blanco, Mr. Leizaola made public another communique in which he denied that we could have had any responsibility for the act. His declaration was based on the following two assumptions:

A. The extreme act of violence, which is a premeditated and perfectly planned killing, does not become the Basque, therefore, E.T.A., could not have participated in the execution of the President of Franco's Government.

B. If E.T.A. had been the executioner, Mr. Leizaola, as President of the Basque Government in Exile, and thus the highest political representative of the Basque people would have been informed of the act; he was not.

It is of great importance to analyze both points in order to understand the true content of the Basque Government and the degree of responsibility of the President's statement insofar as he represents that institution:

A. The acceptance of the first point has been historically harmful to the workers and the rest of the Basque people. Our parents have grown old regretting their past "kindness" and their rejection of violence, which resulted in their defeat. It is important that we understand once and for all that passive resistance and defensive violence by themselves are not useful against the bourgeoisie and its power apparatus in the Spanish state (Franco's dictatorship) (1). The bourgeoisie (also the ruling classes that historically preceded it) has institutionalized violence in the form of exploitation in socioeconomic relations and in the form of oppression in cultural and political relations. The interests of the oligarchy and the promonopolistic sectors of the state are confronted with those of the workers along with the rest of the popular sectors (antimonopolistic), and such a contradiction can be solved only through the definite defeat of one of the two elements in the conflict (2):

(Ed. note: Following are the two notes to Txikia's document on p. 150 of the Spanish publication by Ruedo Iberico.)

(1) In order to define what we mean by defensive violence, it is necessary to delimit three forms of violence:

A. *Defensive Violence.* It is the case of the shootout at Galdakano two years ago. A group of militants killed a Municipal Guard and injured a Civil Guard when both together with other companions tried to arrest them.

It is equivalent to what is commonly known as self-defense.

B. *Violence as an act of retaliation.* The police injured and arrested a militant in Iruña, and subsequently a commando in Azpuitia killed the person in charge of the Political and Social Investigation Bureau of the Civil Guard in that zone. One of the objectives is to warn the state's repressive forces that each one of their acts against the Organization will be met with a strong reply. In this manner, it is likely that the repressive forces will think a little harder before carrying out their operations.

This type of violence can be considered as organized defense.

The execution of Carrero Blanco, as has already been explained in this document, does not exclusively correspond, even in a fundamental way, to that type of violence; but this may be thought of as the case, since the act took place following the recent assassinations of several of our comrades; that is why Mr. Leizaola denies us in his statements the possibility of using this form of violence, and conforming to the legal norms of the bourgeois law, he only recognizes as legal for the Basques (he says nothing with respect to the other peoples) the violence understood in the concept of self-defense.

C. *Offensive Violence*. It is that which is practiced following the necessities designated by a strategy in order to bring about the defeat of the enemy. It includes the types of violence aforementioned whose functions are tactical, with the addition of new ones.

This is precisely where Carrero Blanco's execution fits in.

The Spanish oligarchy not only intends to arrest or kill militant revolutionaries, but also, by way of its own strategy, to methodically practice violence against the Basque People in the form of exploitation and oppression. It is for this reason that the Basque People must have a liberation strategy that includes (in order for it to be successful) the practice of offensive violence.

In summary, to condemn any type of popular violence is brutal nonsense and a clear sign of the inability (on the part of the critic) to give up the ideological perspective of the exploiting class. People do not practice violence just for the sake of it, but because they have an acute need to acquire a human right: the right to freedom in social relations. Violence by the people is merely a reply to oppression: In any of its forms—self-defense, as retaliation, or as an offensive act—it is always defensive when compared to the institutionalized violence practiced by the exploiting class, and in the sense that it is defensive, it is entirely legitimate.

To deny the Basque People, as Mr. Leizaola does, the possibility of using violence in any of its forms, is equivalent to denying them the possibility of liberating themselves; whoever manifests such behavior deserves no other label than of traitor.

(2) In order to prevent erroneous interpretations we must specify that E.T.A. believes the present class struggle in Euskadi to be a confrontation between the monopolistic (Spanish) oligarchy and the Basque People, the latter being comprised of the working class along with social sectors of layers who share antimonopolistic interests in Euskadi. By this definition E.T.A. does not mean to imply that it represents and defends the interests of all the Basque People; this is true only to the extent where the interests of the other layers plainly coincide with those of the working class, which is specifically the class that E.T.A. represents and defends because it is the most exploited and oppressed class, because it is the most numerous and unique, and

because it is in a historical situation where it can spur the progress of the Basque society by eliminating from the latter's bosom every type of national class antagonism and exploitation by man against man.

The oligarchy (and its allies) is a discriminating minority, destined to disappear since it has sufficiently fulfilled the role assigned to it by history. This struggle does not recognize any "moral" or any other standards that may try to regulate it. Passive resistance and defensive violence may be utilized, but once the violence by the exploiting class is institutionalized, our strategy must be comparable if we wish to be successful. In order to achieve victory in any confrontation, we must take the initiative on all levels of the struggle, and violence is one of these levels; the highest and most decisive one in the final analysis.

Mr. Leizaola's statements are the result of a petty bourgeois, humanist cultural ideology that has for years, if not since time immemorial, oriented the political views of the P.N.V., with the effect being none other than the diverting of sectors of the population, fortunately less and less each time, from the only road that leads to the achievement of its objectives.

B. If Mr. Leizaola had given no further proof of his abandonment of the struggle for the socioecenomic, cultural, and political liberation of the Basque People, the sentence previously analyzed would have been sufficient to label him as a traitor. But in addition, he, as well as the Basque Government in general, has demonstrated throughout the past years an absolute lack of activity and a profound estrangement from the true interests of the Basques, which eliminate any doubts with respect to their position. The Basque Government is merely the roving phantom of an institution that has already played out its historical role; today, it can only revive itself by means of a maneuver, on the part of the Spanish oligarchy, in search of the Basque People's integration into the monopolistic system; a maneuver that will involve some Spanish reformist organizations. That is to say, the only function that the Basque Government can perform at the present is that of an instrument for the exploiting class and then only in the case where the latter decided to change the fascist dictatorship for a political system that can be manipulated more effectively against the initiatives of the people. But in order for the oligarchy to assign it such a role, the Basque Government must demonstrate that it is capable of assimilating the remaining patriotic forces, among which we must be included. Apparently, Mr. Leizaola thinks he has achieved his objective, thus the second reason on which he bases his argument that E.T.A. could not be Carrero Blanco's executioner explains itself. Perhaps we should remind him that E.T.A. has defined itself as a Basque Socialist Revolutionary Organization in favor of national liberation and intends to be so in action as well. It has never accepted the authority, much less the paternalism, of the Basque Government, whose form and function is exactly as we have just described; finally E.T.A. will only accept the authority of a Popular Revolutionary Government led by the Working Class of Euskadi.

Now let us continue with the events. After learning about Mr. Leizaola's communique, E.T.A. sent an official delegation to ask that he rectify his declarations. He flatly denied to do so after a heated argument in which he made a display of dialectical infantilism when, in order to justify his denial, he went as far as saying to the members: "Were you in Madrid witnessing the act? No? Well, then how do you know that it was your organization who did it? I had also said that we had not destroyed Gernika, and no one believed me." That is to say, in the first place, that one must visit China in order to verify that they grow rice there and secondly, let us use the proverb: "The misfortune of many is the consolation of fools." Ed. note: a pun on the proverb "Mal de muchos consuelo de todos." Here *todos* (all) is changed to *tontos* (fools).

Immediately, a second delegation was sent accompanied by two P.N.V. members who were to guarantee the authenticity of the delegation as composed by E.T.A. militants. This delegation convinced Mr. Leizaola that he should sign the following declaration, which is a copy of the original French text:

Upon request by representatives of the Basque Organization E.T.A., I must precisely state that said Organization, according to the communique circulated by it, claims responsibility for the operation that caused the death of the Head of State in Madrid, Admiral Carrero Blanco;

That said Organization does not support the Basque Government established in 1936, which continues to function in exile and that there are no existing ties between the one and the other.

Written in Paris, December 22, 1973.

Luis María Leizaola

This statement, which should have been made public in its entirety, was taken by the E.T.A. delegation to the evening newspaper *France-*

Soir, which for unknown reasons published it without the second paragraph, thus creating confusion in the meaning of the first one. (With respect to the second paragraph, the possibility of the Basque Government's request for its omission should not be dismissed.)

2. Undoubtedly, the position taken by the Spanish Communist Party needs special attention. We refer to the declarations made by the Plenum and its President Santiago Carrillo in the magazine "Mundo Obrero," dated December 29, 1973.

The objective of the present chapter is limited to the observation of the positions taken by the different opposition forces with regard to the execution of Carrero Blanco. It isn't intended as an analysis of their political lines. Thus, we shall focus merely on two excerpts from the two declarations mentioned above, although both statements constitute a beautiful meadow where the scythe of criticism will not encounter any cleared land.

> We are against the individual act because we feel that it doesn't solve anything, it doesn't give an outlet, and it can be an obstacle to the progress of the struggle of the masses and the people, in whom exists the possibility of solution.
>
> (From the C.E. Plenum's declaration)

This thesis is as ancient as the betrayal done to the words of Marx and Lenin by many self-titled Marxist-Leninists who in practice are nothing but mere reformists.

No method of struggle, no act by a small group or by the masses, is intrinsically wrong; its validity depends upon its adequacy within the revolutionary process where it is inscribed.

Action for its own sake is adventurism. The subordination of consciousness raising, organization, and elevation of the working masses' level of struggle to small-group activism are unmistakable signs of a petty bourgeois ideology that bases its hopes on the aggressiveness and daring of a small select group, while it disdains the revolutionary potential of the working masses, which is the only one capable of carrying forward the socialist revolution.

But there exists a third type of small group action, whose content is fundamentally divergent and is of an opposite nature with regard to the other two. It is that which aids the aforementioned tasks of consciousness raising, organization, and elevation of the masses' level of struggle, as well as helping these to come nearer to the attainment of power.

To treat the problem of small-group action as Carrillo does is as schematic as saying that rainfall is bad. Rainfall may be good or bad, depending on the conditions that exist when it rains and the results it produces. The same rainfall that may flood cities with the ensuing damage that it causes may also serve to fertilize a field that augured not to yield crops as a result of a drought.

Judging the line of an organization as did Carrillo, it may be said, that an individual act is not a solution; but his interviewer was asking him, not for his opinion concerning E.T.A.'s line of action, but for his thoughts concerning specifically the execution of Carrero Blanco, to which he should have directed his answer. That, however, would have forced him to make a criticism of the action, and the C.P. no longer utilizes that method of knowledge. It is undoubtedly much easier, on a short-term basis, to answer according to dogma; for this reason, Carrillo has preferred to evade the question by resorting to abstract clichés.

An individual act is never neutral, just as any political action is not; it either clears or obstructs the masses' road to power, and it is from this viewpoint that the criticism must be formulated. We know that a single act (or for that matter, one hundred!) is not in itself a total solution to the problems of the exploited masses; but will it help to bring about such a solution? Carrillo does not answer to this point and falls into flagrant contradiction with his former statement:

... the individual act ... can be an obstacle to the progress of the masses' and the people's struggle ...

Notice that he doesn't say: "It's an obstacle," but simply, "it can be an obstacle," in which case he allows for the possibility that it may not necessarily be an obstacle. Since no action is neutral, those that are not obstacles shall be aids, and therefore entirely justifiable.

In other words, Carrillo implicitly recognizes along with us that an individual act can be positive; but then why does he condemn the individual act in general? If he had specifically answered the question asked by his interviewer, he would have avoided such a gross contradiction.

But the answer he avoided was given by the Plenum of the C.E.:

Fellow Countrymen!
Our country enters a critical phase whose importance no one can minimize. The crisis of the dictatorial regime, contained for so long a time, has burst open with the death of Admiral Carrero Blanco.

It is evident that the power crisis is now open. There is a state apparatus that is still standing, but the political system led by the state has been sent into a spin.

After this statement, who would dare say that Carrero Blanco's execution has been negative? We do not believe that anyone can imagine a political system as cruel and repressive to the working class than fascism (1); it follows that the system's going into a spin shall neces-

sarily have positive results for the different peoples in the Spanish State (2).

(1) Someone may perhaps claim that Carrero Blanco's death might serve as a pretext for a sudden attack by the extreme right, which will, upon seizing power by this gesture, harden the line of the fascist regime. In fact, certain rumors to the effect that the Director General of the Civil Guard, Lieutenant General Iniesta Cano, might just try to attempt it, may be correct.

But on what social base in the state can the extreme right depend? Its seizure of power might even cause the political opposition of some sectors of the oligarchy that do not believe in the advantages of fascism and whose economic needs push them toward some sort of liberalization rather than a hardening of the line.

In effect, an extreme right-wing political regime might provoke very quickly a new coup d' état for which the liberal sector of the oligarchy would need some popular support, thus becoming indebted to the people, who would in turn have greater revolutionary possibilities.

Logically, the extreme right has not even counted on sufficient military power in order to attain dominion.

(2) One may oppose the aforementioned political consequences with the paralysis caused in the mass mobilizations that would take place with respect to Process 1001. But what is there of truth in such an objection?

The C.C.O.O. sector, controlled by the Spanish C.P., sent out a feeler in the form of a call to a day of struggle for December 12, adding other reasons for the struggle, such as the high cost of living and the freezing of wages. Its result: We all know what happened—it left much to be desired and it barely consisted of some work stoppages. Such results are not in any way the fault of the peoples of the Spanish state, who throughout recent years have more than proven their great spirit of combat in great spontaneous mobilizations; on the contrary, these are the logical outcomes of whoever proposes reformism and spends all of his efforts in diverting the people from the correct road.

Thus, the execution of Carrero Blanco paralyzed what could not possibly get started at that time. Its balance is highly positive.

... This isn't a menace. But, in effect, if things continue in this fashion, we shall not give up our liberty. Violence in the struggle of the masses may become a necessity, and if the struggle is defined in this terrain, if there is no other choice, we shall take that one. It will be harder, longer, and more painful. We are doing

whatever is possible to avoid it. We call upon everyone, without distinction, to avoid it . . .

So says Carrillo at another point in his declarations. Here is the basis of his anathema toward any individual act. He trusts the possibility that the master might lengthen the slave's chain if the latter is docile enough, although deviously menacing. What he doesn't seem to understand is that, as history has shown time and again, the slave's docility only serves to keep him tied to a chain that is short, and that whenever an exploited social class has achieved any vindication, this only happens through brutal struggle, after which the exploited class wrests its rights from the exploiting class.

Then, to base the elimination of fascism through dialogue and the convergence of interests among the different social sectors of the state is equivalent to sowing seeds in land that hasn't been tilled; it cannot yield any fruit. In order for the fascist system to peacefully give way to a more democratic one, the oligarchy must wish it to be so. This can happen only when a set of economic, political, and other types of reasons force it to do so.

There are those who think that the oligarchy needs a more democratic setup because of its urgent necessity to join the European Common Market; that indeed this is the main reason. But whoever so reasons forgets that no market (and much less the European, to whom Spanish technology as a whole has very little to offer) could have produced the superexploitation of the working class under the necessary protection of the fascist system.

It is possible that the oligarchy may intend to democratize its system of exploitation with a view toward retaining its class privileges, which have been menaced by popular pressure against fascism. Whatever the case may be, only the people's struggle can prepare the political ground to reap the seed of bourgeois democracy. The seed might not even yield fruit, since from the eighteenth century to the present, the terrain has turned rocky. Fascism is not, as some would think, a prebourgeois political system; it is, to the contrary, a system that comes after the bourgeois democratic republic. At any rate, although we do not place too much trust in its possibility, we see no obstacle that would prevent a bourgeois democratic system from forming part of the minimum political program of the working class; on the contrary, it would be convenient to the assimilation of the non-working-class antimonopoly sectors. But it must be kept in mind that any democratic concession from the oligarchy will be gotten only through the continuous struggle, each time more intensely carried out by the entire people; this struggle depends as much on mass struggle as on small group action, especially when the latter supports and creates conditions that are more favorable to the development of the former.

Freedom has never been conceded by the exploiting class to the exploited; it has always been a right wrested from the former. Always through force. It isn't enough to say, "If you do not give me my freedom, I shall fight," because words no longer scare people; it is necessary to fight. It is not a matter of stating that violence in the struggle of the masses "may become a necessity." Indeed, it is already an urgent necessity, and it is the duty of the revolutionary vanguards to understand this and to help the people become aware of it so as to organize in such a way as to carry it on to victory.

> . . . the hand that has so decided it, is as of yet unknown; at any rate, it is the hand of seasoned professionals who are well concealed; it doesn't seem to be that of amateurs who irresponsibly claim paternity for the deed while helping to cover up the authentic perpetrators . . .
>
> (From the declaration of the C.E. Plenum)

> When we stated that the act against Carrero Blanco was the work of professionals and not of amateurs, it was not our intention to degrade E.T.A. We wanted to emphasize that the act had the mark of certain specialized services, rather than that of an organization whose means and possibilities are limited.
>
> It seems that the purpose of choosing December 20, the date of the trial against the leaders of the Workers' Commissions, and of accusing E.T.A., was intended to cover up the real perpetrators of the act, who apparently are not from the left.
>
> (Statements by Santiago Carrillo)

As the proverb says: "Dios los cria y ellos se juntan." (Ed. note: literally, "God makes them and they find each other." In other words, like seeks like.) Thus, the outcome should be of shock to no one. Although they have taken different paths, both the Basque Government and the Spanish C.P. have arrived at the same conclusion: E.T.A. could not be Carrero Blanco's executioner. The reason for this is that the road to treason, as in the case of the road to revolution, is essentially one, although it may have many winding portions, and ends up by uniting those who follow it.

If the leaders of the Spanish C.P. still maintained any bonds with the people, they might have intuitively accepted as logical, as have many of the militants in the base of the party, the fact that E.T.A. executed Carrero Blanco. But it has been a long time since Carrillo's followers have felt the same as the people and this has led them to take a position as ridiculous as that of Leizaola—perhaps, if possible, an even more unpopular one.

And, really, never have such few words contained such a deep contempt for the revolutionary capacity of a people as those of the leadership of the Spanish C.P. toward our people and those of the rest of the Spanish state.

An ex-O.A.S. official, an ex-Sergeant of the French Legion, an I.R.A. specialist, a mining engineer, an electrical technician, an optics technician: All of these people were necessary, according to the official press and the fascist military men, to execute Carrero Blanco; the leadership of the Spanish C.P., with Carrillo at its head, shouts this out in chorus with them.

It is logical that the fascist regime will make statements of this type; it must somehow justify the success of the execution of its leaders in the area of Madrid most intensely guarded by the various police services. But the leadership of the Spanish C.P., what excuse could it have? It's useless to search for one, because it doesn't exist.

The C.P. leadership's contempt for the people even goes as far as considering it incapable of digging a small tunnel, installing an explosive, laying out a cable, and pulling a switch. It is totally logical that those who have such a concept of the people go around preaching pacifism and "national reconciliation," since, if they consider the people incapable of doing such simple things, how could they consider them capable of making a revolution? To make a revolution means to destroy the bourgeois state and to create a proletarian one; the working class must do this and it must take charge of the economic, cultural and political leadership of the country. How could a working class that is incapable of preparing and producing an explosion be capable of taking on the responsibility of such complicated tasks?

Nevertheless and with due justice, we should recognize that probably no member of the Spanish C.P. leadership knows the rudiments of the explosives craft. Perhaps they do not know that the building of a 15-meter tunnel is at the reach of any man not too physically unfit; that in ten minutes one learns to install an explosive like the one utilized in Claudio Coello Street; that to lay out a cable can be done by a child with a ladder; and finally that an oppressed man's need for liberation is enough of an impulse to get him to press the release button. But all of this, far from being an excuse, constitutes an accusation; a very serious accusation against a Party that labels itself as revolutionary and whose ignorance of armed-struggle techniques shows that for a long time it has stopped considering the possibility of armed violence as a necessity.

On the other hand, even if the precise technique for the execution of Carrero Blanco were more complicated, have not people, throughout history, demonstrated the capacity to substitute inadequacies with respect to conventional techniques with courage, limitless creativity, and imagination? How can a group of Marxists, aware of the fact that the working class is the creator of all that exists, consider it incapable of doing such a simple thing? It is simply that the leadership of the Spanish C.P. is Marxist in nothing more than its etiquette, since it forgot long ago the true meaning of Marxism.

Carrillo, you should not ask for E.T.A.s forgiveness; after all, we have known you for a long time. You should seek the forgiveness of the peoples of the Spanish state; try not to underrate them again because they will make the revolution, not you. It isn't enough to say that they have reached adulthood; you must acknowledge this in practice. Your statements show, as do those of Mr. Leizaola (although from another aspect), a total inability to free yourself from the bourgeois frame of thinking. Thus they involuntarily serve as active support of the myth that the masses cannot achieve an accurate technical level in order to carry out revolutionary acts such as that against Carrero Blanco; a myth that must be destroyed before the eyes of the people so as to make them see that the bourgeois state is not unshakeable, that revolution is possible. It is time to understand that the revolution is not a matter of professionalism or amateurism; the revolution is the only solution to the people's need for liberating themselves; and the peoples have always known how to satisfy the needs that have faced them.

3. Let us now look into the positions taken by the groups that have grown out of the split-ups of E.T.A. throughout its brief but hectic history: 6th Assembly (and not "E.T.A.–6th Assembly" as they define themselves) today fused with the L.C.R. and the Spanish Communist Movement (M.C.E.), which, due to the similar content of their criticism, may be considered under one category.

6th Assembly strongly criticizes the position taken by the revisionist parties and morally justifies the act:

> E.T.A. VI–L.C.R. supports the execution of the assassin Carrero Blanco as a legitimate retaliation by E.T.A. V in reply to the assassinations of six of its militants in the last years.

> Zutik No. 62, January '74)

Thank you, but we must remind you that revenge for the assassinated militants has not been the only reason, not even the fundamental one, that has provoked E.T.A. to execute Carrero Blanco.

On the other hand, it isn't a moral judgment what the working class seeks and expects from its vanguards, but a political assessment of the act. L.C.R.–6th Assembly skillfully evades this reply through an overabundance of dialectical gobbledygook.

Let's examine their statement:

> But neither our evaluation of the appropriateness of the retaliation by E.T.A. nor the impressions of great joy shown by the masses for Carrero Blanco's execution escape our firm position against the illusions that can be created in the working class and in sectors of the vanguard by small group activism in general and by this act in particular.

> If it is true that in a period of prerevolutionary maturation—such as the present one—the execution of the Government's President can bring about stimulating effects for the movement, so can it create mirages along the way for the political preparation and organization of the working class in its struggle to destroy the dictatorship.

> In other words (independent of whether it is or it isn't E.T.A. V's concept) it is not through the gradual killing of the regime's capitalists that one can destroy the dictatorship, but through the revolutionary action of the masses.

> (Zutik No. 62, January '74)

E.T.A. accepts these concepts as its own; but there is one aspect missing from the analysis of the revolutionary problem that would have served as a pattern in the possible evaluation of the act. 6th Assembly–L.C.R. has only looked at the action from the point of view of the repercussions that it may have for the organization of the working class. But, in a confrontation, the two opposing parties are dialectically related. That is to say, that the working class not only strengthens itself through consciousness raising and organization, but also through any weakening of the enemy. Many years ago, Lenin cited the extreme heightening of the internal contradictions of the ruling class and the corresponding weakening of its power apparatus as one of the necessary conditions that would indicate the existence of a revolutionary situation. Of course, E.TA. did not seek to achieve such an ambitious objective as the one pointed out by Lenin with this act; but who can doubt that the execution of Carrero Blanco has created many problems for the fascist state and weakened it?

Let us read with respect to this a few lines from the articles published in the French weekly *Le Nouvel Observateur*, dated 12/24–30/73, about Carrero's execution:

Since 1949, Carrero Blanco, in fact, controls the whole country.

Since 1956, he contacted the leaders of Opus Dei, with their principal leader Lopez Rodo, and with Franco's blessings, he secretly prepared the restoration of the Monarchy. He already knew that he would be in charge of continuing Franco's regime after Franco's passing away.

As the Caudillo ages, the factions within Franco's regime start to clash: Opus Dei against Falange. Only Carrero Blanco, accepted by Opus, admitted by Falange because of his devotion to Franco, can prevent the clash and prepare the ground for the future king Juan Carlos, known as the puppet, due to his insignificant role.

In order to weaken the regime, the Franco machinery, the Basque separatists could not have chosen a better target.

And really, can anyone doubt that Carrero Blanco's execution has dealt a strong blow to the Spanish state's fascism; and that it has stirred up the contradictory elements that live within the bosom of the state and that up to the death of the President have been in a numb state? Can anyone doubt the radicalizing effect that it will have on such contradictory elements and the sharpening of their confrontation? Apart from whether a substitute for Carrero Blanco as effective as he in playing the role of unifier and conciliator of the different interoligarchical differences exists or not, are these not going to necessarily be heightened? The liberal sectors that before claimed that it is necessary to give the people freedom in order for them to stop struggling—will they not now defend this position much more persistently? On the other hand, those who preached harshness in order to squash the popular struggle—will they not now seek this harshness more energetically and urgently?

Let us proceed.

> This does not mean in any way that small-group action should be rejected. On the contrary, even when they only serve as examples, the armed activity of the vanguard can and should play a decisive role in the preparation of this process. But to achieve that, it is necessary that at the hour of choosing it, they inscribe themselves in the political education of the proletariat and in the development of its organization in order to prepare that attempt against the dictatorship and against capitalism.
>
> It is precisely this perspective that is missing in E.T.A. V's activism in general and particularly in this concrete action.
>
> (Zutik No. 62, January '74)

This one is probably the most clever attempt throughout the entire text to evade the question by completely distorting the discussion of the problem. Columbus set out to look for a new commercial route to the Far East and discovered America. One thing is looked for, but the result of this search is different from what was originally sought. Whether E.T.A.'s perspective in this action was correct or not (1), that's one problem; whether the results have been positive or not, is a different problem. This latter one is the problem that is precisely evaded.

On the other hand, if certain small-group armed action is positive, why doesn't 6th Assembly–L.C.R. undertake this task?

(1) That E.T.A.'s activism in general has lacked working-class perspective is true, due to the petty bourgeois origins and habits that still plague the organization. To determine whether Carrero Blanco's execution suffers from this same defect is an audacious act on the part of the 6th Assembly–L.C.R. if it doesn't wait for E.T.A. to give an explanation.

Such a judgment may be made only on the basis of the Zutik 64, already published, and on the present document-book.

At the time of judging M.C.E.'s position on Carrero Blanco's execution, we shall observe two issues that are expounded in its official publication *Servir al Pueblo*, the January 1974 issue.

> But the death of Carrero Blanco presents a much deeper problem than that of knowing whether or not he deserved that end. Deserve it he did, no doubt. Now, is the attempt that has killed him a correct type of action or not? Are these the types of action

that will bring about the downfall of the fascist dictatorship?
This is the main problem that puts on the agenda the action that
we are discussing.

We repeat to M.C.E. what we have already told 6th Assembly–
L.C.R. One problem is whether small-group action is correct (a very
profound set of nuances is needed in order to answer this), and another problem is whether this concrete action has been correct, and
for this answer the results of the action must be measured.

Naturally, it is not actions of this type that will bring down the
fascist dictatorship (E.T.A. does not base its strategy on such actions
or on small-group activism in general, as some organizations seem to
accuse us of doing). Now, didn't Carrero Blanco's execution help to
bring about such an objective? That's the question.

Let us see what M.C.E.'s opinion is:

> As for the damage that these attempts may do to the regime,
> we are not anywhere as optimistic as those who believe that
> this is a serious blow capable of creating difficulties to the con-
> tinuation of Franco's regime after Franco's death, because the
> regime might not have someone who could impose the neces-
> sary unity on the different factions that compose it.
>
> The unity of the fascist forces is stronger than their internal
> disunity when it is a matter of the regime's very existence. The
> unity gathered around Franco or Arias Navarro is the unity of a
> class with its state against the people, and it does not depend
> basically on the sympathy, prestige or graces of the leader in
> turn, but on the needs of that class.
>
> The appointment of Arias Navarro as Carrero's successor is a
> good proof that the regime does not need exceptional men, but
> purely and simply disciplined fascists who are obedient to the
> class for whom they operate.

This is where we differ from the analysis of the Spanish Communist
Movement (M.C.E.). We don't know if the demise of Carrero Blanco
will destroy the possibility of continuity of Franco's regime after
Franco's death; it may not destroy it. We do believe, however, that it
will create difficulties for such a continuity (we must also remember
that it was not the only objective, not even one of the concrete objectives).

We are sure that it will heighten the internal contradictions of the
Spanish state; we are equally sure that it represents a parallel
weakening of the state.

Finally, we do not believe that the appointment of Arias Navarro proves that Spanish fascism does not need exceptional men, but simply that it doesn't have them; and logically, somebody has to occupy the post of President of the Government. At any rate, we are sure that an exceptional man is more dangerous than one who lacks such a quality. No one, execpt M.C.E., seems to doubt that Arias Navarro shall not be able to carry out his task at the level of Carrero Blanco.

To conclude, the position taken by M.C.E. is, evidently, one of total skepticism at the achievements of small-group activism as a strategic axis of the Socialist Revolution in the Spanish state (E.T.A. is also very skeptical about it), and the execution of Carrero Blanco concretely. It is on this last point about Carrero Blanco that E.T.A. disagrees entirely, when we consider—we believe this not to be a boast of triumph—that the results of such an action have been highly positive.

> Undoubtedly, it is certain that the choice of the moment and the type of action by E.T.A. V, in the present conditions and capabilities of the movement and of the vanguard, has been at the base of this paralyzation of the battles against Summary 1001; it is true that the meaning of this Summary was of utmost importance for the advancement of the class struggle. But our criticism of E.T.A. V in this respect, shall not obscure that the movement's cessation is basically due to the vanguard's own weakness . . .

Is it true that the execution of Carrero Blanco has put the brakes on the struggles due to Summary 1001? But, as we have stated before, the brakes were put on that which had no possibility of mobilization.

To say that the vanguard's weakness has been the main cause of paralyzation is to say very little indeed. It has been the only cause, for had there existed the possibility of more sensible mobilizations, E.T.A. would have acted in a different manner. On the one hand, it is time to cut out the boastful exultation that follows the moments of great mass mobilizations; on the other hand, it is also time to stop blaming foreign agents for the failures of a great many directives promoted by the vanguard. It is time to admit that the majority of huge mass mobilizations have been spontaneous and have resulted from the superexploitation to which the peoples of the state have been subjected, and not from the vanguard's direction and organization of them, as some are wont to boast. We have simply followed them and claimed their victories. Perhaps in this manner we may get a truer picture of the social situation in the Spanish state and a better assessment of our own forces, which will give our directives more accuracy.

The only organizations to whom the masses listen (fortunately, less and less) are the reformist and revisionist parties; and the masses can expect very little from those who, through mistrust of them, only educate them in the area of labor claims. He who sows wheat should not expect to reap apples.

On the other hand, the revolutionary movement is still too young, weak, and fragmented to have a firm basis. We will not gain anything by shouting victory to the point of believing that when the train moves it is because it has us as its engine. The truth is that lately the train has moved only and almost always, as we say, in front of us. Then, when the train is standing still, we stand on our heads, and despite all our efforts it hardly moves; in our blindness, instead of practicing self-criticism we place all or part of the blame on foreign agents who have little or nothing to do with the immobility of the train.

E.T.A. considers that Summary 1001 would not have produced very significant mobilizations; what must be judged is whether or not the positive aspects of the action are an improvement upon the hypothetically paralyzed mobilizations.

In sum, we affirm that all of the criticism of the 6th Assembly–L.C.R. is composed of "one of lime and one of sand." Different and partial aspects of the action are isolated from each other and then they are criticized, sometimes in contradictory fashion (good as a reprisal; negative as a brake on the mobilization of the masses with regard to Summary 1001). But an evaluation of the action as a whole, with all of its aspects interrelated, is consistently avoided. The conscious or unconscious cause of this insufficient criticism is none other than simple opportunism.

To give it a negative evaluation is to automatically find oneself confronting the people, the working class included, of course, for whom it has been a double lesson (on the one hand, the destruction of the myth that one cannot fight the fascist power apparatus; on the other hand, the recognition of their own strength) and a psychological liberation. To give it a positive evaluation means to break with the already outworn argument that E.T.A. is a petty bourgeois organization and therefore incapable of analyzing its actions from a working-class perspective. Although they affirm that E.T.A. is an ideologically and politically heterogeneous organization, they are bent on denying that such heterogeneity can allow analyses and actions, although these may be isolated, which will serve exclusively the working class.

Finally, the 6th Assembly–L.C.R., just as all "revolutionary" organizations (unfortunately) across the Spanish state, considers itself to be the best, the only one suited to lead the working class in the revolutionary process. On the other hand, it recognizes (according to its already-quoted statements) the need for certain armed activities by small groups (even if it doesn't determine which); and if 6th Assembly–L.C.R., considering itself to be the best organization, does not develop this type of activity, it supposes that such types of action—if carried out—serve interests foreign to the working class. It is what is called—or how should we call it?—professional jealousy.

We shall point out, finally, although briefly, among the positions that are unconditionally in solidarity with the execution of Carrero Blanco, that of the *Movimiento Libertario* (Libertarian Movement), which was expressed in the January 1974 issue of its official publication, *Frente Libertario:*

To end the year, the active resistance—punished so much everywhere, especially since last June's Constitution drawn by the Government presided by Carrero—could not have expected a better reward.

Sentimentally, one would have wished for the execution—so often sought and so often foiled—of the one most responsible for the national misfortunes, the traitor Franco, but politically, today it is of greater importance the execution of his right-hand man and projected successor, the Admiral. Considering it in this manner, without waiting for the present issue to come out, as soon as the event became known to us, this editorial staff sent the following communiqué to the foreign press agencies:

Frente Libertario Anarcho-Syndicalist organ of the emigration and militant publication of the Libertarian Movement that operates within Spain, declares its full solidarity and sends warmest greetings to the authors of the act effected against the sinister Carrero Blanco.

In opposition to the contemporizing declarations of the Spanish C.P. and other political groups that parade themselves as representatives of the opposition, we understand and proclaim that this execution constitutes an act of liberation for the working class and for all of the people oppressed by the Spanish state.

By slaying Carrero Blanco, the ones responsible for the act have directly attacked Franco, his Police and his Army, thus proving that there cannot be any "civil peace" in Spain under a dictatorial power founded under an ultra-authoritarian conception of order.

Cheers for direct action against Franco's regime!

APPENDIX IV

Police Information Bulletin 7/74

EXCERPT FROM "INFORMATION BULLETIN No. 7/74," RE-PORT FROM THE SPANISH POLICE TO THE P.I.D.E. (POR-TUGUESE POLICE)

The desire to make it possible to print this set of documents has been one of the reasons for the delay in publishing this documentary book.

During the coup in Portugal, the working class took by assault the General Headquarters of the Portuguese political police (P.I.D.E.) and in a secret file in the Director's office were found various interesting documents of the fascist police organizations of Spain, South Africa, and Brazil.

The documents of the Spanish police were written in Bilbao and spoke exclusively of E.T.A.—ideology, structure, practice, diverse incidents, etc. In short, they are documents of alarm and at the same time seekers of help for the destruction of the revolutionary movement in general and in particular, for the destruction of E.T.A.

This document, of which we publish only the excerpt related to this book, has been obtained through bonds of revolutionary solidarity between the Basque and the Portuguese Peoples.

THE ASSASSINATION OF THE PRESIDENT OF THE GOVERNMENT ADMIRAL DON LUIS CARRERO BLANCO BY E.T.A. 5TH ASSEMBLY TERRORISTS

THE FACTS

The Assassination and Its Preparation

At 9:30 last December 20, a violent explosion was produced on Claudio Coello Street, a few feet away from its intersection with

Maldonado Street, which reached the "Dodge Dart" automobile, license plate PMM 16.4L6, occupied by Mr. President of the Government Don Luis Carrero Blanco, who was accompanied by the Police Inspector Don Juan Antonio Bueno Fernández, and as driver, Don José Luis Pérez Mojeda, an employee of the Ministries' Parking Lot.

The intensity of the explosion was such that the heavy Dodge flew up into the air, crashed against the cornice of the Jesuits' building, flew over the roof, and landed on the second-floor terrace that faces the patio.

The explosion also reached the President's escort car, occupied by the Inspectors Don Rafael Galiana del Río, Don Miguel Alonso de la Fuente, and the driver. The three were injured (the first one seriously, the other two slightly). It reached a taxi (the taxi driver was also seriously injured), as well as several people who received injuries of varying degrees. Some 20 parked cars were greatly damaged, as well as some buildings on Claudio Coello Street and neighboring blocks.

When the cloud of dust was dispersed, the magnitude of the incident became manifest. Those in the escort car, injured, looked for the President's missing car, which was located moments later, with the resulting shock, on the interior terrace of the Jesuits' building.

Immediately its occupants were recovered—the President, the Police Inspector, and the driver—and were quickly taken to the Francisco Franco Health Center; Mr. Carrero Blanco and Mr. Bueno Fernández were admitted dead on arrival; three hours later, the driver, Mr. Pérez Mojeda, died.

The other injured parties were taken into care and were hospitalized in the same health center.

An enormous hole, 12 meters in diameter and several meters deep, was produced in the roadway along with breaks in the water and gas pipelines. This, along with the confusion of the first few moments, made it difficult to determine the origin or the cause of the explosion, but once the accumulated debris at the entrance of house No. 104 of Claudio Coello Street was cleared away, it was confirmed that a narrow tunnel about a meter and a half deep had been constructed perpendicular to the building and extending to the center of the street from the basement of this house. Through the same tunnel various electrical cables were seen that extended along the exterior of the site of the building, together with the telephone cables and followed the length of the block of the designated street toward Diego de León Street.

The report furnished in the first few moments by technical personnel of the Artillery Armory (we shall concern ourselves with the written report later) showed that the constructed tunnel had been used to place very potent explosives that were difficult to determine at the time because the burned ground in the funnel of the hole had been subjected to the flow of water; that the charge could have been set off by electrical contact originating at the end of the cable, located at Diego de León Street; that in their opinion, the charge had been placed lengthwise and by the manner in which the tunnel and the charge had been prepared, it was evident that the authors were experts in handling explosives; that the calculated charge of dynamite that was placed at the end of the tunnel was 250 kg.

So as not to miss the hit and force the President's car to go through the middle of the road in Claudio Coello Street, exactly over the explosive charge, a car, an Austin model 1300 was double-parked; this car was damaged by the explosion and recovered by the City Police. A plastic can containing approximately 8 kgs. of a product easily identified as "plastic-explosive" was found hidden in the trunk.

We shall deal later with the results of the analysis of the explosive, as well as with the identity of the owner of that vehicle, license plate No. M-893,948.

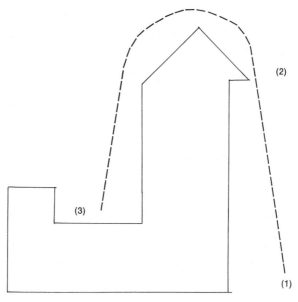

The vehicle of the President of the Government, with its three occupants inside, was hurled up in the air by the explosion (1), collided with the top edge (2) of the five-story building, cleared the roof-top and landed on the terrace (3) that surrounds the interior patio, folding into the shape of a "V."

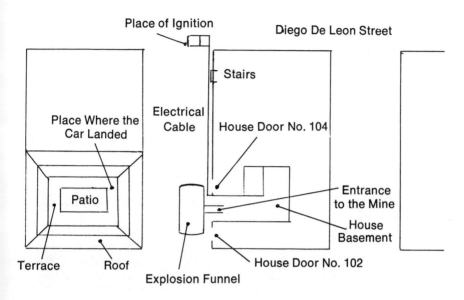

Place of Ignition

Diego De Leon Street

Stairs

Place Where the
Car Landed

Electrical
Cable

House Door No. 104

Patio

Entrance
to the Mine

House
Basement

Terrace   Roof

House Door No. 102

Explosion Funnel

Maldonado Street

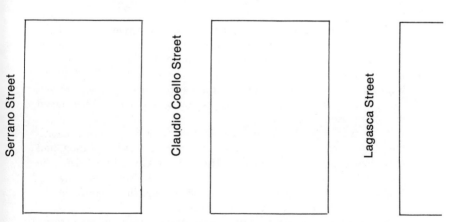

Serrano Street

Claudio Coello Street

Lagasca Street

Juan Bravo Street

POLICE INVESTIGATIONS

Without delay, they took as a starting point the right side of the basement of house No. 104 Claudio Coello Street, which was the beginning point of the tunnel where the explosives were placed.

This basement had been for sale during a period of time, and in the middle of November it was acquired by an individual who through D.N.I. No. 2,621,463, which he presented, claimed to be:

—ROBERTO FUENTES DELGADO, Adult, Single, Resident of Madrid, Living at No. 1 Mirlo Street.

He gave as down payment 80,000 pesetas and agreed to pay the rest of the sum in monthly installments.

Upon occupying the premises, repeated blows were heard coming from inside; the superintendent thought this was due to some repair work or improvement that was being done and she so informed the neighbors of the right side of the mezzanine, who were the most disturbed by the noises; in her desire to know the nature of the work, she tried to investigate by way of a window adjacent to Claudio Coello Street, but the vision was obstructed by a sheet; the windows and shutters were also shut.

On the eve of December 18, the individual occupying the basement informed the concierge that an electrician would appear in person a few hours later. The electrician, when he arrived, entered the premises by using a key that he already possessed; he left minutes later, but not before telling the superintendent that his work would be finished the following day. Precisely, on the nineteenth, at about 8:30 P.M., supplied with a ladder, the electrician in question arrived again; the superintendent doesn't know how long the electrician stayed in the premises.

The buyer of the basement, according to what the superintendent's husband asserted, had claimed that his profession was sculpturing, and upon being questioned as to the nature of the blows heard daily, he answered that he was finishing a piece of work. The couple agreed that at times, a strange odor would come through the windows of the patio; this was corroborated by several neighbors.

In the process of identification, upon the examination of pictures, the superintendents, in a categorical way, without any doubts, specified that the person they knew as Roberto Fuentes Delgado, buyer of the premises, was the person who among the photographs corresponded to

————, and the one who was supposedly the electrician was identified as————.

On his part, the owner of the property, who through a contract written by a lawyer sold that dwelling in the middle of last November to Roberto Fuentes Delgado (according to evidence in the D.N.I. that he presented), with some doubts recognizes————, as the person to whom he made the sale, adding that he claimed to be studying Industrial Professionalism and that he was thinking of using the premises to study sculpturing or modeling.

The authentic photograph of Roberto Fuentes Delgado that is on file at the D.N.I. archives, was shown to the superintendent of house No. 104 Claudio Coello Street, and to the others who participated in the sale; all agree that it is a different person.

The true owner of the D.N.I. Roberto Fuentes Delgado, lives and works in Burgos and lost his identification card many years ago; therefore, the one used in the apartment in question was a false one.

TECHNICAL REPORTS

*Concerning the Place of the Incident and the Characteristics
of the Explosive.*

1. Gathered Information. In the place of the explosion, the existence of an elliptical crater may be observed, whose upper and lower axes are 19 and 9 meters respectively, with a depth at the center estimated at 2.50 meters.

On the right-side basement of the building 104, one can see the entrance to a mine tunnel, which was the entrance to the charge. The tunnel is 6 meters long, with a rectangular section .80 meters wide and .60 meters in height.

In the basement, devices such as slow fuses, quick fuses, and electrical charges were found as well as other material used in the operation—tools, electric batteries, a lantern, insulating tape, etc.

A double electric cable, 2.5 mm. wide, was fastened to the window facing the street; it was connected to a copper terminal that supposedly was connected to the starter used in the explosion.

This cable was spread the length of the block of Claudio Coello Street, in the direction of Diego de León, to the corner where the ignition system was installed; this system consisted of two flashlight batteries of 1.5 volts, connected in series with a switch, normally used in domestic electrical installations, also connected in series. The cable was provisionally placed over door hinges.

At this last point, there was a ladder leaning against the wall; it was similar to those used by operators of the Telephone or Electric Companies, which served as an observation post to watch for the signal that would set off the charge. Also found was an electrician's bag with various materials.

After studying the vicinity and the funnel produced by the explosion, the type of explosive used has not been determined, since the funnel was destroyed by water as a result of the rupture of pipelines, which prevented any access to the fire chamber.

2. Conclusion. From the facts already stated and from observations made, the following conclusions have been arrived at:

A. The preparation of the attempt was carefully planned and studied and also included the requirement of a reference point on the wall of the building opposite to the one already referred to, that could have served as a guide at the moment of setting off the explosion.

B. The work done for the success of the explosion had to be long and hard, since the dimensions of the mine tunnel only permitted one person to work in a horizontal position and with a great limitation of his movements, judging by the nearly 3 cubic meters of removed earth. These circumstances and the nature of the tunnel allow us to judge that those involved were skilled in mining, well-digging, etc.

C. In order to secure the desired results, a long charge, about 6 to 8 meters in length, was placed in the direction of the vehicle's path, and displaced 1.5 meters in relation to the middle of the roadway; from this it may be concluded that the traffic on the road had been previously studied. In this manner, the vehicle would be hit even if allowances were made for possible defects in the operation. Nevertheless, the car was hit full flush, judging from the distance traveled into the air, for in any other case it would have traveled forward or backward after the thrust, in the direction of Claudio Coello Street.

D. Since the type of explosive used is not known, the exact amount of the charge cannot be ascertained. Nevertheless, with the sole intention to draw an estimate, it is judged that 200 kgs. of explosive were placed in five charges of 40 kgs. each for a crater the size of the one produced to be possible. This charge,

transformed into explosive plastic, would be equivalent to 190 kgs. of "XP" used in the Army or to 304 kgs. of regular dynamite.
E. As an igniting system, the electric one was used, by way of electric batteries and charges as a means of providing the spark; taking into consideration the precariousness of the system, it is thought that a minimum number of charges was used.

About the Explosive Found in the Austin 1300 M-893,948 Automobile.

1) The explosive found in the trunk of the vehicle was contained in a plastic can 20 x 18 x 28 cm with a circular mouth of 9 cm in diameter; it occupied a little more than ⅔ of the deposit and together with the container it weighed 9.250 kg.
2) In an organic analysis it has been found that it is a rubber-type explosive, molded like the plastic explosives; it is of a dark yellow color with brown seams, a bitter almond smell, and a noticeable discharge.
It had been placed in the form of a hollow charge. To achieve this, cardboard was placed at the bottom of the container in the form of an almost quadrangular pyramid, with its base facing down; the height of this cardboard was 7.5 cm. and the middle sides of the base measure 16 and 8 cm.
3) Judging from the information gathered from the organic analysis and the elements found in the chemical analysis (incomplete), we can think of a plastic explosive of the rubber type, of a homemade nature; if presented in the form of a cone, several of them might form a shapeless mass, be put in the receptacle, and be given the shape of a hollow charge.
The results of the analysis disclose the following components of the explosive:

Ammonium nitrate	59.88%
Nitroglycerine, or more likely, Nitroglycol	27.76%
Nitrocellulose	1.35%
Dinitrotoluene and trinitrotoluene plus volaties	5.87%
Sawdust and other insolubles	2.60%

This composition coincides significantly with that foreseen in the first report; with the one of the explosive Rubber 2E-C (officially named Gelamonite 1-D), which is made by the Spanish Union of Explosives and whose composition is the following:

Ammonium nitrate	61.50%
Nitroglycerine/Nitroglycol	28.00%
Nitrocellulose	1.20%
Dinitrotoluene	7.00%
Sawdust	2.30%

NOTE: As will be observed when reading the document, the names of the individuals considered by the police as suspects have been eradicated from the documents in this text.